Foreword

It gives me great pleasure to write this Foreword ω Ρhilip ⸺ the ⸺ *Maritime Blockade: Past, Present, and Future.* I have had the good fortune of collaborating with Phil on a number of projects and publications over the past decade, and it is very pleasing indeed that amongst the many calls upon his time and expertise, he has been able to research and write this fine book.

Phil's inquisitive, methodical, and historical approach to the law applicable in situations of armed conflict at sea is clearly evident throughout this work. He takes the reader on an analytical journey from the theoretical and operational foundations of maritime blockade law, through incidences of its practice, to a critical analysis of its continuing applicability and status in the context of twenty-first-century international humanitarian law. In particular, his analysis and conclusions as to the issue of starvation in cases of maritime blockade—with his associated finding that the current legal regime is wanting—is a welcome reinvigoration of debate as to an often fundamental, concerning, and legally very challenging consequence of maritime blockade.

This book is also important for the markers it proposes as reference points for a discussion about the future shape of the law of maritime blockade. Whilst acknowledging the continuing importance and effectiveness of maritime blockade as a method of warfare, this recognition and analysis of its clear susceptibility to critique is central to Phil's argument. To this end, his proposals for reconceptualizing blockade law in the twenty-first century, incorporating the traditional concepts and purposes of blockade, while addressing the issues of humanitarian access and relief, merit close attention and will hopefully spark further and broader discussion. As Professor Wolff Heintschel von Heinegg, Phil's doctoral supervisor, has noted, the role of rigorously argued proposals for nunaced, updated guidelines as a catalyst for progressive development in the sometimes arcane field of the law of naval warfare can not be understated.

This book is the first significant treatise on the law of maritime blockade published in several decades. Its contribution to the understanding of blockade law, and the law of naval operations in general, makes it a most welcome resource for students, teachers, and practitioners of naval operations law.

Rob McLaughlin
Director, Australian Centre for the Study of Armed Conflict
Australian Defence Force Academy
University of NSW, Canberra
25 October 2017

Series Editors' Preface

Even within the context of the rather overlooked area of the Law of Armed Conflict/International Humanitarian Law, the law of naval warfare (as it is still, somewhat anachronistically known) the part of that law which relates to blockades, has, until recently, not received the attention it deserves. Still less has there been a comprehensive monograph on point. That is not to say that the issues raised are not relevant in the modern world, as the revival of interest in the area that has surrounded the Israeli blockade of Gaza, and the controversy that surrounds it, in particular since the interdiction of the *Mavi Marmara* and other ships in this context in 2010.

The incident was the subject of significant comment at the legal and political level. The debates on point sometimes raised as much heat as light. It was also the subject of international legal attention by various conflicting commissions of inquiry, and a petition by flag States of the interdicted vessels to the International Criminal Court (ICC), requesting that it become involved. This request has led to complex litigation in that Court, exposing dissensus between its various organs, as the Prosecutor and the Pre-Trial Chamber involved were quite clearly uncomfortable with each other's approach to whether it ought to be investigated.

This, perhaps, should not be a surprise, in that the issues involved in blockades involve, in addition to legal issues, difficult political, economic, and humanitarian considerations. Therefore, objective legal analysis of this contentious area is extremely important to provide a common framework for discussion of what are often deeply divisive. This is particularly the case owing to the fact that, in spite of blockade's relationship to the law of neutrality, in addition to the complex interplay of those functions, it can often be the subject of unneutral comment.

Dr. Drew's study is a careful study the legal aspects of blockade, primarily, in the 20th and 21st century, and as such is both important and welcome. Beginning with an impressive knowledge of history, in the pre-modern era of international law, it moves on to the First Word War, in which extensive use of blockades was made. The work also evaluates practice coming from World War II, the UN Charter era (including cold-war conflicts such as Korea and Vietnam), and situations, such as Gaza, where the Security Council has not been involved, as well as Iraq, Bosnia, and Libya, where the UN has taken coercive action. The study covers the Law of Armed Conflict/Humanitarian Law, both treaty-based and customary, and, importantly, International Human Rights Law. It is based on the author's many years of practice and experience, followed by detailed scholarly engagement of the area.

As this book's subtitle, and its contents make clear, it is grounded in history, practice, and looks to the future. Whilst critical (with a small 'c', hence not in the sense of the Critical Legal Studies movement identified, for example, with David Kennedy and Martti Koskenniemi) Dr. Drew adopts a constructive approach to the development of the law of blockade, hence the suggestions with which it concludes, which are a set of guidelines to further guide the evolution of law and practice in the area. We are delighted to have this book in the Series.

The Editors

Acknowledgements

This book is the final step in a process that began during a dinner in Rhode Island in 2012. On that evening, Professor Doctor Wolff Heintschel von Heinegg agreed to accept me as a doctoral student. I am indebted to him for his encouragement and sage guidance throughout the development and defence of my dissertation, and ultimately, this book. I would also like to thank Professor Marco Milanovic and Professor Michael Schmitt, both of whom were kind enough to review my drafts and offer invaluable insight and guidance.

I owe special thanks to my friend and colleague, Professor Rob McLaughlin of the Australian Defence Force Academy, who encouraged me to undertake my doctoral degree, and provided me with invaluable assistance and advice throughout. Rob is a true friend, and a valued mentor.

Finally, my greatest gratitude goes to my family; Kelsey, Emilia, and particularly my wife Christa, for your love, encouragement, and support. Thank you.

Phillip Drew
Canberra, Australia
October 2017

Contents

Table of Cases

Table of Legislation

1

Introduction

The period since the end of the Second World War has seen a remarkable evolution in international law, particularly in the fields of International Human Rights Law (IHRL) and International Humanitarian Law (IHL). In the years following the war, with the devastation of the conflict fresh in their minds, the world's leaders engaged in a number of diplomatic conferences and processes aimed at ensuring 'that armed force shall not be used, save in the common interest ... [and that] ... respect for the obligations arising from treaties and other sources of international law can be maintained'.[1] Concomitantly they commenced a series of diplomatic initiatives that resulted in the creation of the United Nations Charter, the development of universal conventions on human rights,[2] and a large-scale overhaul of the law of armed conflict.[3] In terms of IHL, the crowning achievement of the last quarter of the twentieth century was the adoption of The Protocols Additional to the Geneva Conventions of 1949, particularly Additional Protocol One[4] (Additional Protocol 1). There can be no argument that the ratification of the Protocols by the majority of the world's states signalled a quantum advance in humanitarian protection.[5] In spite of the general advances made towards the protection of civilians against the effects of armed conflict however, one area of the law of armed conflict stands alone for having not been brought into the modern era—the law of maritime blockade.

'The purpose of establishing a blockade is to deny the enemy the use of enemy and neutral vessels or aircraft to transport personnel and goods to or from enemy

---

[1] Charter of the United Nations (adopted 24 October 1945) 1 UNTS XVI, preamble (hereafter UN Charter).

[2] See, for example, Universal Declaration of Human Rights (adopted 10 December 1948) UNGA Res 217 A(III) (hereafter UDHR).

[3] For the purpose of this book, the terms 'the law of armed conflict' and 'international humanitarian law' will be used interchangeably.

[4] International Committee of the Red Cross (ICRC), Protocol Additional to the Geneva Conventions of 12 August 1949, and relating to the Protection of Victims of International Armed Conflicts (Protocol I) (8 June 1977) 1125 UNTS 3, art 35(1) (hereafter AP1).

[5] As of 31 March 2017 there were 174 states party to AP1. ICRC online: ICRC <https://ihl-databases.icrc.org/ihl/INTRO/470> accessed 13 May 2017. Although a number of states, such as the United States, Israel, Pakistan, and India, are not party to the treaty, much of its provisions are recognized as being representative of Customary International Law. See ICRC, *Customary International Law Study* (Cambridge University Press, 2009).

territory.'[6] It is, as Sir William Scott described in 1799, 'a sort of circumvallation around a place, by which all foreign connexion and correspondence is, as far as human force can effect it, to be entirely cut off. It is intended to suspend the entire commerce of that place'.[7] As such, blockades are most effective when employed against states that rely on maritime commerce for much, if not all, of their trade and sustenance. Insofar as the primary goals of a maritime blockade are to prevent a state from being militarily replenished and to isolate its economy, a blockade can undermine the ability of the targeted state to maintain not only its war effort, but its civilian population as well. As will be discussed in Chapter 6, a lengthy blockade conducted against a modern, industrialized economy, or against a country that is not self-sustaining in food production, can cause severe shortages of foodstuffs and other items necessary for the survival of the civilian population.

There are three principal theories in this work; first, because there is no codified law of blockade, and there is no universally accepted model of blockade that extends beyond the basic rules for the establishment of a blockade, there is no such thing in international law as a universally accepted 'law of blockade'. Second, because maritime blockade is an indiscriminate method of warfare, wide-scale starvation of civilian populations as a consequence of blockade operations may constitute arbitrary deprivation of life. Third, it is submitted that the time has come for states to critically assess the current status of blockade law, and to develop new models and procedures that comply with twenty-first-century humanitarian law.

The first part of this book is dedicated to an overview of the history and practice of the inter-related concepts of contraband, neutrality, and blockade. Through historical examination of the evolution of the law of blockade, this work demonstrates that there is no consistent practice or standard *opinio juris* regarding the total corpus of this method of warfare or the law that defines and regulates it.

Reviewing the humanitarian effects from some of the most devastating blockades in history, the second part of the work examines the existing framework for blockade and argues that in its current form it violates the IHL principle of distinction. Arguing that in most situations the economy of a state cannot be considered to be a military objective within the meaning of article 52.2 of Additional Protocol 1, it is contended that the wilful starvation of a civilian population during a blockade is analogous to the deliberate targeting of civilians in kinetic operations. As a result, such action on the part of a blockading force constitutes an indiscriminate attack that can, in the event of civilian deaths, be considered an arbitrary deprivation of life.

In making this point, this book advances the notion that contemporary efforts to reduce the effects of blockade through the use of the proportionality test, as outlined in article 57(2)(b) of Additional Protocol 1,[8] are of little value. In support of this position the mechanisms of Part IV of Additional Protocol 1 are explored, and

---

[6] Wolff Heintschel von Heinegg, 'The Current State of the Law of Naval Warfare: A Fresh Look, the San Remo Manual' (2006) 82 Int'l L Stud 270, 276 (hereafter Heintschel von Heinegg, 'Current State').

[7] *The Vrow Judith* [1799] 1 C Rob 150, 151–2 (hereafter *Vrow Judith*).

[8] AP1 (n 4) art 57.2(b).

the argument is posited that because economies are generally not considered to be military objectives, any operations directed at them as a whole are unlawful. Hence, because such operations are unlawful *ab initio*, the proportionality test cannot be employed. In the alternative the author contends that even if the economy can be considered to be a military objective, any operation aimed at destroying it would be one of 'those which employ a method or means of combat which employ a method or means of combat which cannot be limited ... and is of a nature to strike military objectives and civilian objects without distinction'.[9] The argument is further developed that even if a blockade does not violate the principle of distinction at first blush, it is impossible to anticipate with any accuracy the expected harm that may be caused to a civilian population in cases where the destruction of a state's economy is the aim of an operation. Thus, in such situations it impossible to employ the proportionality test, which requires that forces engaging in operations 'refrain from deciding to launch any attack which may be expected to cause incidental loss of civilian life, injury to civilians, damage to civilian objects, or a combination thereof, which would be excessive in relation to the concrete and direct military advantage anticipated'.[10]

The work also explores the notion that there is a deliberately imposed gap in humanitarian protection in article 49.3 of Additional Protocol 1 that permits states to engage in blockade operations without having to apply, or consider, the humanitarian protections as laid out in Part IV of Additional Protocol 1. This view is confirmed through an examination of committee notes and travaux preparatoires for the Additional Protocols as well as official statements made by governments since the Protocols have been in force. It is contended that as a result of this humanitarian gap, and the confusion that exists with respect to the state of the law regarding humanitarian assistance and access in maritime blockade, the law in this area remains unclear, and thus wide open to challenge.

The final part of the book, in the form of an appendix, offers a suggested model for contemporary blockade. Taking into account the historical development of the law, the perceived strengths and weaknesses of the current body of the law, and incorporating humanitarian principles and guarantees, this model advocates a continuing role for maritime blockade as a method of warfare, but suggests a legal construct in which it would be unlawful to deliberately cause starvation of the targeted state's civilian population.

Defining Maritime Blockade

While legal definitions of naval blockades attempt to be precise, the range of activities that have historically fit under this rubric are vast indeed.[11]

---

[9] Ibid, art 51.4.   [10] Ibid, art 57.2(b).
[11] Bruce A. Elleman and S.C.M. Paine (eds), *Naval Blockades and Seapower: Strategies and Counter-Strategies 1805–2005* (Routledge, 2006) 4 (hereafter Elleman, *Sea Power*).

In the absence of a multinational convention, international law pertaining to any topic can be ambiguous, and therefore subject to a variety of interpretations. This is the challenge that faces any student of the law of maritime blockade; in spite of some four centuries of practice, maritime blockade has defied convention, with the inevitable result that the scope, application, and legal parameters of blockade remain unresolved and, for many, confusing.[12]

There is a myriad of definitions for the term 'maritime blockade'.[13] The majority of those that do exist describe blockade as a method of naval warfare that is only operative in armed conflict.[14] While historically there existed a concept of 'pacific blockade',[15] the notion that a blockade can be classified as peaceful ignores the underlying reality that the establishment of a lawful blockade permits the blockading state's navy to use force to interdict shipping and prevent all maritime traffic from sailing into or out of a place. Insofar as any such interference would constitute a breach of the requirement under article 2(4) of the Charter of the United Nations to 'refrain ... from the threat or use of force against the territorial integrity or political independence of any state',[16] a blockade cannot, by any modern standard, be considered to be a pacific action.[17]

While there is no universally accepted definition of maritime blockade, an examination of several contemporary definitions[18] informs that maritime blockades share the following common characteristics:

- they are *in bello* operations conducted by naval forces of a belligerent against its opponent's coastlines;[19]

---

[12] The confusion surrounding blockade and similar interdiction methods is illustrated in the discussion of the relationship between blockade and contraband in Maurice Parmalee, *Blockade and Sea Power: The Blockade of 1914–1919 and its Significance for a World State* (Hutchison and Co, 1924).

[13] For the purpose of this book, 'blockade' refers only to the traditional method of warfare by which a belligerent naval power prevents egress or ingress of all maritime vessel or air traffic to or from the ports of a blockaded state. It does not include any restrictions on land transport or any other form of economic or political isolation of a state. 'Maritime Blockade' and 'Naval Blockade' are synonymous. Although the author acknowledges and accepts that an air blockade is synonymous to a naval blockade, and is subject to the same legal regime, the focus of this thesis is on maritime operations. That being stated, it is recognized that in order to be effective, any naval blockade must include denial of over-flight and air access to areas that are being subjected to maritime blockade.

[14] Wolff Heintschel von Heinegg, 'Naval Blockade' [2000] 75 Int'l L Stud 203, 205 (hereafter Heintschel von Heinegg, 'Blockade').

[15] John Westlake, 'Pacific Blockade' [1909] 25 LQ Rev 13.

[16] United Nations, Charter of the United Nations, 24 October 1945, 1 UNTS XVI (hereafter UN Charter).

[17] Robert W. Tucker, *The Law of War and Neutrality at Sea* (United States Government Printing Office, 1957) 287 (hereafter Tucker, *Neutrality*). Absent a UNSC Resolution authorizing such action, any such use of force constitutes a violation of section 2(3) and (4) of the UN Charter.

[18] See, for example, *Australian Defence Force, Executive Series Law of Armed Conflict* (Canberra, Defence Publishing Service, 2006) 6–18; *US Naval War College Commander's Handbook on the Law of Naval Operations* (Newport, US Naval War College 2007) 7–26 (hereafter *Commander's Handbook*); UK Ministry of Defence, *The Manual of the Law of Armed Conflict* (Oxford University Press, 2004) 363 (hereafter, *UK Manual*); German Navy *Kommandanten-Handbuch* [*German Handbook*] 154.

[19] James Kraska, 'Rule Selection in the Case of Israel's Naval Blockade of Gaza: Law of Naval Warfare or Law of the Sea?' (2010) 13 Yearbook of International Humanitarian Law 367, 388 (hereafter Kraska, 'Rule Selection').

- they block all 'vessels and/or aircraft of all nations ... from entering or exiting specified ports, airfields, or coastal areas belonging to, occupied by, or under the control of an enemy nation';[20]
- they are 'directed to the exercise of economic pressure on an adversary,[21] [and its armed forces][22] with the goal of halting all maritime trade, neutral and enemy, contraband and non-contraband, alike';[23] and
- they are enforced by 'condemnation of [the] ship and ... cargo, [of anyone] who attempts to [trade with] the beleaguered enemy'.[24]

Because one of the key characteristics of maritime blockade is the interdiction of maritime trade, blockades are often confused with other types of maritime interdiction operations, specifically those of siege, embargo, and the belligerent right to intercept and seize vessels and their cargoes under the law of contraband. Much of the confusion surrounding the relationship between blockade and contraband, in particular, is directly attributable to the construct of the Declaration of London[25] and the fact that it did not provide a definition for either of the actions. As a result, the drafters of the Declaration made it very easy for uninitiated readers to regard blockade and contraband as being inherently similar, rather than as two separate and distinct legal schemes.

To assist in understanding what a maritime blockade is, it is helpful to briefly describe and differentiate the other common types of interdiction operations with which blockade is often confused.

Siege

Derived from the old French word '*sege*', meaning 'to sit',[26] siege is a military operation in which belligerent forces surround a city or other geographical location, and stop all contact between that location and the world around it. Employed as a method of warfare throughout history, sieges are tactical operations that are typically conducted against fortified cities or garrisons. With a focus on attrition, sieges

---

[20] *Commander's Handbook* (n 18) 7–26.

[21] George I. Phillips, 'The Declaration of Paris: 1856' (1918) 34 LQ Rev 63, 230 (hereafter Phillips, 'Declaration of Paris').

[22] Heintschel von Heinegg, 'Naval Blockade and International Law' in Bruce Elleman and S.C.M. Paine (eds), *Naval Blockades and Seapower: Strategies and Counter-strategies 1805–2005* (Taylor & Francis Group, 2006) 10 (hereafter Heintschel von Heinegg, 'Seapower').

[23] William R. Kennedy, 'Some Points in the Law of Blockade' (1908) 9:2 Journal of the Society of Comparative Legislation 239.

[24] J.E.G. Montmorency, 'The Principles Underlying Contraband and Blockade' (1916) 2 Problems of the War: Papers Read Before the Society in the Year 1916 21, 29.

[25] Declaration Concerning the Laws of Naval War (1909) 208 Consol TS 338 (hereafter Declaration of London).

[26] 'Sege', OED Online. <http://www.oed.com/viewdictionaryentry/Entry/11125> accessed 12 May 2017.

generally include bombardment, assaults, and the forced starvation of the besieged location.

The genesis of blockade lies in siege operations; early maritime blockades were simply the seaward aspect of the besiegement of port cities.[27] As warfare, maritime commerce, and technology evolved over the years, however, blockade emerged as a distinct method of warfare that now has only a few similarities with its origins. A brief examination of the characteristics of modern blockade shows that blockade operations differ from siege warfare in three principal ways:

i. Blockade is a strategic operation with strategic goals: the aim of a blockade is two-fold; first it seeks to cut off the blockaded state from being re-supplied with military goods or personnel. Secondly, it seeks to cut off the coastal state (or region) from all maritime commerce, whether inbound or outbound. In this manner blockade is a form of economic warfare that aims to cause significant disruption to the targeted state's economy in order to reduce its ability to wage war.[28] Siege, on the other hand, is a limited tactical operation that is designed to isolate a limited geographical area, such as a city, so that it will capitulate.[29]

ii. Insofar as the primary goal of a siege is to surround and destroy a military garrison, a siege generally includes the bombardment of the besieged locale. In this manner the destruction of the garrison can be accomplished through a mixture of kinetic attacks and, if necessary, the eventual starvation of the defending force.[30] In the case of blockade, vessels of the blockading force rarely engage land-based targets. Rather, the focus of the blockading force is on stopping all maritime traffic from reaching the blockaded area.

iii. Blockades interfere with neutral commerce: the essence of blockade is that it stops all maritime traffic from conducting trade with the blockaded area. In this manner, blockade will prevent neutrals from engaging in their general right to trade and carry on international relations with whomever they choose. Siege, on the other hand, is a land-based operation that effects only local trade and has little or no impact on the rights of neutral states.

Contraband

Similar to blockade in many respects, contraband operations are aimed at interdicting maritime trade. The law of contraband, which applies only during armed conflict, permits a belligerent the right to intercept 'goods which are ultimately destined for territory under the control of the enemy and which may be susceptible for use in armed conflict'.[31] As such, the focus of the law of contraband is the interdiction and

---

[27] Heintschel von Heinegg, 'Blockade' (n 14) 205.   [28] Ibid.
[29] Roy Gutman and David Rieff (eds), *Crimes of War* (W.W. Norton and Co, 1999) 336.
[30] *UK Manual* (n 18) 87–8.
[31] Louise Doswald-Beck (ed), *San Remo Manual on International Law Applicable to Armed Conflicts at Sea* (Cambridge University Press, 1995) 215 (hereafter SRM).

seizure of goods that are categorized as contraband. Under this construct, goods that are not listed as contraband are not subject to intercept or seizure by the belligerents.

Whereas the emphasis of contraband rests on the nature of the goods being imported, 'blockades by contrast, are not targeted against particular material'.[32] Rather, the focus of blockade is to cut off all maritime traffic from a blockaded area. To this end, when a blockade is established, there is no such thing as contraband; the nature and quality of the cargo being interdicted are irrelevant.

Sanctions and Embargoes

Sanctions and embargoes[33] are targeted actions that ban or restrict trade or other commercial activity between an embargoed state and other countries. Often imposed as a response to objectionable military, political, or economic actions undertaken by the targeted country, sanctions are 'a tool for coercing target governments ... in a measured way that supplements diplomatic reproach without the immediate introduction of military force'.[34] Insofar as the focus of embargoes is on items or activities that are enumerated in lists developed by the government, organization, or body that has authorized the embargo action, embargoes closely resemble contraband operations; with the important distinction that contraband operations are acts of war while embargoes generally are not.

With the notable exception of embargoes that are sanctioned by the United Nations Security Council (UNSC), the imposition of an embargo does not provide the sanctioning state or body with the right to interfere or intervene against all vessels conducting trade with the embargoed state. Rather, embargoes not sanctioned by the Security Council apply only to citizens and corporations of those countries that agree to participate in the sanctions.[35]

In most cases embargoes apply to commercial activity, with enumerated goods such as weapons, munitions, vehicles, luxury items, or other similar commodities being subjected to trade restrictions or prohibitions. In other cases, such as the European Union's boycott that was focused on Iran's oil exports,[36] the sanctions may include actions such as travel restrictions and the freezing of assets. The operative theory of sanctions is that if they can be implemented and maintained at the right intensity for the right period of time, they will cause the embargoed government to modify its conduct.

---

[32] Michael N. Schmitt, *Blockade Law: Research, Design and Sources* (William S. Hein and Co, 1991) 3 (hereafter Schmitt, *Blockade Law*).

[33] The terms 'sanctions' and 'embargoes' can be used interchangeably.

[34] Gary Clyde Hufbauer et al, *Economic Sanctions Reconsidered*, 3rd edn (Peter G. Peterson Institute for International Economics, 2007) 5.

[35] Steve Chan and A. Cooper Drury, 'Sanctions as Economic Statecraft: An Overview' in Steve Chan and A.Cooper Drury (eds), *Sanctions as Economic Statecraft: Theory and Practice* (Palgrave, 2000) 5–7.

[36] EC, Council Decision 2012/35/CFSP of 23 January 2012 amending Decision 2010/413/CFSP concerning restrictive measures against Iran [2012] OJ, L 19/22.

While the right to conduct blockade or contraband operations is implicit in the law of armed conflict, embargo activities that involve enforcement require specific legal authorization before navies may conduct interdiction operations against vessels in international waters.[37] One such authorization can be granted by means of a resolution of the UNSC,[38] which has the unique power to bind all members of the United Nations. Alternatively, bilateral or multilateral agreements such as the Proliferation Security Initiative (PSI)[39] may permit enforcement action to be taken by and against all states party to the agreement. Where neither of such authorities is provided, sanctions regimes may only be enforced by states acting against their own flagged vessels or nationals.[40] It follows, therefore, that unless there is a UN sanction regime in place, an embargo cannot be enforced against vessels whose flag states are not party to the sanctions regime.

Table 1 provides a comparison of the principal types of maritime interdiction operations. It spells out the characteristics of the operations, the regimes under which they operate, the legal bases for their establishment, and the types of cargoes/vessels that can be subjected to interdiction and/or seizure.

Definition of Blockade

Unlike all other forms of interdiction operations, the establishment of a blockade automatically includes the authority for the imposing power to use force to stop the movement of all maritime traffic into and out of a blockaded area. Thus, while maritime blockade may share a combination of characteristics with other forms of maritime interdiction, it differs from them in that at its core it is a purely military operation designed to cut a state off from all maritime commerce. It is a violation of

---

[37] Although governments cannot impose financial penalties against foreign persons for evading sanctions regimes, they are free to pass legislation to punish their own citizens and/or corporations that do. For example, US persons or companies violating the trade embargo or sanctions against Iran are liable to criminal penalties including monetary fines up to $1 million, freezing and/or seizure of assets, and imprisonment of up to twenty years. See US Department of the Treasury, 'An overview of O.F.A.C. Regulations involving Sanctions against Iran' <http://www.cfr.org/iran/overview-ofc-regulations-involving-sanctions-against-iran/p13029> accessed 13 May 2017.

[38] In the case of sanctions passed by the UNSC acting under Chapter VII of the UN Charter, the UNSC may impose a complete restriction against maritime trade and traffic, authorizing participating states to take 'all necessary measures' to enforce compliance. In such cases, participating forces are authorized to stop, board, search, and, where appropriate, seize vessels attempting to breach the sanctions, no matter their flag.

[39] See US Department of State, 'Proliferation Security Initiative: Statement of Interdiction Principles' <http://www.state .gov/t/isn/c27726.htm> accessed 13 May 2017. Note that PSI does not provide a separate legal basis for the boarding of vessels in international waters. Rather, the authority to conduct PSI boarding is found in the bilateral agreements that are signed by participating states. Thus, a vessel conducting boarding operations in accordance with PSI cannot conduct a boarding against a vessel flagged in a state that is not a party to the PSI regime.

[40] See, for example, HM Treasury Office of Financial Sanctions Implementation: Monetary Penalties for Financial Sanctions Breaches Guidance. UK Government < https://www.gov.uk/government/uploads/system/uploads/attachment_data/file/637102/Monetary_penalties_for_breaches_of_financial_sanctions.pdf.> accessed 13 May 2017.

Table 1.1 A comparison of the principal types of maritime interdiction operations

	Blockade	Embargo/Sanctions	Law of Contraband
Purpose	1. To interdict any seaborne activity that may provide assistance to the military of the blockaded state. 2. To cause damage to the enemy's economy with the intent of compromising its war effort.	To use economic pressure to persuade a state to change its policies or conduct.	To stop items that are susceptible for military use from reaching an enemy.
Legal regime and authority for action	Armed conflict—Blockades are belligerent actions aimed at interdicting all maritime traffic, irrespective of its cargo.	Peace—Each embargo is subject to enabling legislation, bilateral agreement, Security Council Resolutions, etc.	Armed conflict—the Law of Contraband is a justification for interdiction of prohibited goods carried on vessels that are destined for enemy ports during periods of armed conflict.
Enforced by	Belligerent naval assets.	Government vessels/officials of state(s) participating in the sanctions regime.	Belligerent naval assets.
Enforced against	All vessels and cargoes, whether contraband or not, destined to or departing from blockaded ports.	Vessels carrying embargoed goods to or from sanctioned ports as specified by enabling legislation, international agreement, or UNSC resolution, etc. In case of national/regional sanctions, government vessels may only conduct visit and search against own state flagged vessels, or others according to agreement with flag state.	Neutral vessels carrying items of a military nature that are destined for the enemy of the belligerent.
Penalty for breach	Condemnation of vessel and cargo. Vessels and/or cargo may be brought before a prize court in the seizing state.	Dependent upon enabling legislation, UNSC Resolution, etc. Generally, vessels are turned back.	Vessels and/or cargo are seized and brought before a prize court in the seizing state.

the right of freedom of the seas, but one is permitted to be conducted during armed conflict under the *lex specialis* of IHL.

Having considered the discussion above, for the purposes of this book, the following definition of Blockade will be used:

Maritime Blockade is a method of warfare by which a belligerent party or parties to an armed conflict seek to prevent all unauthorized vessels and aircraft (enemy, neutral and friendly) from entering or exiting specified ports, airfields, or coastal areas belonging to, occupied by, or under the control of an opposing force or forces.

2

Maritime Neutrality Law

> War without neutrals has not been recorded in the history of mankind. Wars accompanied by violations of neutrality, on the part of either belligerents or neutrals, are the only wars fought to date.[1]

Insofar as the objective of a maritime blockade is to block all maritime traffic from entering or exiting a blockaded area, it affects the rights of neutrals more so than does any other form of maritime warfare. Consequently, in order to properly understand blockade law, some familiarity with the law of neutrality and how it applies in the maritime domain during armed conflict is required.

Neutrality is the legal framework that regulates the relationships between states that are 'engaged in armed conflict and those that are not participating in that conflict'.[2] Operational only in times of armed conflict, it is a temporal relationship characterized by impartiality between third states and the belligerents to the conflict.[3] The fundamental aspect of neutrality is that it provides explicit recognition under international law that so long as neutrals respect and adhere to the general principles of neutrality, and do not engage in activities that are harmful to one or more of the parties to the conflict, they generally remain subject to peacetime rules governing international relations and trade. That is to say, they are entitled to continue friendly relations with all states, with the exception that their relations with belligerents must be adapted to comply with the rights and duties imposed by the law of neutrality.

During an armed conflict belligerents are obligated to respect the status of neutrals. To this end, belligerents may not conduct military activities, including the transportation of weapons and personnel through neutral territory, nor engage in military operations in neutral territorial waters, or otherwise attempt to gain advantage through interference with neutral states' rights and obligations.[4] In return, and in order to preserve their status, neutral states must not engage in any

---

[1] George Politakis, *Modern Aspects of the Laws of Naval Warfare and Maritime Neutrality* (Keegan Paul International, 1998) 345 (hereafter Politakis, *Modern Aspects*).

[2] UK Ministry of Defence, *The Manual of the Law of Armed Conflict* (Oxford University Press, 2004) 19 (hereafter *UK Manual*).

[3] Hersch Lauterpacht, *International Law: Volume 5, Disputes, War and Neutrality, Parts IX–XIV* (Cambridge University Press, 2004) 648 (hereafter Lauterpacht, *International Law*).

[4] The laws of neutrality that emerged from customary law in the nineteenth century were codified in several of the Hague Conventions of 1907, including; No III, Convention Relative to the Opening

activity that will provide a military advantage to one belligerent over another. Correspondingly, neutrals have the duty to prevent the use of their territories as places of sanctuary or as bases of operations by belligerent forces of any side.[5] This corresponding set of rights and duties is the central foundation of the law of neutrality. In return for abiding by the laws of neutrality, neutral vessels are permitted to exercise freedom of movement and operation on the high seas without hindrance from belligerent warships, so long as the neutral vessels are not carrying contraband, attempting to breach a blockade, or engaging in some other form of un-neutral act.[6]

The Development of Modern Maritime Neutrality Laws

While the basic principles of freedom of the seas during peacetime have been in existence for millennia, the rights of neutrals to engage in maritime trade with one or more belligerent parties to a conflict remained largely unsettled until the middle of the nineteenth century.[7] Created in response to the emerging importance of maritime commerce to the world's economies in the 1700s and 1800s, the principles and laws of maritime neutrality were developed to address the conflicting interests between neutral states that 'insist[ed] upon continued freedom of commerce for [their] subjects despite the existence of war, and the [desire] of . . . belligerent[s] to prevent neutral subjects from affording assistance to the military effort of an enemy'.[8]

The genesis of contemporary maritime neutrality law can be traced to Empress Catherine II of Russia and her Declaration of Armed Neutrality in 1780,[9] which was created in reaction to confrontational British policies and practices towards neutral shipping in European waters. At the time, England, which was engaged

---

of Hostilities (requiring notice to neutrals of a state of war); No V, Convention Respecting Rights and Duties of Neutral Powers and Persons in Case of War on Land; No VI, Convention Relating to the Status of Enemy Merchant Ships at the Outbreak of Hostilities; No VII, Convention Relating to the Conversion of Merchant Ships into War-Ships; No XI, Convention Relative to Certain Restrictions with Regard to the Exercise of the Right of Capture in Naval War; and No XIII, Convention Concerning the Rights and Duties of Neutral Powers in Naval War. Hague Conventions, 18 October 1907, 205 Cons TS 395 (entered into force 26 January 1910). (Please note that subsequent references to the Hague Conventions will provide the Convention number only, for example, Hague XIII.)

[5] Hague XIII (n 4) art 5.

[6] Committee on Maritime Neutrality, 'Final Report: Helsinki Principles on Maritime Neutrality: Report of the 68th Taipei, Taiwan Conference, 24–30 May 1998' in Dietrich Schindler and Jiri Toman (eds), *The Laws of Armed Conflicts: A Collection of Conventions, Resolutions, and Other Documents*, 4th rev edn (Martinus Nijhoff, 2004) 1425–30, art 5.1.2 (hereafter Helsinki Principles).

[7] See Paris Declaration Respecting Maritime Law—1856 (adopted 16 April 1856), Martens, Nouveau Receuil Général, 1st ser, vol XV, UK, HC, c. in *Sessional Papers*, vol 66 (1856) (hereafter Paris Declaration).

[8] Robert W. Tucker, *The Law of War and Neutrality at Sea* (United States Government Printing Office 1957) 182 (hereafter Tucker, *Neutrality*).

[9] James Brown Scott, *The Armed Neutralities of 1780 and 1800: A Collection of Official Documents Preceded by the Views of Representative Publicists* (Oxford University Press, 1918) 273 (hereafter Scott, *Armed Neutralities*).

in war against several European powers, 'claimed the right to capture enemy property of every kind on the high seas, wherever it was seized, and whatever the nationality of the ships carrying it—enemy or neutral'.[10] The British policy, which was affirmed in the declaration of war against France on 17 March 1778, and through several subsequent Orders in Council, authorized the Royal Navy to intercept and seize all goods destined for the enemy, wherever such goods were found. The broad application of the policy brought England into disagreement with the Russian Empress who was displeased that neutral Russian merchant vessels and goods destined for France and Spain were being captured by the Royal Navy and British privateers. In her Declaration of Armed Neutrality, Catherine decreed the following:

1. That neutral vessels may navigate freely from port to port and along the coasts of nations at war;

2. That the effects belonging to subjects of the said powers at war shall be free on board neutral vessels, with the exception of contraband merchandise;

3. That as to the specification of the above mentioned merchandise, the Empress holds to what is enumerated in the 10th and 11th articles of her treaty of commerce[11] with Great Britain, extending her obligations to all the powers at war;

4. That to determine what constitutes a blockaded port, this designation shall only apply to a port where the attacking power has stationed vessels sufficiently near and in such a way as to render access thereto clearly dangerous; and

---

[10] George I. Phillips, 'The Declaration of Paris: 1856' (1918) 34 LQ Rev 63, 63 (hereafter Phillips, 'Declaration of Paris').

[11] See Scott, *Armed Neutralities* (n 9) 329. Articles 10 and 11 of the Anglo-Russian Treaty of 1766 provided the following:

Article 10
The subjects of the two high contracting Parties shall be,liberty to go, come, and trade freely with the states, with which one or other of the parties shall,this or,any future period be engaged in war, provided they do not carry warlike stores to the enemy. This liberty, however, not to extend to places actually blocked up, or besieged, either by sea or land.,all other times, and with the single exception of warlike stores, the aforesaid subjects may transport to these places all sorts of merchandise, as well as passengers, without the least impediment. In the searching of merchant ships, men of war and privateers shall behave as favorably, as a state of actual war can possibly permit towards the most friendly neutral Powers, observing, as far as may be, the principles and maxims of the law of nations, that are generally acknowledged.

Article 11
All cannon, mortars, firearms, pistols, bombs, grenades, bullets, balls, fuses, flint, stones, matches, powder, saltpeter, sulphur, breastplates, pikes, swords, belts, cartouch-bags, saddles and bridles, beyond the quantity that may be necessary for the use of the ship, or beyond what every man serving on board the ship, and every passenger ought to have, shall be accounted ammunition or warlike stores, and if found shall be confiscated according to law, as contraband goods, or prohibited effects, but neither the ships nor passengers, nor the other merchandises found,the same time, shall be detained or hindered from prosecuting their voyage.

    5. That these principles shall serve as a rule for proceedings and judgements as to the legality of prizes.[12]

Despite British diplomatic efforts to dissuade European states from joining Catherine's coalition, her efforts ultimately prevailed; by the end of 1783, Sweden, Denmark, Prussia, Portugal, the Ottoman Empire, the Holy Roman Empire, and Holland had joined the Neutral League.[13]

    Whereas Empress Catherine's first armed neutrality marked an important milestone in the initial development of neutrality laws, much credit for the evolution of neutrality law can also be accredited to Thomas Jefferson, who, as US Secretary of State, addressed the issue during the French Revolutionary War against the first coalition in 1793. At that time, the United States was neutral, and was facing French demands to permit French vessels to use its bases from which to conduct operations against British interests in North America. In a letter rejecting France's request, Jefferson outlined his government's understanding of the concept of neutrality, stating that:

… a neutral nation must, in all things relating to the war, observe and enact impartiality towards the parties; that favours to one to the prejudice of the other would import a fraudulent neutrality, of which no nation would be the dupe; that no succour should be given to either unless stipulated by treaty, in money, arms, or anything else directly serving favour … that if the U. S. have a right to refuse the permission to arm vessels and raise men within their ports and territories, they are bound by the laws of neutrality to exercise that right, and to prohibit such armaments and enlistments; … we hold it certain that the law of nations and the rules of neutrality forbid our permitting either party to arm in our ports.[14]

Notwithstanding the progress made through the League of Armed Neutrality and Jefferson's decree, the lack of consensus respecting the scope of the law of neutrality continued to be a major source of disagreement between the powers of Europe.[15] The creation of an alliance between Britain and France during the Crimean War in 1853 was a turning point in maritime neutrality law. In that conflict, Britain and France joined forces against Russia, cooperating in hostile and the exercise of belligerent rights over private property at sea.[16] Realizing that they could not operate as allies in the face of their divergent policies, the British and French sought

---

    [12] Ibid, 273.

    [13] The signatories to the first League of Armed Neutrality agreed to protect neutral shipping and commerce from interference by parties to the conflict, that is; Spain, France and Britain. See Scott, *Armed Neutralities* (n 9) 255–6, 340–1, 381–4.

    [14] Paul Leicester Ford, *The Works of Thomas Jefferson*, federal edn, vol 7 (G.P. Putnam's Sons, 1905) 804. For further information on US neutrality during the Anglo-France War see *Proclamation 4— Neutrality of the United States in the War Involving Austria, Prussia, Sardinia, Great Britain, and the United Netherlands Against France April 22, 1793*. The Presidency Project <http://www.presidency. ucsb.edu/ws/index.php?pid=65475&st=&st1=> accessed 13 May 2017 (hereafter Proclamation of Neutrality 1793).

    [15] For a particularly good overview of the diplomatic rivalries surrounding neutrality at sea in the eighteenth century, see Richard Pares, *Colonial Blockade and Neutral Rights 1739–1763* (Clarendon Press, 1938) especially Chapter 4 (hereafter Pares, *Colonial Blockade*).

    [16] H.W. Malkin, 'The Inner History of the Declaration of Paris' (1927) 8 BYIL 1, 13.

consensus on the points of neutral goods and neutral vessels.[17] Likely influenced by the Swedish and Norwegian proclamations of Neutrality on 2 January 1854,[18] the improbable allies issued a proclamation to neutral sates on 28 March 1854, which read in part:

To preserve the commerce of neutrals from all unnecessary obstruction, [the Allies are] willing, for the present, to waive a part of the belligerent rights appertaining to [them] by the law of nations ... [The Allies] will waive the right of seizing enemy's property laden on board a neutral vessel, unless it be contraband of war ... It is not [our] intention to claim the confiscation of neutral property, not being contraband of war, found on board enemy's ships; and [we] further declare, that being anxious to lessen as much as possible the evils of war, and to restrict its operations to the regularly organized forces of the country, it is not [our] present intention to issue letters of marquee for the commissioning of privateers.[19]

The importance of the Anglo-French proclamation of 1854 to the development of maritime neutrality law cannot be overstated; for the first time in history, the two largest naval powers in Europe expressed their intention to respect the concept of 'free ships, free goods'. This fundamental change in policy, which reversed several hundred years of practice, served as an impetus for the great powers to codify principles of neutrality as part of the Paris peace conference. The resulting Paris Declaration of 1856[20] provided, in part, that:

...
2. The neutral flag covers enemy's goods, with the exception of contraband of war; and
3. Neutral goods, with the exception of contraband of war, are not liable to capture under enemy's flag; ...[21]

---

[17] Prior to 1853, the British policy was that enemy goods on a neutral ship could be captured but that neutral goods on an enemy ship would be released, whereas the French would seize neutral goods on an enemy ship but would not capture enemy goods on a neutral vessel. In other words the French test for seizure of goods was based on the nationality of the ship, while the British test was focused on the nationality of the goods.

[18] On 2 January 1854, Sweden, which was allied with Denmark and Norway, addressed identical communications to the actual and possible belligerents. See Charles H. Stockton, 'The Declaration of Paris' (1920) 14:3 AJIL 356, 357 (hereafter Stockton, 'Declaration of Paris').

[19] Foreign Office, *British and Foreign State Papers, Vol. 46* (William Ridgway, 1856) 48. The UK proclamation was supported by the 'British Order in Council in Furtherance of Her Majesty's Declaration of March 28, 1854, Respecting the Trade of Neutrals and British Subjects—April 15, 1854'.

[20] Paris Declaration (n 7).

[21] Ibid. As the ICRC points out, 'On the conclusion of the Treaty of Paris on 30 March 1856 which ended the Crimean War (1853–56), the Plenipotentiaries also signed the present Declaration. It is the outcome of a modus vivendi which was adopted between France and the United Kingdom in 1854 and was originally intended for the Crimean War. Both Powers recognized that they would not seize enemy goods on neutral vessels nor neutral goods on enemy vessels. The belligerents furthermore proclaimed that they would not issue letters of marque. The Declaration of Paris confirmed these rules and added to them the principle that blockades, in order to be binding, must be effective. Virtually all of the major maritime states acceded to the Declaration.' Countries such as Spain and the United States did not become party to the declaration because they argued that the property rights of neutrals were inviolable. The United States, however, declared in 1861 that it would abide by the principles of the Declaration, and continues to do so. See ICRC, 'Declaration Respecting Maritime Law. Paris, 16 April 1856' <http://www.icrc.org/ihl.nsf/INTRO/105> accessed 13 May 2017.

The Paris Declaration was a ground-breaking initiative in numerous respects. Ultimately ratified or acceded to by fifty-five states,[22] it represented the first time in history that nations convened in peacetime to create a multilateral treaty to regulate warfare. In this respect, it was a catalyst for the codification of the laws of war, a process that continues to the present day.[23] With the intention of making 'things during a state of war as easy and as little disturbing as possible to neutrals engaged in *bona fide* neutral trade',[24] the Paris Declaration's primary accomplishment was the affirmation of the general right of neutrals to engage freely in commerce without the threat of seizure of their property by belligerents, so long as the neutrals refrained from engaging in the carriage of contraband.

While the concept of 'free ships, free goods' was set out in the Paris Declaration, there remained significant disagreement as to what obligations neutral states must abide by in order to claim and retain neutral status. Although no international consensus was forthcoming in the middle of the century, the issues respecting the rights and responsibilities were addressed in the bilateral Treaty of Washington of 1871.[25] The Treaty's framework included instructions for neutral governments in article VI, which stated that:

A neutral Government is bound—

First: —To use due diligence to prevent the fitting out, arming or equipping, within its jurisdiction, of any vessel which it has reasonable ground to believe is intended to cruise or to carry on war against a Power with which it is at peace; and also to use like diligence to prevent the departure from its jurisdiction of any vessel intended to cruise or carry on war as above, such vessel having been specially adapted, in whole or in part, within such jurisdiction, to warlike use.

Secondly: —Not to permit or suffer either belligerent to make use of its ports or waters as the base of naval operations against the other, or for the purpose of the renewal or augmentation of military supplies or arms, within such jurisdiction, to warlike use.

Thirdly: —To exercise due diligence in its own ports and waters, and, as to all persons within its jurisdiction, to prevent any violation of the foregoing obligations and duties.[26]

Although the Washington Treaty was a bilateral pact, binding only the United States and Great Britain, it made a substantial contribution to the development

---

[22] ICRC, 'Treaties and States Parties to Such Treaties: Declaration Respecting Maritime Law, Paris, 16 April 1856' <http://www.icrc.org/applic/ihl/ihl.nsf/states.xsp?xp_viewstates=XPages_NORMstatesParties&xp_treatySelected=105> accessed 13 May 2017.

[23] The Declaration of Paris signified a quantum shift in international relations and the laws of war. It signified the first time that states, without being influenced by ongoing hostilities, agreed to terms that could affect long-held rights during hostilities. It served as a catalyst and model for subsequent law of armed conflict treaties, including the Convention for the Amelioration of the Condition of the Wounded in Armies in the Field (1864) (First Geneva Convention), the Declaration Renouncing the Use, in Time of War, of Explosive Projectiles Under 400 Grammes Weight (1868) (St Petersburg Declaration), and the Final Acts of the 1899 and the 1907 Hague Peace Conferences.

[24] Phillips, 'Declaration of Paris' (n 10) 64.

[25] United Kingdom and the United States of America, Treaty for an Amicable Settlement of all Causes of Differences Between the United States and Great Britain (8 May 1871) 17St, 863, USTS 133 (hereafter the Treaty of Washington).

[26] Ibid.

to maritime neutrality law by setting out in writing the generally accepted rules of neutrality.

Hague XIII

The primary concepts set out in the Washington Treaty provided the basis for the development of Hague Convention (XIII) Concerning the Rights and Duties of Neutral Powers in Naval War—1907.[27] Hague XIII was but one of the conventions created during the 1907 Peace Conference, a forum that had the optimistic goal of achieving consensus on arms limitation and an established system of arbitration that would replace war.[28] Although these principal objectives were not realized, the 1907 Peace Conference did reach agreement on numerous matters relating to the law of naval warfare and maritime neutrality, most aspects of which are contemporarily regarded as declaratory of the rules of international law.

Hague XIII marked a significant advancement in the law of neutrality, not only for its affirmation of neutral rights, but also for establishing the parameters within which belligerents and neutrals must conduct their affairs vis a vis one another. Most specifically, it set out the following duties and obligations for neutral states:

1. impartiality;
2. abstention from providing any form of assistance to a belligerent that would assist it in the prosecution of war;
3. restrictions on the use of neutral ports and territorial seas;[29] and
4. obligations of the neutral party to 'prevent any violation of the provisions of the above Articles occurring in its ports or roadsteads or in its waters'.[30]

Neutral Trade

Some people are aghast that neutrals went on trading with the enemy during both world wars. That is explicitly allowed, however, by the Hague rules. The only restrictions they impose are (1) that the neutral state, as distinguished from private merchants of death, may not sell munitions to the belligerents, (2) that whatever restrictions on trade are imposed are even handed as between the warring states.[31]

---

[27] Hague XIII (n 4) art 7. The provisions outlining rights and obligations of neutrals, as spelled out in Hague XIII, remain unchanged to this date.

[28] Lydia de Beer (ed), *The Hague Conventions: A Compilation of Documents* (Wolf Legal Publishers, 2011) 103.

[29] Hague XIII (n 4) arts 1–24.   [30] Ibid, art 25.

[31] Detlev F. Vagts, 'The Traditional Legal Concept of Neutrality in a Changing Environment' (1998) 14 American International University Law Review 83, 93.

The requirement for a neutral state to treat the belligerents with impartiality and to abstain from assisting either belligerent in the prosecution of a conflict is a fundamental principle of neutrality law. It follows, therefore, that a neutral state must not provide weapons, warships, aircraft, ammunition, or other war materials either directly or indirectly to a belligerent power. Although there is a ban on state-to-state assistance, there are no corresponding restrictions on trade between neutral corporations and belligerents. The right of neutral businesses to continue free trade with belligerents is reflected in both Hague V[32] and Hague XIII,[33] which specifically state that:

A neutral power is not bound to prevent the export or transport, on behalf of one or other of the belligerents, of arms, munitions of war, or, in general, of anything which can be of use to an army or a fleet.[34]

While it is now accepted that the trading activities of private neutral merchants do not alter the status of the neutral state vis a vis the belligerents, such was not always the case. The development of this concept did not occur until the late eighteenth century, and was largely influenced by the United States,[35] which championed the cause of private merchants, manufacturers, and traders by advocating that its merchants should be permitted to continue friendly relations with belligerent parties to an armed conflict in which the United States was not involved. The notion that the activities of nations could be separated from those of their nationals was not universally accepted. In the eyes of many, particularly the British, the concept of neutral commerce was considered to be a Franco-American initiative that had 'made an honest doctrine of neutrality impossible'.[36]

As the concept of neutral commerce was emerging, there was a growing consensus that 'if the neutrals had a right to a free exercise of their ordinary commerce, the belligerents were equally entitled to defend themselves against the damage which might arise'.[37] The acknowledgement that there were limitations on neutral commercial rights was incorporated into international law in the Declaration of Paris of 1856[38] which provided, at article 3, that 'Neutral goods, *with the exception of contraband of war*, are not liable to capture under enemy's flag'.[39]

The corollary to article 3 of the Declaration of Paris was that belligerent vessels had a right to interdict neutral vessels that were engaged in carrying contraband, and that neutral states undertaking trade with belligerents were required

---

[32] Hague V (n 4).   [33] Hague XIII (n 4).

[34] Note that Hague XIII, art 7 uses the word 'bound' in place of the Hague V, art 7 words 'called upon'.

[35] Christine Sternberg Patrick and John C. Pinheiro (eds), *The Papers of George Washington, Presidential Series, vol. 12, 16 January 1793–31 May 1793* (University of Virginia Press, 2005) 472–4.

[36] J.E.G. De Montmorency, 'The Principles Underlying Contraband and Blockade' (1916) 2 Problems of the War 21.

[37] Pares, *Colonial Blockade* (n 15) 240. Maddison's 'Memoire Containing a Review of the British Doctrine Which Subjects to Capture a Neutral Trade Not Open in Time of Peace', written in 1806, provides an excellent overview of the principal philosophies surrounding neutral trade.

[38] Paris Declaration (n 7) art 2.   [39] Ibid, art 3 (author's emphasis).

to acquiesce to such interdiction. Guidance for the capture of neutral vessels was included in the Declaration of London[40] as follows:

A vessel carrying goods liable to capture as absolute or conditional contraband may be captured on the high seas or in the territorial waters of the belligerents throughout the whole of her voyage...[41]

The contraband system, as set out in the Declaration of London, established that the liability of capture of a neutral vessel destined for enemy ports was dependent not upon the character of the vessel per se, but rather on the category of goods it was carrying.[42] That is to say, so long as goods destined for an enemy port were not 'liable to capture as absolute or conditional contraband',[43] those goods, and the neutral vessels carrying them, should not be subject to seizure, except in situations of blockade.

In spite of the advances made in maritime neutrality law during the late nineteenth and early twentieth centuries, the laws of neutrality were largely ignored during the world wars, both by belligerents[44] and neutrals alike.[45] Irrespective of the disregard displayed towards neutrality during the two wars, nations have continued to support and advocate for the existence of maritime neutrality laws.

Modern Principles of Maritime Neutrality

The cornerstone for the modern law of maritime neutrality is found in Hague Convention XIII, which, more than a century after its inception, continues to be the principal treaty governing the rights and obligations of neutrals during international armed conflict. While Hague XIII contains some twenty-six rules, Professor Robert Tucker is widely credited for having condensed those rules into four fundamental principles; impartiality, abstention, prevention, and acquiescence.[46]

---

[40] London Declaration Concerning the Laws of Naval War (1909) 208 Consol TS 338 (not entered into force) (hereafter Declaration of London).

[41] Ibid, art 37.

[42] Ibid, arts 22–44 'Contraband of War'. Note that the items listed as contraband in the Declaration of London reflect the tools of warfare of the early twentieth century. While a modern list would likely exclude many of the items listed in the Declaration and include more modern weapons, the overall concept remains the same. Contraband consists of materials that are useful to a belligerent in war.

[43] Ibid, art 3.

[44] The development of unrestricted submarine warfare by the German Navy, particularly after 1 February 1917, signified a blatant disregard for the rights of neutral traders.

[45] The United States' support of the United Kingdom through the 'Lend-lease Program' and 'Destroyers for Bases Program' between 1939 and its entry into the war in December 1941 is generally seen as a flagrant violation of the United States' obligations under neutrality law.

[46] Tucker, *Neutrality* (n 8) 202, fn 14.

Impartiality

The positive duty of impartiality, as laid out in the preamble to Hague XIII,[47] is intrinsically intertwined with that of abstention. Simply stated, the principle of impartiality requires that a neutral state must show no favour or discrimination in its relations with the belligerents. In accordance with this principle, neutral governments are required not only to 'apply impartially to the two belligerents the conditions, restrictions, or prohibitions made by it in regard to the admission into its ports, roadsteads, or territorial waters, of belligerent war-ships or of their prizes',[48] but any other privileges or restrictions as well.

The essence of impartiality is equal treatment, but not necessarily equal effects. As Tucker notes, 'It is entirely possible—and in many instances almost inevitable—that the strict fulfillment by a neutral of its obligations will result in the greater discomfort and disadvantage of one side in a war'.[49] Hence, a nation can maintain its neutrality even while engaging in activity that, although equal in application, causes more harm to one side than the other.

As is the case with the duty to abstain from supplying goods and services to the belligerents, the duty of impartiality applies only to acts that can be attributed to the neutral state, and not to the private acts of its subjects.[50] As a general rule, private individuals remain free to engage in whatever activity that they may wish,[51] so long as those activities do not fall within the prohibitions provided in Hague V and/or Hague XIII. Having said that, however, state practice since the adoption of Hague Conventions has modified this approach somewhat.

Over the past century, the separation of states from private armaments industries within their borders has largely disappeared. Contemporary international arms trade is usually heavily regulated and controlled by states, and the various conventions to which they have become party. Insofar as corporations normally may not export arms or weapons to other states without their home state's authority, it is now generally accepted that a state that grants permission to supply any sort of war materials to one of the belligerents to a conflict is engaging in non-neutral activity.

---

[47] The preamble to Hague XIII (n 4) provides, in part, that 'it is, for neutral powers, an admitted duty to apply these rules impartially to several belligerents'.

[48] Hague XIII (n 4) art 9.

[49] Tucker, *Neutrality* (n 8) 204. For example, an oil-rich neutral nation may prohibit oil exports to both belligerents. In the case where one of the belligerents is self-sufficient in oil and the other is not, the duty of impartiality will be fulfilled, even though its effect will not be equal.

[50] Ibid, 206.

[51] In accordance with Hague V (n 4), citizens of a neutral country may cross the frontier individually to offer their services to one of the belligerents without jeopardizing the neutrality of the sending state, so long as the sending state has not permitted the belligerent to recruit or establish formed units in the neutral's territory.

Abstention

The duty of abstention dictates that a neutral party must not provide any of the belligerents with goods or services that may assist either directly or indirectly in the war effort. In terms of maritime neutrality, 'the supply, in any manner, ... of war-ships, ammunition, or war material of any kind whatever, is forbidden'.[52] As has been noted, and as reflected in Hague XIII, article 7, a neutral government's obligation of abstention applies only to the activities, goods, and services over which the government has control. Hyde interprets the obligation to abstain broadly to include such activities as 'the loaning of money, or the extension of credit, or ... placing ... various government agencies at the disposal of a belligerent in such a way as to aid it directly or indirectly in the prosecution of the war'.[53]

Prevention

Hague XIII states that in order to maintain neutrality, neutral states must prevent three specific activities from occurring within their jurisdiction or in areas over which they exercise control. They must:

1. take measures to prevent fitting out or arming of vessels which a government believes are intended for belligerent use;
2. take similar measures to prevent the departure of vessels intended for belligerent use, if the vessels have been locally adapted to warlike use;[54] and
3. restrict the use of neutral territorial waters, ports and roadsteads.[55]

The duty of prevention stands as an exception to the notion that a neutral government need not concern itself with the commercial activities of is citizenry vis a vis the belligerents. The most apparent of the duties of prevention is that of preventing vessels from being built or armed for delivery, either directly or indirectly, to a belligerent.[56] This restriction is limited in its scope, in that it does not extend beyond the fitting out and supplying of armed vessels.

---

[52] Hague XIII (n 4) art 6.
[53] Charles Cheney Hyde, *International Law, Chiefly as Interpreted and Applied by the United States*, vol 3, 2nd edn (Little, Brown and Company, 1922) 2231 (hereafter Hyde, *International Law*).
[54] Herbert W. Briggs, 'Neglected Aspects of the Destroyer Deal' (1940) 34:4 AJIL 569, 577.
[55] Hague XIII (n 4) arts 12–25.
[56] One of the earliest adjudicated cases of violation of neutrality occurred during the American Civil War as a result of the British failure to prevent armed vessels from being built by private interests in the United Kingdom and delivered through intermediaries to the Confederate Navy. The ALABAMA, which was the most infamous of the vessels, is credited with having destroyed sixty-four ships during the twenty-two months that it served before being sunk off Cherbourg in 1864. The British, who had declared neutrality in the US Civil War on 14 May 1861, denied any responsibility for the vessels, stating that they had not been outfitted with arms in Britain. The case went to arbitration as part of the Treaty of Washington. On 14 October 1872, the arbitration was settled and the United Kingdom was ordered to compensate the United States in the amount of £15.5 million. The decision of the Geneva Arbitration was ultimately codified in Hague XIII, article 9. See J.C. Bancroft Davis, 'Geneva Arbitration' in John J.

In addition to the requirements to prevent vessels from being supplied to belligerent forces, a neutral government must prevent its waters, ports, and roadsteads from being misused by belligerent war-ships.[57] To that end, the neutral is required to ensure that a belligerent does not conduct operations in its waters,[58] does not replenish arms or ammunition in its ports,[59] does not, other than in exceptional circumstances, remain in port for more than twenty-four hours,[60] or conduct repairs beyond the minimum required to make their vessels seaworthy.[61] Furthermore, a belligerent vessel refuelling in a neutral port may only take on enough fuel to reach the nearest port in its own country.[62]

Acquiescence

Concomitant with the right of neutral merchants to engage in trade is the right of belligerents to stop war materials from reaching their foes. While neutral merchants are not prohibited from engaging trade with belligerents, they do so at their own peril, with the risk that their cargo and/or vessels may be seized. To that end, in non-neutral waters belligerents are permitted to stop neutral vessels to verify their cargo and destination,[63] and the neutral state is obliged to permit such interdiction to occur.[64]

Lalor (ed). *Cyclopædia of Political Science, Political Economy, and the Political History of the United States* (Maynard, Merrill & Co. 1899). Library of Economics and Liberty <http://www.econlib.org/library/YPDBooks/Lalor/llCy497.html> accessed 9 October 2017. See also Tom Bingham, 'The Alabama Claims Arbitration' (2005) 54:1 International and Comparative Law Quarterly 1.

[57] Hague XIII (n 4) art 9. A neutral Power must apply impartially to the two belligerents the conditions, restrictions, or prohibitions made by it in regard to the admission into its ports, roadsteads, or territorial waters, of belligerent war-ships or of their prizes. Nevertheless, a neutral Power may forbid a belligerent vessel that has failed to conform to the orders and regulations made by it, or which has violated neutrality, to enter its ports or roadsteads.

[58] Hague XIII (n 4) art 2.   [59] Ibid, art 18.   [60] Ibid, art 12.   [61] Ibid, art 17.

[62] Ibid, art 19. The case of the GRAF SPEE, a German battleship during the Second World War, is of interest. The GRAF SPEE, which had engaged in battle against three British cruisers, entered the waters of neutral Montevideo in order to have repairs done. Knowing that by the dictates of Hague XIII the ship would either have to leave the neutral port as soon as she was made seaworthy, or be interred for the remainder of the war, the Royal Navy vessels waited just outside of Montividean waters for the GRAF SPEE. Not wanting to sacrifice his crew to what he perceived to be certain death, the hand of the Royal Navy's cruisers, and not wanting to surrender his ship to British-friendly Montevideo, the Captain of the vessel scuttled the ship just outside of the port. See 'GRAF SPEE' online: Encyclopaedia Britannica <http://www.britannica.com/EBchecked/topic/240653/Graf-Spee> accessed 9 October 2017.

[63] See 'Award of the Arbitral Tribunal of the Permanent Court of Arbitration,the Hague in the Case of the French Mail Steamer "Carthage"' (1913) 7:3 AJIL 623–9.

[64] Tucker, *Neutrality* (n 8) 253. Note that while neutral merchant vessels are generally obligated to obey belligerent orders in order to maintain neutral status, enemy merchant vessels do not have any obligation to obey belligerent orders. Rather, enemy merchant vessels, their cargoes, and crews are generally subject to capture at all times anywhere outside of neutral waters. See also Louise Doswald-Beck (ed), *San Remo Manual on International Law Applicable to Armed Conflicts at Sea* (Cambridge University Press, 1995) (hereafter SRM).

Neutrality in the Twenty-first Century

In the years immediately following the Second World War, the concept of neutrality was considered by many to be obsolete. This position was founded on the premise that when the Security Council passes a resolution that calls upon all member states to take action under a Chapter VII resolution, 'Member states no longer possess, in principle, the freedom either to refrain from actively participating in a war that has taken on the character of a United Nations enforcement action, or—should they not be called upon by the Security Council to take military measures—to observe the duty of impartiality as laid down by the traditional law'.[65] The theory behind this position is that under a UN Security Council resolution that calls for 'all reasonable measures' to be taken to restore international peace and security, there can be only two categories of states; those that are being admonished by the Security Council, and those that form the world community upon whose behalf the Security Council is taking action.

Although it can be contended that neutrality is not relevant in the era of the Charter of the United Nations, this argument is based on the mistaken presumption that the only armed conflicts that can occur are those in which the United Nations Security Council has become seized of the matter. The reality of modern armed conflict, however, is that many conflicts are conducted outside of the ambit of the Charter, without direction or involvement of the Security Council.[66] In these cases, the traditional *jus in bello*, of which the law of neutrality is a part, applies.

In the face of globalization, and the existence of large alliances (such as NATO) in which states share resources and facilities, some have advocated for a category of 'non-belligerency'. Under this concept, states can continue to provide weaponry and indirect military assistance to one side in a conflict, all the while claiming that they are not participating in the conflict. Such 'benevolent neutrality', as Professor Heintschel von Heinegg points out, is a myth; a country is either neutral, whereby it abides by the rights and obligations of neutrality law, or it is not.[67]

The importance of strict observance of neutrality laws cannot be overstated. It is by virtue of this body of law that neutral states can continue friendly relations with both sides of the conflict. Given that many modern economies depend heavily on foreign trade, the ability of states to continue trading through conflict regions is essential to the world economy. The demise of neutrality law in favour of a vague concept such

---

[65] Tucker, *Neutrality* (n 8) 171.

[66] See *Legality of the Threat of Use of Nuclear Weapons Opinion*, Advisory Opinion [1996] ICJ Rep 226, 257 (hereafter *Nuclear Weapons Case*) where the court stated that 'as in the case of the principles of humanitarian law applicable in armed conflict, international law leaves no doubt that the principle of neutrality, whatever its content, which is of a fundamental character similar to that of the humanitarian principles and rules, is applicable (subject to the relevant provisions of the United Nations Charter), to all international armed conflict'.

[67] Wolff Heintschel von Heinegg, ' "Benevolent" Third States in International Armed Conflicts: The Myth of the Irrelevance of the Law of Neutrality' in Michael Schmitt and Jelena Pejic (eds), *International Law and Armed Conflict: Exploring the Faultlines* (Martinus Nijhoff, 2007) 543.

as 'benevolent neutrality' could create a system in which there could be degrees of neutrality. Such a development could completely subvert the existing framework and replace it with a regime that is imprecise and open to subjective interpretation. As Professor Heintschel von Heinegg has observed, 'states should … think twice before departing from the essentials of neutrality law'.[68]

---

[68] Ibid.

3

The Law of Contraband

From the earliest times the belligerent has endeavoured to shut off his opponent from outside help, and it was in accordance with such an obvious course
that Roman Emperors and Popes forbade or banned the supply by enterprising
contractors of arms and necessaries of war to barbarians or heathens.[1]

Derived from the Latin word '*contrabannum*' meaning 'against a proclamation or
declaration',[2] contraband is defined as, 'goods, [under neutral cartage], which are
ultimately destined for territory under the control of the enemy and which may be
susceptible for use in armed conflict'.[3] As is the case with the law of neutrality, the
law of contraband has application only during armed conflict, and affects only the
relationships as between neutral carriers and belligerents. In modern armed conflict
it provides the only legal basis in international law, outside of the law of blockade and
United Nations-imposed embargoes, under which a belligerent vessel may visit and
search a neutral vessel that is otherwise sailing on the high seas in compliance with the
provisions of the United Nations Convention on the Law of the Sea (UNCLOS).[4]

History of Contraband

Just as the law of neutrality recognizes that neutrals have the right to continue
commerce with states engaged in armed conflict, it has always provided belligerents the right to prevent their enemies from being supplied with the necessities of war. Hence, the law explicitly acknowledges the right of belligerents
to intercept neutral vessels and seize any materials of war that are destined for
enemy ports.[5]

---

[1] J.E.G. De Montmorency, 'The Principles Underlying Contraband and Blockade' (1916) 2
Problems of the War 25.
[2] *Funk and Wagnall's Standard Dictionary: International Edition* (Funk and Wagnalls, 1971) 283.
[3] Louise Doswald-Beck (ed), *San Remo Manual on International Law Applicable to Armed Conflicts at
Sea* (Cambridge University Press, 1995) 215 (hereafter SRM).
[4] United Nations Convention on the Law of the Sea (adopted 10 December 1982) 3163 UNTS 94
(hereafter UNCLOS).
[5] Paris Declaration Respecting Maritime Law—1856 (adopted 16 April 1856), Martens, Nouveau
Receuil Général 1st ser, vol XV, UK, HC, c. in *Sessional Papers* vol 66 (1856) para 2 (hereafter Declaration
of Paris).

The Law of Maritime Blockade: Past, Present, and Future. Phillip Drew. © Phillip Drew 2017. Published
2017 by Oxford University Press.

Throughout the history of naval warfare, neutral merchants have traded with belligerents under the threat of confiscation of their goods, irrespective of the goods' nature or purpose. Although modern rules of neutrality recognize that neutral merchants are not subject to the same restrictions as neutral governments vis à vis trading with belligerents, such has not always been the case. Indeed, until the early 1600s, trade by neutral merchants with belligerents was regularly subjected to interference not only by belligerent parties, but by their own sovereigns as well.[6]

As maritime trade grew exponentially through the seventeenth and eighteenth centuries, and the economies of many European states became increasingly dependent on maritime commerce, the wholesale interference with neutral trade that had heretofore been common was becoming no longer tenable. With this in mind, legal philosophers of the period, including Gentili, Grotius, and Vattel, set their minds to the issue. Addressing the conflict between the rights of the suspicious belligerent to ensure that the enemy was not provided with unhindered access to the necessities of war, and the rights of other states to engage freely in trade, Grotius introduced the concept of contraband to modern international law in his seminal work, *The Law of War and Peace*, in 1625.[7]

Grotius laid out a system that categorized contraband into three classes of goods, stating:

First, we must make distinctions with reference to the things supplied. There are some things, such as weapons, which are useful only in war; other things which are of no use in war, as those which minister to pleasure; and others still which are of use both in time of war and at other times, as money, provisions, ships, and naval equipment.[8]

The advent of the notion of 'classes of goods' signalled a new era in the seventeenth-century law of neutrality. This maturation of the law delineated goods under neutral cartage that would be subject to seizure by belligerents from those items that would not.

The term 'contraband' was introduced into international law in the Treaty of Southampton,[9] concluded between England and Holland in 1625, during their war against Spain. The treaty described goods that could be seized as follows:

All contraband merchandise, such as ammunition, ships, weapons, sails, ropes, gold, silver, copper, iron, lead, and the like, from wherever they may be carried, to Spain, and other lands

---

[6] For example, in 1522 Francis I of France and Archduchess Margaret of the Netherlands, in signing their treaty of neutrality, 'expressly stipulated that the neutral sovereign should himself punish those of his subjects who supplied the enemy' with prohibited goods. In other words, the early laws of neutrality made no distinction between the neutral state and the neutral merchant. See Harold Pyke, *The Law of Contraband of War* (Clarendon Press, 1915) 34, 48, and 220 (hereafter Pyke, *Contraband*).

[7] Hugo Grotius, *The Law of War and Peace, Book III*, translated by Jean Barbeyrac (The Liberty Fund Inc, 2005).

[8] Ibid, 602.

[9] Treaty of Offensive and Defensive Alliance Between the United Netherlands and Great Britain, 17 September 1625, art 20 (hereafter Treaty of Southampton).

under the control of the King of Spain and his adherents, will be of good prize, with the ships and men who will carry them.[10]

By a proclamation of the following year, 'corn, grain, victuals of all sorts, together with a number of articles enumerated as munitions of war, if destined for a Spanish port',[11] were included as contraband, falling under Grotius' category of *ancipitus usus*,[12] or, as it is commonly referred to in modern terms, 'conditional contraband'.

Although it was introduced as a form of maritime interdiction in the mid-1600s, the scope and meaning of 'contraband' remained undefined until the early twentieth century, with the result that 'the rules relating to contraband [were] to be deduced from the practice and opinion of nations as evidenced in unilateral acts by states and the decisions of their national prize courts'.[13] Consequently, the term 'contraband' was used in the Declaration of Paris in 1856 without the parties to the treaty having a common understanding as to its meaning.[14]

The matter of contraband was included as part of the agenda for the 1907 Hague peace conference; however, because of significant disagreements within the fourth committee, which was responsible for the subjects of contraband and blockade, the issue was not settled.[15] Instead, the principal naval powers agreed to consider the topic in a series of naval conferences to be held in London in 1908 and 1909.

By invitation, the ten greatest naval powers of the early twentieth century[16] were summoned to the London Naval Conference in 1908. One of the primary goals for the delegations was the development of a universal law of contraband. Although consensus had eluded the delegates to the peace conference the previous year, the participants at the London Conference were able to reach agreement on the main provisions of the law of contraband. The resulting product was the twenty-three

---

[10] Ibid (translated from original).

[11] R.G. Marsden, 'Naval or Victualling Stores: The Right of Pre-Emption' (1902) 4:1 Journal of the Society of Comparative Legislation 45, 47.

[12] 'Of Doubtful use; an article that may be used for a civil or peaceful, as well as military or war-like, purpose.' See Henry Campbell Black et al, *Black's Law Dictionary*, 6th edn (West Publishing Co, 1990) 86.

[13] Pyke, *Contraband* (n 6) 12.

[14] The Declaration of Paris (n 5), provided as follows: '3. Neutral goods, with the exception of contraband of war, are not liable to capture under enemy's flag.' There was no definition section in the Declaration, nor was there a differentiation between absolute and conditional contraband.

[15] The fourth committee was responsible for dealing with the questions of contraband and blockade. During deliberations the committee was presented with a number of options on how to deal with contraband, the most significant of which was the British suggestion that the concept of contraband should be abolished in favour of absolute protection of neutral shipping from belligerent interference. While a large majority of the delegates (26 to 5) of the fourth committee voted in favour of the British proposal, France, Russia, the United States, Germany, and Montenegro voted against it. Given the requirement for unanimity, the committee determined that it would not be able to complete its report during the time allotted. For a very good overview of the work of the committees to the second peace conference see A. Pearce Higgins, *The Hague Peace Conferences and Other International Conferences concerning the Laws and Usages of War. Texts of Conventions with Commentaries* (Cambridge University Press, 1909).

[16] The London Naval Conference, convened on 4 December 1908, was attended by Delegates from Germany, the United States of America, Austria–Hungary, Spain, France, Great Britain, Italy, Japan, the Netherlands, and Russia.

articles on contraband which formed the core of the second chapter to the London Declaration Concerning the Laws of Naval War—1909.[17]

Although the London Declaration never entered into force,[18] many of its provisions relating to contraband are recognized as being reflective of customary international law. Indeed, other than the fact that some of the items enumerated in articles 22[19] and 24[20] have been relegated as obsolete due to technological advances, the general principles outlined in chapter two remain valid, particularly with respect to the categories of absolute and conditional contraband.

[17] London Declaration Concerning the Laws of Naval War (1909) 208 Consol TS 338 (not entered into force) (hereafter Declaration of London).

[18] Ibid, art 68 provided that the Declaration would be effective only upon ratification. The British House of Lords refused to approve the declaration and thus, Great Britain did not ratify. Since Britain was the major naval power at the time, and had hosted the conference, the other signatories refused ratify as well. As a result, the declaration never came into effect.

[19] Ibid, art 22 provided that: 'The following articles may, without notice, be treated as contraband of war, under the name of absolute contraband:

    (1) Arms of all kinds, including arms for sporting purposes, and their distinctive component parts.
    (2) Projectiles, charges, and cartridges of all kinds, and their distinctive component parts.
    (3) Powder and explosives specially prepared for use in war.
    (4) Gun-mountings, limber boxes, limbers, military wagons, field forges, and their distinctive component parts.
    (5) Clothing and equipment of a distinctively military character.
    (6) All kinds of harness of a distinctively military character.
    (7) Saddle, draught, and pack animals suitable for use in war.
    (8) Articles of camp equipment, and their distinctive component parts.
    (9) Armour plates.
    (10) Warships, including boats, and their distinctive component parts of such a nature that they can only be used on a vessel of war.
    (11) Implements and apparatus designed exclusively for the manufacture of munitions of war, for the manufacture or repair of arms, or war material for use on land or sea.'

[20] Ibid, art 24 provided: 'The following articles, susceptible of use in war as well as for purposes of peace, may, without notice (*), be treated as contraband of war, under the name of conditional contraband:

    (1) Foodstuffs.
    (2) Forage and grain, suitable for feeding animals.
    (3) Clothing, fabrics for clothing, and boots and shoes, suitable for use in war.
    (4) Gold and silver in coin or bullion; paper money. (5) Vehicles of all kinds available for use in war, and their component parts.
    (6) Vessels, craft, and boats of all kinds; floating docks, parts of docks and their component parts.
    (7) Railway material, both fixed and rolling-stock, and material for telegraphs, wireless telegraphs, and telephones.
    (8) Balloons and flying machines and their distinctive component parts, together with accessories and articles recognizable as intended for use in connection with balloons and flying machines.
    (9) Fuel; lubricants.
    (10) Powder and explosives not specially prepared for use in war.
    (11) Barbed wire and implements for fixing and cutting the same.
    (12) Horseshoes and shoeing materials.
    (13) Harness and saddlery.
    (14) Field glasses, telescopes, chronometers, and all kinds of nautical instruments.'

Essentially, the categories of contraband as described by Grotius some 400 years ago, and incorporated into the Declaration of London, have endured the test of time: absolute contraband consists of those goods which by their nature, design, purpose, or use are essential war goods, such as tanks, aircraft, ships, weapons, and munitions; and, conditional contraband is comprised of those items of dual nature which, while in their primary design and use are created for peaceful purpose, may be converted for military use.

In addition to the categories of absolute and conditional contraband, the Declaration of London also created, at article 28, a class of items that were to become known as 'free goods'.[21] Included under article 28 were goods such as raw materials for textiles, fertilizers, building materials, agricultural machinery, soaps, and paint.[22] Article 29[23] specifically required that 'Articles serving exclusively to aid the sick and wounded' were not to be treated as contraband.

The Declaration of London established separate rules for the handling of the two principal categories of contraband. In accordance with article 30,[24] absolute contraband on board a neutral vessel was liable to seizure if destined for enemy or enemy-occupied territory, irrespective of whether the shipment was direct or through an intermediary. Thus, in the case of absolute contraband, the ultimate destination of the articles was determinative of liability for capture.[25] Conditional contraband, on the other hand, was only liable to capture by a belligerent if found on a vessel destined directly for enemy armed forces or a government department located in enemy or enemy-occupied territory. Under this regime, conditional contraband was not subject to the doctrine of continuous voyage.[26]

Contraband in the World Wars

At the dawn of the First World War in 1914, the major belligerent powers indicated their general intent to abide by most of the provisions of the unratified Declaration of London, specifically as they related to contraband and blockade.[27] Within

---

[21] Ibid, art 28.

[22] Ibid, art 28. Article 29 declared that medicines and medical goods were not to be treated as contraband.

[23] Ibid, art 29.

[24] Ibid, art 30 provided that 'Absolute contraband is liable to capture if it is shown to be destined to territory belonging to or occupied by the enemy, or to the armed forces of the enemy. It is immaterial whether the carriage of the goods is direct or entails transhipment or a subsequent transport by land.'

[25] As will be discussed, the concept of ultimate destination implies that the doctrine of continuous voyage applies to the goods on board a neutral vessel.

[26] See Declaration of London (n 17) art 35, which provided, 'Conditional contraband is not liable to capture, except when found on board a vessel bound for territory belonging to or occupied by the enemy, or for the armed forces of the enemy, and when it is not to be discharged in an intervening neutral port. The ship's papers are conclusive proof both as to the voyage on which the vessel is engaged and as to the port of discharge of the goods, unless she is found clearly out of the course indicated by her papers, and unable to give adequate reasons to justify such deviation.'

[27] See, for example, George R.I., Proclamation 4 August 1914 (1914) London Gazette 6163.

months of the commencement of the war, however, the rules were being modified
by the powers as they sought to isolate one another from access to foreign markets
and supplies.

The circumstances of the First World War proved a significant challenge to the
legal regimes that had been negotiated just a few years before. The emerging doctrine of total war revealed some of the underlying weaknesses of the contraband system, chief amongst which was the near impossibility of developing comprehensive
contraband lists that could remain relevant in the face of technological advances and
the complete mobilization of belligerents' economies in support of the war effort.[28]

A practical solution to the problem of contraband lists was provided by the United
States Navy in 1917, with the publication of its *Instructions for the Navy of the United
States Governing Maritime Warfare.*[29] Rather than employing the model of identifying individual items of contraband found in the Declaration of London, the 1917
Naval Instructions instead adopted a system under which contraband was identified
by the function of the item.[30] By implementing this approach the belligerents were
able to establish their contraband lists by classification of goods, making the lists
much more flexible and less likely to be rendered obsolescent by the constant technical advances that were transforming means and methods of warfare in the early
twentieth century.

As was the case at the beginning of the First World War, initial British intentions at the dawn of the Second World War were to establish classes of contraband.

---

[28] The sheer number of UK Orders in Council and Proclamations regarding contraband during the
First World War is illustrative of the impracticality of listing contraband items. Indeed, as a conflict
progresses, and it becomes increasingly evident that certain items are desperately required by an enemy,
the opposing belligerent will inevitably add such items to their lists of contraband.

[29] *Instructions for the Navy of the United States Governing Maritime Warfare: June 1917*
(Washington: Government Printing Office, 1917) (hereafter 1917 Naval Instructions).

[30] Ibid. It must be noted that para 24 of the 1917 Naval Instructions did not differentiate between
absolute and conditional contraband. Rather, the instructions established different criteria for seizure
based on class and destination of goods. Notably, foodstuffs not destined for the military were not considered contraband, as illustrated in para 24 which provided that:

> 24. The articles and materials mentioned in the following paragraphs (a), (b), (c), and (d),
> actually destined to territory belonging to or occupied by the enemy or to armed forces of
> the enemy, and the articles and materials mentioned in the following paragraph (e) actually
> destined for the use of the enemy Government or its armed forces, are, unless exempted by
> treaty, regarded as contraband.
> (a) All kinds of arms, guns, ammunition, explosives, and machines for their manufacture
>   or repair; component parts thereof; materials or ingredients used in their manufacture;
>   articles necessary or convenient for their use.
> (b) All contrivances for or means of transportation on land, in the water or air, and machines
>   used in their manufacture or repair; component parts thereof; materials or ingredients
>   used in their manufacture; instruments, articles or animals necessary or convenient for
>   their use.
> (c) All means of communication, tools, implements, instruments, equipment, maps,
>   pictures, papers and other articles, machines, or documents necessary or convenient for
>   carrying on hostile operations.
> (d) Coin, bullion, currency, evidences of debt; also metal, materials, dies, plates, machinery
>   or other articles necessary or convenient for their manufacture.
> (e) All kinds of fuel, food, foodstuffs, feed, forage, and clothing and articles and materials
>   used in their manufacture.

The British contraband list of 1939[31] was a brief but wide-ranging list delineating the categories of contraband along the lines of those set out in the paragraph 24 of the 1917 Naval Instructions.[32] German and French contraband lists were published shortly thereafter, with similar provisions, with the notable exception that the German Prize Law Code of 28 August 1939 stated that conditional contraband is not liable to capture if discharged in a neutral port, on condition of reciprocal procedure on the part of the enemy.[33]

Virtually all of the good intentions with respect to abiding by the recognized laws of contraband and neutrality disappeared quickly. As the struggle for Europe intensified, and the reliance of the belligerents upon trade for their very survival increased, the laws were stultified. Practice during the Second World War is well summarized in the following paragraph from the US Naval Commander's Handbook:

The practice of belligerents during the Second World War collapsed the traditional distinction between absolute and conditional contraband. Because of the involvement of virtually the entire population in support of the war effort, the belligerents of both sides tended to exercise governmental control over all imports. Consequently, it became increasingly difficult to draw a meaningful distinction between goods destined for an enemy government and its armed forces and goods destined for consumption by the civilian populace. As a result,

[31] George R.I., Proclamation 4 September 1939, *A Proclamation Specifying the Articles to be Treated as Contraband of War* (1939) London Gazette 6051. The 1939 British contraband list read as follows:

'Absolute Contraband
  (a) All kinds of arms, ammunition, explosives, chemicals, or appliances suitable for use in chemical warfare and machines for their manufacture or repair; component parts thereof; articles necessary or convenient for their use; materials or ingredients used in their manufacture; articles necessary or convenient for the production or use of such materials or ingredients.
  (b) Fuel of all kinds; all contrivances for, or means of, transportation on land, in the water or air, and machines used in their manufacture or repair; component parts thereof, instruments, articles, or animals necessary or convenient for their use; materials or ingredients used in their manufacture; articles necessary or convenient for the production or use of such materials or ingredients.
  (c) All means of communication, tools, implements, instruments, equipments, maps, pictures, papers and other articles, machines, or documents necessary or convenient for carrying on hostile operation; articles necessary or convenient for their manufacture or use.
  (d) Coin, bullion, currency, evidences of debt; also metal, materials, dies, plates, machinery, or other articles necessary or convenient for their manufacture.
Schedule II.

Conditional Contraband
  (e) All kinds of food, foodstuffs, feed, forage, and clothing and articles and materials used in their production.'

[32] The British contraband list in the 4 September 1939 Proclamation was not well received by neutral states. Italy, the Netherlands, and the Soviet Union were amongst those that made official representations to the British, condemning their practice. The Italian government noted, 'The measures adopted by the British Government in this field appear to be, and are, contrary to the letter and the spirit of international law, which lays down within well-defined limits the rights of belligerents in order to safeguard the interests of third states and the freedom of their legitimate trade'. See *Correspondence with the Italian Government Regarding the Exercise by His Majesty's Government in the United Kingdom of their Belligerent Rights at Sea* (1940) Cmd. 6191, 2.

[33] Robert W. Tucker, *The Law of War and Neutrality at Sea* (United States Government Printing Office, 1957) 270(n) (hereafter Tucker, *Neutrality*).

belligerents treated all imports directly or indirectly sustaining the war effort as contraband without making a distinction between absolute and conditional contraband.[34]

Modern Concepts of Contraband

The conclusion of the Second World War in 1945 did not bring an end to the law of contraband. Although often confused with the regime of sanctions and embargoes as practised under the United Nations,[35] the law of contraband remains a valid and separate aspect of the law of naval warfare.

As with most bodies of the law of armed conflict, the law of contraband has undergone significant revision during the past several decades. A review of major naval manuals reflects a movement towards collapsing all contraband into one category.[36] This trend echoes the practice followed in times of total war, such as was experienced during the world wars, when the belligerents declared so many items to be absolute contraband that any classification into categories became pointless.

In spite of the apparent post-war movement away from the classification of contraband by some of the world's naval powers, and statements in some manuals, including the San Remo Manual[37] and the *Manual on International Law applicable to Air and Missile Warfare*,[38] to the effect that the classification of contraband has become obsolete, the notion that there should be only one category of contraband is not universally accepted. Addressing the crux of the issue directly in 1952, Lauterpacht stated that 'although belligerents must be free to take into consideration the circumstances of the particular war, as long as the distinction between absolute and conditional contraband is upheld it ought not to be left altogether to their discretion to declare any articles they like to be absolute contraband'.[39] In making this statement, Lauterpacht was addressing the fundamental concern of neutral traders; that of knowing what articles may be subject to capture, and where on the oceans a cargo may or may not be seized.

---

[34] *US Naval War College Commander's Handbook on the Law of Naval Operations* (US Naval War College 2007) 7–6 (hereafter, Commander's Handbook).

[35] Much of the confusion related to contemporary operations arises from the regular use of the term 'contraband' to describe items under embargo or subject to sanctions. While the use of 'contraband' in such instances is not wrong per se, it does result in some believing that the law of contraband and the laws surrounding sanctions are one and the same.

[36] The most recent version of the USNWC Commander's Handbook and the San Remo Manual do not mention the distinction between absolute and conditional contraband. The German Commander's Handbook states (at 142) that, 'The traditional differentiation between absolute and conditional contraband ... is no longer relevant today', while the Australian Manual on the Law of Armed Conflict, whilst acknowledging the declining importance of the distinction, still distinguishes between the classifications (at 6–15).

[37] Louise Doswald-Beck (ed), SRM (n 3) 216–17.

[38] *HPCR Manual on International Law Applicable to Air and Missile Warfare* (Cambridge University Press, 2013) Rule 60 (hereafter AMW). Of note, many of the primary contributors to the SRM are also the main authors of the AMW.

[39] H. Lauterpacht, *Oppenheim's International Law*, 7th edn (Longmans Green and Co, 1952) 803 (hereafter Lauterpacht, *Oppenheim's*).

Writing more recently, Bothe argued that a 'distinction must be made between absolute and conditional contraband'.[40] While acknowledging that a state does have some discretion in determining which goods are essential for its enemy to wage war, Bothe condemns the practice of creating unnecessarily expansive lists of absolute contraband, contending that, 'Absolute contraband is goods which must by their very nature be considered as essential for war, and must be distinguished from conditional contraband'.[41] As Lauterpacht has noted, when developing a contraband list, the question that a state must honestly ask itself is, 'whether, in the special circumstances of a particular war, or considering the development of the means used in making war, the article concerned is by its character destined to be made use of for military, naval, or air-fleet purposes because it is essential to those purposes. If not, it ought not to be declared absolute contraband.'[42]

As is the case with the law of blockade, the law of contraband is governed chiefly by customary law. Consequently, there is uncertainty as to its scope and function. The fact that some states maintain the distinction between types of contraband while others apparently no longer do so reflects one of the most prevalent themes in the contemporary law of maritime warfare; that of ambiguity.

In considering the question of whether there should be categories of contraband, one must query whether the abandonment of the principle is warranted, necessary, or for that matter, helpful. Recognizing that contemporary armed conflicts are generally limited in nature and scope, and that the likelihood of total war engulfing the world in the future is small, it is incumbent upon decision makers to determine whether and to what extent the experiences and practices of the world wars should influence the evolution of the law of contraband. In particular, consideration should be given to whether the fundamental principles of contraband that were agreeable to the major maritime powers in 1909 might remain valid in the context of twenty-first-century law of naval warfare.

While it is readily acknowledged that the construct of the contraband provisions in the Declaration of London was fundamentally flawed, it does not necessarily follow that the concept of classification of contraband is of no value. Understanding that at the core of the law of contraband lies the dichotomy of the rights of a neutral to conduct trade and the desire of a belligerent to ensure that its enemy is cut off from access to the necessities of war, a measure of certainty for both parties is essential.

A Model for Twenty-first-Century Contraband

In spite of the apparent move away from separate classifications of contraband in recent decades, there exist in international law, and particularly in international business law, good reasons to maintain distinct categories of contraband. Understanding that the overwhelming proportion of world commerce is transported by sea, it is

---

[40] Michael Bothe, 'The Law of Neutrality' in Dieter Fleck (ed), *The Handbook of International Humanitarian Law*, 3rd edn (Oxford University Press, 2008) 598 (hereafter Bothe, 'Neutrality').
[41] Ibid.   [42] Lauterpacht, *Oppenheim's* (n 39) 803.

crucial for trade to continue in times of armed conflict. It is equally important that unless a blockade is in effect, interdiction of trade should be kept to a minimum. While it is essential that weapons and other implements of war should be subject to interdiction and seizure as contraband, the over-use of contraband has the potential to severely impact legitimate trade. Hence, the adoption of a single category of contraband that does not delineate between the intended use and function and consumer of the items serves little military purpose. In this regard, it is a regressive measure.

International instruments such as the Treaty on the Non-Proliferation of Nuclear Weapons,[43] the Chemical Weapons Convention (CWC),[44] the Proliferation Security Initiative,[45] and the Wassenar Arrangement[46] provide evidence that the concept of absolute contraband exists in contemporary international law. These conventions and agreements identify classes of goods that, by their very nature, are designed for war fighting *strictu sensu*. Additionally, classes of goods, such as those identified at sub-paragraphs 24(a), (b), (c), and (d) of the 1917 Instructions Governing Naval Warfare,[47] would undoubtedly be considered contraband as well.[48]

With relatively minor modifications, a new classification of 'Absolute Contraband' for the twenty-first century could be developed, with the understanding that the class could be modified as required to incorporate advances in technology and or weaponry not previously anticipated. In order to be effective, however, the class of 'Absolute Contraband' could not be subject to change by individual states. Rather, such designation could only be subject to amendment by an international body, such as the United Nations Security Council or another specialized organization.[49] In such manner, the creation of unnecessarily expansive lists of absolute contraband by one or more of the belligerents, as occurred during the world wars, could be prevented.

A universal enumeration of absolute contraband would also provide assurance to neutral traders and belligerents alike, allowing each to know at all times those classes of items which, in times of armed conflict, will always be subject to seizure upon proof of enemy destination. Ideally, such items would be subject to the doctrine of continuous voyage and, given that any carrier should have knowledge of the nature of absolute contraband, the vessel(s) and cargo involved would be liable to forfeiture.

---

[43] 1968 Treaty on the Non-Proliferation of Nuclear Weapons (1973) 729 UNTS 161 [NPT].

[44] Convention on the Prohibition of the Development, Production, Stockpiling and Use of Chemical Weapons and on their Destruction 1974 UNTS 45 (hereafter CWC).

[45] US Department of State, 'Proliferation Security Initiative: Statement of Interdiction Principles' <http://www.state .gov/t/isn/c27726.htm> accessed 13 May 2017.

[46] See Wassenaar Arrangement on Export Controls for Conventional Arms and Dual-Use Goods and Technologies. The Wassenaar Arrangement <http://www.wassenaar.org> accessed 13 May 2017.

[47] 1917 Naval Instructions (n 29) 149.

[48] As discussed, the British Contraband Proclamation of 4 September 1939 was based on the 1917 US Naval Instructions. Unfortunately, as the war progressed, those lists, along with many of the laws of maritime warfare, were disregarded, with the ultimate result being that virtually all vessels with enemy destination, or intercepted within certain zones, were subject to being sunk on sight.

[49] Of note, the CWC (n 44) included the development of a specialized body, the Organization for the Prohibition of Chemical Weapons (OPCW), which is responsible for investigating, monitoring, and overseeing the destruction of chemical weapons.

At the opposite end of the spectrum from absolute contraband is the class of commodities known as 'free goods'. Whilst free goods were originally considered to be items that did not fall under the umbrella of absolute or conditional contraband, the essence of 'free goods' has changed, particularly since the coming into force of Additional Protocol 1. The concept was given life in the San Remo Manual,[50] which described the category as goods, which consist of those items that must never be declared contraband; covering items which are generally humanitarian in nature and are required for the survival of the civilian population. Free goods are exempt from seizure.[51]

Between free goods and absolute contraband lie those items that may be classified either as conditional contraband or non-contraband. As goods that are 'susceptible of use in war as well as for purposes of peace',[52] conditional contraband should consist of such items if they are obviously, or are reasonably expected to be, destined for the military or a related belligerent government department, and can assist in the war effort. Under such a scheme, belligerent governments would be permitted to develop lists of conditional contraband with the proviso that the lists would be subject to requirements of public notification, and ultimate seizure would be subject to the review of prize courts.[53] Seizure of conditional contraband, as per the case of *The Kim*, which held that, 'If the ships or goods are sent to the destination of a neutral port, only the better to come to the aid of the enemy, there will be contraband of war, and confiscation will be justified',[54] would be subject to the same rules and procedures as absolute contraband, with the exception that in the case of conditional contraband, only the cargo would be subject to forfeiture. Non-contraband destined to enemy ports, although subject to the belligerent right of inspection, would not be liable to seizure.

The issue of contraband and how it should be dealt with has eluded codification for more than a century. Although it is impossible to provide an exhaustive list of items that should be classified as absolute contraband, the Naval Instructions of 1917, combined with the various conventions that outlaw and/or restrict certain weapons, could provide a solid foundation for identifying those items that should always be considered in the category of 'absolute'. While states should have the

---

[50] The SRM was prepared during the period 1988–94 by a group of legal and naval experts participating in their personal capacity in a series of Round Tables convened by the International Institute of Humanitarian Law. The purpose of the Manual is to provide a contemporary restatement of international law applicable to armed conflicts at sea. The Manual includes a few provisions which might be considered progressive developments in the law, but most of its provisions are considered to state the law which is currently applicable. See International Committee for the Red Cross, online: ICRC, <https://ihl-databases.icrc.org/ihl/INTRO/560?OpenDocument>last accessed 9 October 2017.

[51] SRM (n 3) para 150.   [52] Declaration of London (n 17) art 24.

[53] Wolff Heintschel von Heinegg, 'Visit, Search, Diversion and Capture in Naval Warfare: Part 1, The Traditional Law' 29 Cdn YBIL 283. Prize courts are domestic courts. When a vessel is seized, it must be taken to the prize court in the country of the seizing power where the decision is made to either condemn the cargo and or vessel, or to return it or compensate the owner. While an international prize court would arguably be seen as less biased than domestic courts, past attempts to establish such a court have failed.

[54] 'British Prize Court Decisions: *The Kim, The Alfred Nobel, The Bjornsterjne Bjornson,* and *The Fridland*' (1915) 9:4 AJIL 979, 994.

authority to classify certain other items as absolute contraband, such classification should only be done for items that may be objectively considered to make a direct contribution to the war-fighting effort. Any goods that do not fall squarely within that limited classification should be considered to be either conditional contraband, non-contraband, or free goods. Such an initiative would serve to protect the legitimate rights and concerns of the belligerents, all the while protecting the rights of neutrals to conduct trade with the various parties.

4

The Historical Practice of Blockade

As with the law of contraband, maritime blockade has evolved in the context of a struggle between belligerent and neutral rights. Based upon the premise that a blockading force can degrade its enemy's ability to sustain its war effort by cutting it off from maritime commerce, blockade has the specific purpose of stopping all shipping traffic from entering or leaving the blockaded state's harbours or ports. As such, the history of blockade has been 'formed through the process of assertion [by belligerents], followed by acceptance or rejection [by neutrals]'.[1]

Blockade practice over the last four centuries has been characterized by a lack of common understanding on all but the most basic principles, and widespread disagreement over the more contentious practices, such as continuous voyage, distance blockade, and humanitarian access.[2] A failed attempt by the international community to codify the law of blockade in the early twentieth century[3] left the law and practice of blockade in a state of ambiguity. Inconsistent practice, and a continuing disagreement over the scope and geographical parameters of the practice, has left maritime blockade mired in the archaic framework of pre-First World War naval operations and practice.

The Early History and Practice of Blockade

> The modern doctrine of blockade and the associated principles of contraband have evolved over centuries, remaining basically constant in the principles invoked but continuously changing as to structural details.[4]

From the sieges of the early Peloponnesian conflicts of the fifth century BC through to the siege of Constantinople of 1453, naval forces were commonly employed to support ground forces in their siege operations against port cities. This early form of blockade generally had the limited tactical objective of causing the capitulation

---

[1] Michael G. Fraunces, 'The International Law of Blockade: New Guiding Principles in Contemporary State Practice' (1992) 101 Yale LJ 893, 895 (hereafter Fraunces, 'Blockade').

[2] See discussion in Douglas Guilfoyle, 'The Mani Marmara Incident and Blockade in Armed Conflict (2011) 81:1 BYIL 171, 199–201.

[3] London Declaration Concerning the Laws of Naval War (1909) 208 Consol TS 338 (not entered into force) (hereafter Declaration of London).

[4] James F. McNulty, 'Blockade: Evolution and Expectation' (1991) 62 Int'l L Stud 172, 172 (hereafter McNulty, 'Blockade').

The Law of Maritime Blockade: Past, Present, and Future. Phillip Drew. © Phillip Drew 2017. Published 2017 by Oxford University Press.

of a besieged port, and rarely disrupted maritime traffic outside of the immediate vicinity of the cordoned area.[5]

The sixteenth and seventeenth centuries were a time of significant change in Europe. The discovery and colonization of the new world, and increasing trade across the continent led to significant changes to European commerce.[6] Correspondingly, mercantilism and access to maritime trade routes began to emerge as vital components of many of Europe's economies.[7] Understanding that access to maritime trade was essential to sustaining economic growth, the major trading nations invested heavily in naval power and developed new methods to protect their trading interests, and when necessary, interfere with those of others.[8] It was under this atmosphere that the ancient tactic of seaward sieges began a transformation to the new form of maritime warfare known as blockade.[9]

The Development of Blockade as a Distinct Method of Warfare

The Dutch era (1584–1689)

The Dutch blockade against Flemish ports in 1584 is generally recognized as the beginning of the modern practice of maritime blockade.[10] By *placaat* that year, the Dutch sovereign announced that, all Flanders Ports under the control of Spain were, 'under siege from the sea, ... that no commerce would be allowed entry,'[11] and that any merchants undertaking to 'carry to the Spaniards provisions or any other goods whatsoever'[12] would be treated as enemies.

Although similar in many respects to traditional besiegement by sea, the Dutch initiative to interdict all vessels attempting to trade in the areas controlled by Spain represented a radical change in naval strategy in three fundamental aspects. First, whereas the purpose of siege is to use a mixture of bombardment and isolation to force the capitulation of the besieged locality, the Dutch blockade extended beyond single ports to the entirety of the coastline, and was not merely the seaward aspect of accompanying landward siege against a specific location. Rather, the focus of the Dutch blockade was more strategic, with the aspiration of cutting large areas

---

[5] Michael Schmitt, 'Aerial Blockades in Historical, Legal and Practical Perspective' (1991) 2 USAF Acad J Legal Stud 21, 24 (hereafter Schmitt, 'Aerial Blockades').

[6] George I. Phillips, 'Economic Blockade' (1920) 36 LQ Rev 227, 227 (hereafter Phillips, 'Economic Blockade').

[7] Carl Kulsrud, *Maritime Neutrality to 1780* (Little, Brown and Company 1936) 238–43 (hereafter Kulsrud, *Maritime Neutrality*).

[8] John Brewer, *The Sinews of Power: War, Money and the English State, 1688–1783* (Alfred A. Knopf, 1989) 168.

[9] McNulty, 'Blockade' (n 4) 174–5.

[10] Thomas David Jones, 'The International Law of Blockade—A Measure of Naval Economic Interdiction' (1983) 26 Howard LJ 759, 765.

[11] John Westlake, *The Collected Papers of John Westlake on Public International Law* (Cambridge University Press, 1914) 325 (hereafter Westlake, *Collected Papers*).

[12] John Westlake, *International Law: Part Two—War* (Cambridge University Press, 1907) 170 (hereafter Westlake, *International Law: Part Two*).

of coastline off from access by the Spanish military and denying them any replenishment or access to maritime trade.[13] Secondly, while a seaward siege generally included the bombardment of the besieged locality, many of the Dutch ships conducting a blockade were stationed along the coast with the primary goal of interdicting shipping. Thirdly, while a siege rarely encompassed an area larger than a city, the Dutch action was directed against the entirety of the Spanish coastline. This evolution in practice marked the commencement of the modern era of blockade.[14]

As a leading European naval power during the seventeenth century, the Netherlands was the principal force in the development of nascent blockade doctrine. The development of the Dutch blockade strategy was reflected in the words of Hugo Grotius, who wrote in 1624:

[I]f I am unable to protect myself without intercepting the goods which are being sent to the enemy, necessity ... will give me a right to intercept such goods ... If ... the enforcement of my right shall be hindered by the supplying of these things, and if he who supplied them has been in a position to know this (for example, in case I should be holding a town under siege or keeping ports under blockade, and a surrender or the conclusion of peace should already be in anticipation), then he will be liable to me for injury ... his goods may be seized, and ownership over them may be sought, for the purpose of recovering damages.[15]

Grotius' articulation of blockade is noteworthy for three primary reasons. First, it recognized the concept of blockade as an action that may be carried out either as part of a siege, or as a separate maritime operation conducted independently from any land operation. Secondly, Grotius appeared to imply that a blockade must be 'backed up by real naval strength as opposed to fictitious blockades laid on only by *placaat*'.[16] Thirdly, Grotius did not impose any geographical parameters on the act of interception; rather, he noted only that a right to intercept arises when a party attempts to provide supplies to a blockaded place.

In 1630, some six years after Grotius introduced his theories on blockade, the Dutch embarked on their second campaign to blockade Flemish ports. Wary of the increasing power of Britain's Royal Navy, and with a desire to see Britain remain uninvolved in its conflict with Spain, the Dutch government sought advice from its Admiralty as to the legality of engaging in the operation. Relying heavily on the works of Grotius, the Admiralty advised that blockades were legal acts of war, noting that just as a landward siege may cut off neutral trade to a besieged location, so too may a blockading force interdict neutral shipping attempting to reach blockaded ports.[17] Consequently, when the *placaat* was issued on 9 July 1630, it proclaimed that, 'the Flanders coast was blockaded and that neutral ships found at any distance from Flanders intending to call at those ports would be subject to condemnation. Further, the *placaat* proceeded to state that ships which succeeded in passing the

---

[13] McNulty, 'Blockade' (n 4) 174.　　　[14] Ibid.

[15] Hugo Grotius, *The Law of War and Peace, Book III*, translated by Jean Barbeyrac (The Liberty Fund Inc. 2005) 602.

[16] Westlake, *Collected Papers* (n 11) 326.

[17] See Westlake, *International Law, Part Two* (n 12) 251.

blockade into Flanders ports would remain subject to confiscation wherever intercepted on the outward voyage.'[18]

Of significant importance in the *placaat* of 1630 was the restatement of the notion that a belligerent could capture any neutral vessel bound for a blockaded port, irrespective of its distance from the port. Equally noteworthy in the development of the new stratagem was the pronouncement that vessels outbound from a blockaded area would be subject to interception until such time as they reached a safe port.[19] These two concepts set out the fundamental principles that established blockade as a distinct form of naval warfare.

The *placaat* of 1630 provoked the ire of Europe's neutral powers. France, Britain, and a number of other maritime trading states of the time objected to the Dutch action, decrying it as a violation of neutral rights.[20] However, the objections to the new practice were not long-lived. Once it became expedient for the protesting states to engage in similar action during their periods of conflict, they did so with vigour.[21]

The British era (1689–1815)

> When Britannia ruled the waves, one of the most efficient tools of her leadership was the blockade.[22]

While it is fair to credit the Dutch for having been the originators of modern blockade, it is the British who deserve recognition for having developed the doctrine from its early form at the beginning of the eighteenth century into the model that was largely accepted as the customary norm at the commencement of the First World War.[23]

England's first foray into maritime blockade was in 1689, at the commencement of the Second Hundred Years War. Cooperating with the Dutch, the British engaged in a blockade against France and all of its possessions.[24] This action marked a significant departure for the British who had traditionally decried blockade as unlawful interference against neutral trade. Once Britain had adopted blockade as a method of warfare, however, there was no turning back. Unlike the Dutch who had not consistently applied the doctrine that they had created,[25] the British did not waiver in their practice. As Britain emerged as the dominant European naval power of the eighteenth century it became the leading force in the development of the law and practice of blockade.[26]

The evolution of blockade progressed rapidly as a result of the persistent conflicts between England and France during the eighteenth and early nineteenth centuries.

---

[18] Westlake, *Collected Papers* (n 11) 327.

[19] Placaat of 1630, in Westlake, *International Law, Part Two* (n 12) 199.

[20] Philip Jessup, *Neutrality: Its History, Economics and Law, Vol I, The Origins* (Columbia University Press, 1935) 113 (hereafter Jessup, *Neutrality*).

[21] McNulty, 'Blockade' (n 4) 175.   [22] Ibid, 176.   [23] Ibid, 182.

[24] For a discussion regarding the diplomatic process behind the establishment of the blockade see G.N. Clark, *The Dutch Alliance and the War Against French Trade 1688–1697* (The University Press, 1923) 31–3.

[25] McNulty, 'Blockade' (n 4) 175.   [26] Ibid, 176.

As an island nation England was acutely aware that its survival in the industrial age depended on its ability to maintain its trading routes and its access to foreign goods. With a primary objective of disrupting each other's economies, the British and French struggled to deny one another access to maritime trade, both along each other's domestic coasts and in their overseas territories. Chief amongst the tactics employed was maritime blockade.

The other states of Europe felt the effects of the endless series of blockades through a significant decline in trade and the collapse of industries that were dependent on overseas commerce.[27] The impediment of continental trade subsequently evoked the ire of the major neutral powers, specifically Prussia, the Netherlands, Russia, Denmark, and Sweden, all of which objected to what they considered to be excessive interference with their neutral trading rights. While these powers generally did not object to the belligerent right to intercept contraband en-route to enemy ports, they did object to the fact that this new doctrine of blockade permitted the interdiction of bona fide commercial trade between neutrals and the belligerents. The continental powers also expressed their displeasure with the British practice of declaring blockades over vast areas in which they could not possibly impose their will.[28] The main complaint against these so-called 'paper blockades' was that by simply declaring an area to be under blockade, a belligerent could legally seize neutral vessels and their cargoes found in that area. It was the complaint of neutrals that if a state wished to declare a blockade over an area, then it should be required to dedicate sufficient force to the operation so as to make the blockade apparent and effective.[29]

In reaction to British practices, the northern European neutral maritime powers established the League of Armed Neutrality,[30] as proposed by Empress Catherine of Russia. With respect to blockade, Empress Catherine's declaration contained two key provisions. The first was 'That Neutral vessels may navigate freely from port to port and along the coasts of nations at war'.[31] This was a direct rebuttal of the British stipulation that vessels trading between enemy ports must first call at a British port for inspection. The second key principle, which is directly related to the first, was found in Empress Catherine's fourth point: 'That to determine what constitutes a blockaded port, this designation shall apply only to a port where the attacking Power has stationed its vessels sufficiently near and in such a way as to render access thereto clearly dangerous'.[32] This rejoinder to so-called 'paper blockades' reflected

[27] François Crouzet, 'Wars, Blockade, and Economic Change in Europe, 1792–1815' (1964) 24:4 The Journal of Economic History 567, 568.

[28] Kulsrud, *Maritime Neutrality* (n 7) 238–43.

[29] A.A. Richmond, 'Napoleon and the Armed Neutrality of 1800. A Diplomatic Challenge to British Sea Power' (1959) 104 Journal of the Royal United Service Institution 186, 190.

[30] See Isabel de Madariaga, *Britain, Russia and the Armed Neutrality of 1780* (Yale University Press, 1962) ch 7.

[31] Encyclopedia of the New American Nation, 'Armed Neutralities: The League of Armed Neutrality' <http://www.americanforeignrelations.com/A-D/Armed-Neutralities-League-of-the-armed-neutrality.html> accessed 13 May 2017.

[32] James Brown Scott, *The Armed Neutralities of 1780 and 1800: A Collection of Official Documents Preceded by the Views of Representative Publicists* (Oxford University Press 1918) 273 (hereafter Scott, *Armed Neutralities*) 274.

the neutrals' discontent with the fact that Britain's enforcement of blockades was irregular and that its blockade policies gave the Royal Navy carte blanche to interfere with neutral trade.

Ultimate victory over France and Napoleon by the European powers in 1815 brought a century of international conflict to an end, and with that, an interlude in the development of blockade doctrine. By that point, five general principles of blockade, although not fully respected or practised by any single one of the parties, had emerged:

(1) proper establishment;

(2) adequate notice;

(3) effective enforcement;

(4) impartial application; and

(5) respect for neutral rights.[33]

Although amongst the major naval powers there was general agreement on the broader aspects of blockade, disputes with respect to a number of the operational details of blockade persisted.[34] The unsettled status of the law eventually provided the major powers with the impetus to develop a standardized body of law. The catalyst for reaching agreement presented itself in the form of the Crimean War, in which the two traditional foes of the eighteenth century, France and England, found themselves united against a common enemy; Russia.

Blockade in the late nineteenth century (1856–1909)

While the four decades of European peace that had commenced in 1815 brought pause to the evolution of the law of blockade, the Crimean War provided new impetus to continue with its development. At the core of the new initiatives was the requirement for Britain and France to resolve some of their divergent maritime policies regarding neutrality, contraband, and blockade.

For the century and a half preceding the outbreak of the Crimean War, England and the continental powers had been at odds with respect to their policies concerning blockade and neutral carriage. 'England had always maintained the right to seize enemy goods not contraband on neutral vessels, as she considered the destruction or the crippling of an enemy's commerce and her trade, however carried on, as a legitimate and proper objective in maritime war.'[35] The continental Europeans, on the other hand, had always held that other than with the case of contraband, enemy goods on neutral vessels and neutral goods under the enemy's flag were not liable to capture. Additionally, as has been mentioned above, Britain had hitherto

---

[33] Fraunces, 'Blockade' (n 1) 895.

[34] Robert W. Tucker, *The Law of War and Neutrality at Sea* (United States Government Printing Office, 1957) (hereafter Tucker, *Neutrality*).

[35] Charles H. Stockton, 'The Declaration of Paris' (1920) 14:3 AJIL 356, 358.

disregarded European objections to its practice of establishing blockades, 'backed by just sufficient naval force as to permit the barest claim to efficiency'.[36]

A fundamental shift in British policy towards the recognition of the require-ment for blockades to be effective was outlined in the British Order in Council of 15 April 1854.[37] In addition to making significant concessions regarding neutral carriage, the Privy Council paid particular heed to the requirement of effectiveness by stating:

Her Majesty … must maintain the right of a belligerent to prevent neutrals from breaking any effective blockade which may be established with an adequate force against the enemy's forts, harbours, or coasts.[38]

The creation of the Order in Council brought an official end to Britain's practice of declaring paper blockades. This concession, made to create a common policy frame-work under which allied navies could cooperate, was one of the first steps in the development of universally accepted principles for the law of blockade.[39]

The Declaration of Paris (1856)

Three years of brutal conflict on the Crimean Peninsula were brought to an end with the conclusion of the Treaty of Paris in March 1856,[40] part of which was the Declaration of Paris,[41] a convention aimed at governing future naval warfare. Ratified by all the countries that had participated in the Crimean War,[42] and acceded to by most European and South American naval powers,[43] the Declaration established a set of rules whose principal goals were to regulate the relationship between neutrals and belligerents during conflict. Particularly, the Declaration provided that:

1. Privateering is, and remains, abolished;

2. The neutral flag covers enemy's goods, with the exception of contraband of war;

3. Neutral goods, with the exception of contraband of war, are not liable to cap-ture under enemy's flag;

4. Blockades, in order to be binding, must be effective, that is to say, maintained by a force sufficient really to prevent access to the coast of the enemy.[44]

---

[36] McNulty, 'Blockade' (n 4) 176.
[37] Victoria R.I., Order in Council of 15 April 1854, (1854) London Gazette 21544, 1208.
[38] Ibid.   [39] McNulty, 'Blockade' (n 4) 178.
[40] General Treaty of Peace Between Great Britain, Austria, France, Prussia, Russia, Sardinia, and Turkey, 30 March 1856 in Edward Herstlet, *The Map of Europe by Treaty: Political and Territorial Changes Since the General Peace of 1814* (Butterworths, 1875) 1250.
[41] Paris Declaration Respecting Maritime Law—1856 (adopted 16 April 1856), Martens, Nouveau Receuil Général 1st ser, vol XV, UK, HC, c. in *Sessional Papers* vol 66 (1856) para 2 (hereafter Paris Declaration).
[42] Henry Sumner Maine, 'Naval or Maritime Belligerency' *International Law: A Series of Lectures Delivered Before The University of Cambridge 1887* [unpublished], online: < http://archive.org/stream/internationallaw00mainuoft/internationallaw00mainuoft_djvu.txt> accessed 9 October 2017.
[43] Declaration of Paris (n 41) signatories list.   [44] Ibid, art 4.

The Declaration of Paris was a turning point in international law. It represented the first time in history that an international treaty was negotiated and subsequently opened to ratification or accession to other states; thus beginning the era of codified laws of war.[45]

While the Declaration of Paris represented a substantive advancement in the law of naval warfare, the broad and ambiguous language used in its construction proved to be problematic when tested during the American Civil War, particularly in the context of the Union government's blockade of Confederate ports, a strategy that tested the relationship between the United States and the United Kingdom. The significant disputes that arose between the two powers during this timeframe exposed critical problems in the law of blockade, providing incentive for the issue to be revisited in a new forum. The opportunity for review of naval operations law presented itself at the Second Hague Peace Conference of 1907.

The Declaration of London (1909)

At the invitation of Great Britain, the world's ten largest naval powers convened in London from 4 December 1908 until 26 February 1909. A follow-on to the Second Hague Peace Conference of 1907, the conference was convened to deal with the following matters:

(a) Contraband, including the circumstances under which particular articles can be considered as contraband; the penalties for their carriage; the immunity of a ship from search when under convoy; and the rules with regard to compensation where vessels have been seized but have been found in fact only to be carrying innocent cargo;

(b) Blockade, including the questions as to the locality where seizure can be effected, and the notice that is necessary before a ship can be seized;

(c) The doctrine of continuous voyage in respect both of contraband and of blockade;

(d) The legality of the destruction of neutral vessels prior to their condemnation by a prize court;

(e) The rules as to neutral ships or persons rendering 'unneutral service';

(f) The legality of the conversion of a merchant-vessel into a war-ship on the high seas;

(g) The rules as to the transfer of merchant-vessels from a belligerent to a neutral flag during or in contemplation of hostilities; and,

---

[45] The Paris Declaration was eventually signed by the majority of naval powers, with the exception of Spain and the United States. Although it was passed through the British House of Commons there was, and remained until 1899, significant opposition to the Declaration in the British houses of parliament. Those who opposed the Declaration were loath to surrender what they considered to be the long-held irrefutable right in maritime warfare to seize enemy property wherever found at sea. For an interesting review of the debates surrounding the Declaration see 'The Declaration of Paris', *The Saturday Review*, 22 July 1876, 96–7.

(h) The question whether the nationality or the domicile of the owner should be adopted as the dominant factor in deciding whether property is enemy property.[46]

The agenda for the London Conference was ambitious. Achieving consensus on the issues placed before the plenipotentiaries was no simple task; divergent views on many of the subjects were deep-rooted and mired in several centuries of antagonistic practice. Ultimately, however, broad agreement was achieved, with the delegates agreeing that the rules that they had formulated corresponded 'in substance with the generally recognized principles of international law'.[47]

The resulting product of the meetings was the Declaration Concerning the Laws of Naval War,[48] a wide-ranging accord that codified of the general principles of blockade and contraband, set out the parameters of un-neutral service and established the rules for a naval prize court. Importantly, the Declaration of London codified the five basic requirements for the lawful establishment of a blockade:

1. It must be properly established,[49]

2. It must be maintained by a force that is sufficient to prevent access to the enemy coastline;[50] that is to say, it must be effective;

3. It must be declared and properly notified.[51] A declaration of blockade is made either by the blockading Power or by the naval authorities acting in its name. It specifies:

   (1) The date when the blockade begins;

   (2) the geographical limits of the coastline under blockade;

   (3) the period within which neutral vessels may come out;[52]

4. It must respect the rights of neutrals;[53] and,

5. It must be applied impartially to the ships of all nations,[54] including merchant vessels of the belligerent as well as all neutral vessels.[55]

Although it was signed by all of the parties to the London peace conference,[56] the Declaration was met with significant opposition in the United Kingdom. Concerned that the British negotiators had conceded too many rights, particularly with respect to blockade, the declaration was denounced by, 'the Imperial Maritime League, . . . [and] an extended list of commercial associations. [Faced with] dwindling support in the House of Commons, an atmosphere of suspicion and mistrust toward European powers, and a belief that a war with Germany was on the horizon, the

---

[46] Ibid, xix.   [47] Declaration of London (n 3) Preamble.   [48] Ibid, 89.
[49] Ibid, arts 1 and 18.   [50] Ibid, art 2.   [51] Ibid, art 8.   [52] Ibid, art 9.
[53] Ibid, arts 17, 18, and 19.   [54] Ibid, art 5.
[55] Significantly, the five requirements set out in the Declaration of London continue to be the core of principles of blockade.
[56] See 'Treaties and States Parties To Such Treaties: Declaration Concerning the Laws of Naval War. London, 26 February 1909', International Committee of the Red Cross <http://www.icrc.org/applic/ihl/ihl.nsf/states.xsp?xp_viewstates=XPages_NORMstatesSign&xp_treatySelected=255> accessed 13 May 2017.

House of Lords defeated The Naval Prize Bill on 12 December 1911'.[57] Parliament's failure to ratify the Naval Prize Bill was fatal to the Declaration of London.[58] In addition to extinguishing the opportunity for a multilateral treaty on blockade, the failure of the Declaration of London also stopped Hague XII—Convention Relative to the Creation of an International Prize Court[59] in its tracks.[60] This court, which would have been the first truly international court, could have provided the very legal interpretation and guidance that the nations were seeking when they convened in London in 1908.[61]

As a result of Britain's rejection of the Declaration of London, the only attempt in history to create a treaty to govern maritime blockade died on the parliamentary drafting table. Consequently, as the European powers spiralled towards war, the status quo of nineteenth-century naval law, with its attendant disputes and uncertainties, remained as the framework for the law of maritime blockade.

Blockade in the Modern Era (1914–Present)

First World War (1914–19)

> [I]t is well known that the war destroyed any pretence of a law of maritime rights.[62]

As had been foreseen by the British House of Lords when they rejected the Naval Prize Bill,[63] a pan-European conflict war was looming on the horizon as the world entered the second decade of the twentieth century. As the possibility of war grew more ominous during the summer of 1914, neutral countries, particularly the United States, sought assurances that the belligerents would, for sake of clarity and understanding, respect and apply the operational provisions that had been negotiated in the development of the Declaration of London.[64]

The United States' concerns were somewhat alleviated by the Royal Proclamation on 4 August 1914,[65] in which Britain signalled its intent to abide by the Declaration

---

[57] UK HL Debates 12 December 1911 vol 10 cc809–95, 895.

[58] Declaration of London (n 3) art 71, provided that 'The present Declaration, which bears the date of 26 February 1909, may be signed in London up till 30 June 1909, by the Plenipotentiaries of the Powers represented,the Naval Conference'.

[59] See D. Schindler and J. Toman, *The Laws of Armed Conflicts*, 3rd edn (Martinus Nijhoff, 1988) 825–36.

[60] 'Naval Prize Bill and the Declaration of London' (1912) 6:1 AJIL 180, 180 (hereafter Naval Prize Bill).

[61] Ibid, 181.

[62] Jack L. Goldsmith and Eric A. Posner, *The Limits of International Law* (Oxford University Press, 2005) 51.

[63] Naval Prize Bill (n 60) 226.

[64] The Secretary of state to Ambassador W.H. Page, telegram. Department of State, Washington, 6 August 1914. JSTOR Internet Archive <http://archive.org/stream/jstor-2212241/2212241_djvu.txt> accessed 13 May 2017.

[65] George R.I., Proclamation (4 August 1914) London Gazette, 6163.

of London during the coming conflict.[66] Following the lead of the British, the Austrians and Germans, on 13 August[67] and 22 August 1914[68] respectively, affirmed they would apply the Declaration of London, so long as its provisions were respected by other belligerents.

The characterization of the First World War as a colossal and bloody war of attrition fought on the muddy battlefields of Europe, belies the fact that the strategic goals of the belligerents were nothing short of the complete and unconditional defeat of their enemies. Central to this stratagem were the policies of unlimited naval warfare and maritime blockade. Commencing from the very first days of the War, the German Navy engaged in a campaign of mine warfare, proclaiming that 'during the state of war in which the German Empire finds itself, the necessity will arise ... of blockading with mines the points of departure for attacks on the part of hostile fleets against Germany, and the ports of shipment, departing and arriving, of troop transports'.[69] Within weeks, the United Kingdom's Order in Council of 22 August[70] signalled the country's intention to depart from the Declaration of London by proclaiming that:

(5) Notwithstanding the provisions of Article 35[71] of the said Declaration, conditional contraband, if shown to have the destination referred to in Article 33,[72] is liable to capture to whatever port the vessel is bound and at whatever port the cargo is to be discharged.[73]

In advising the United States of its decision to broaden the scope of the doctrine of continuous voyage, Britain explained its position regarding articles 34 and 35 of the *Declaration* as follows:

The peculiar conditions in the present war due to the fact that neutral ports such as Rotterdam are the chief means of access to a large part of Germany and that exceptional measures have been taken in the enemy country for the control by the Government of the entire supply of

---

[66] Ibid. The lists contained in the 4 August 1914 proclamation mirrored those of the Declaration of London, with the exception that in the Proclamation, aeroplanes, balloons, and their component parts were included as absolute contraband.

[67] See 'Supplement: Diplomatic Correspondence Between the United States and Belligerent Governments Relating to Neutral Rights and Commerce' (1915) 9:3 AJIL 1,1 (hereafter Diplomatic Correspondence).

[68] Ibid, 2.

[69] 'Note Verbale from German Foreign Ministry to United States Ambassador to Berlin, 7 August 1914' in *Papers Relating to the Foreign Relations of The United States, 1914. Supplement, The World War* (United States Government Printing Office, 1928) 454(fn).

[70] United Kingdom Privy Council (22 August 1914) London Gazette, 6673.

[71] Declaration of London (n 3) art 35. Conditional contraband is not liable to capture, except when found on board a vessel bound for territory belonging to or occupied by the enemy, or for the armed forces of the enemy, and when it is not to be discharged in an intervening neutral port. The ship's papers are conclusive proof both as to the voyage on which the vessel is engaged and as to the port of discharge of the goods, unless she is found clearly out of the course indicated by her papers, and unable to give adequate reasons to justify such deviation.

[72] Ibid, art 33. Conditional contraband is liable to capture if it is shown to be destined for the use of the armed forces or of a government department of the enemy state, unless in this latter case the circumstances show that the goods cannot in fact be used for the purposes of the war in progress. This latter exception does not apply to a consignment coming under art 24(4).

[73] United Kingdom Privy Council (22 August 1914) London Gazette, 6674.

foodstuffs have convinced His Majesty's Government that modifications are required in the applications of Articles 34 and 35 of the Declaration. These modifications are contained in paragraphs 3 and 5 of the accompanying Order in Council.[74]

Taking their lead from the United Kingdom, France and Russia followed suit,[75] declaring on 27 August and 3 September respectively that they would apply the Declaration of London with the exact modifications adopted by the United Kingdom.[76]

In response to the pronouncements of the allied powers, the United States declared that it would 'insist that the rights and duties of the Unites states and its citizens in the present war be defined by the existing rules of international law and the treaties of the United States'.[77] Although the United Kingdom attempted to assuage neutral concerns by partially withdrawing the 22 August Order in Council on 29 October 1914,[78] the United States remained steadfast in its position that the Declaration of London should be applied in its entirety. Faced with significant losses due to allied contraband rules, particularly those relating to the application of the doctrine of continuous voyage, the Americans continued their protests, demanding that neutral rights be recognized and respected.[79]

Through the winter of 1914–15, rhetoric and belligerent action on the high seas escalated. In response to extensive German mining activity the British declared, on 2 October 1914, that an area of the north sea of approximately 3,000 square miles extending from the northern approaches to the English Channel towards Germany would be mined.[80]

---

[74] Diplomatic Correspondence (n 67) 4.   [75] Ibid, 5–6.   [76] Ibid, 5.
[77] Ibid, 7.   [78] George R.I., Proclamation 29 October 1914, London Gazette 8756.
[79] The British were generally less than receptive to American complaints about interference with neutral trade. Although not wanting to alienate the United States, Britain stood fast to its position that it was facing a new type of warfare that required new tactics and strategies. On 10 February 1915, Lord Grey wrote a long letter to the United States, outlining Britain's position. In suggesting that the Americans were engaging in hypocrisy he noted in part,

> No better instance of the necessity of countering new devices for despatching contraband goods to an enemy by new methods of applying the fundamental principle of the right to capture such contraband can be given than the steps which the Government of the United States found it necessary to take during the American Civil War. It was at that time that the doctrine of continuous voyage was first applied to the capture of contraband, that is to say, it was then for the first time that a belligerent found himself obliged to capture contraband goods on their way to the enemy, even though,the time of capture they were enroute for a neutral port from which they were intended subsequently to continue their journey. The policy then followed by the United States Government was not inconsistent with the general principles already sanctioned by international law, and met with no protest from His Majesty's Government, though it was upon British cargoes and upon British ships that the losses and the inconvenience due to this new development of the application of the old rule of international law principally fell.

See William Bayard Hale, *American Rights and British Pretensions on the Seas: The Facts and the Documents, Official and Other, Bearing upon the Present Attitude of Great Britain toward the Commerce of the United States* (Robert M. McBride & Company, 1915) 114.
[80] 'Telegram from British Minister of Foreign Affairs to British Ambassador to Washington, 2 October 1914' in *Papers Relating to the Foreign Relations of The United States, 1914. Supplement, The World War* (United States Government Printing Office, 1928) 460 (hereafter Foreign Relations 1914).

Responding to the United Kingdom's belligerency, Germany moved to further cut Britain off from its crucial maritime supply lines. On 4 February 1915 the German Admiralty notified the United States that sea-lane access to Britain was to be blocked to all enemy merchant vessels, that such vessels would be sunk on sight, and that the safety of neutral vessels operating in the area could not be guaranteed.[81] This proclamation signalled the commencement of unrestricted submarine warfare, under which merchant vessels and passenger ships alike were liable to be sunk on sight, with no provisions made to ensure the safety of passengers or crew.[82]

The British countered the German proclamation by joining with France in an escalation of economic warfare in which the countries were to 'prevent commodities of any kind from reaching or leaving or leaving Germany, [holding] themselves free to detain and take into port ships carrying goods of presumed enemy destination, ownership, or origin'.[83]

The expansion of the Royal Navy's interdiction measures aroused considerable anger in neutral countries, many of which enjoyed strong trading links with Germany, including in particular the United States, the Netherlands, Denmark, and Sweden.[84] British Foreign Secretary Sir Edward Grey responded to neutral complaints by stating that the measures that had been implemented were 'no more than an adaptation of the of the old principles of blockade to the circumstances with which we are confronted',[85] noting that 'if the blockade can only become effective by extending it to enemy commerce passing through neutral ports, such an extension is defensible and in accordance with principles which have met with general acceptance'.[86] The British prize court lent its support to the government's policy in the case of '*The Kim*'.[87] Acknowledging that 'in these days of easy transit,' a blockade

---

[81] The text of the German proclamation read in part:

The Waters surrounding Great Britain and Ireland, including the whole English Channel are hereby declared to be comprised within the area of war and all enemy merchant vessels found in those waters after the eighteenth instant will be destroyed although it may not always be possible to save crews and passengers. Neutral vessels expose themselves to danger within this zone since in view of the misuse of the neutral flag ordered by the British Government on January thirty-first and of the contingencies of maritime warfare it cannot always be avoided that neutral vessels suffer from attacks intended to strike enemy ships.

See 'Telegram from US Ambassador to Germany to the Secretary of State' in *Papers Relating to the Foreign Relations of The United States, 1915. Supplement, The World War* (United States Government Printing Office, 1928) 94 (hereafter Foreign Relations 1915).

[82] The German Navy was compelled to abandon its policy for a short time as a result of an American ultimatum to cut off diplomatic ties after the sinking of the French passenger vessel '*The Sussex*' on 24 March 1916. After a nine-month hiatus, however the Kaiser reinstated the policy of unrestricted submarine warfare on 9 January 1917. The return to unrestricted warfare, which resulted in renewed attacks on US vessels, was the primary factor that persuaded the Americans to declare war on Germany in April 1917.

[83] Edgar Turlington, *Neutrality: Its History, Economics and Law in Four Volumes: III the World War Period* (Columbia University Press, 1936) 48 (hereafter Turlington, *Neutrality*).

[84] Foreign Relations 1914 (n 80) 260.   [85] Turlington, *Neutrality* (n 83) 63.

[86] Diplomatic Correspondence (n 67) 168.

[87] 'British Prize Court Decisions: *The Kim, The Alfred Nobel, The Bjornsterjne Bjornson*, and *The Fridland*' (1915) 9:4 AJIL 979, 994.

could be rendered ineffective by rail or other means of land transportation, the court held that:

[I]t is a truism to say that international law, in order to be adequate, as well as just, must have regard to the circumstances of the times, including the circumstances arising out of the particular situation of the war, or the condition of the parties engaged in it ... [T]he doctrine of continuous voyage, or transportation, both in relation to carriage by sea, and to carriage by overland, had become part of the law of nations at the commencement of the present war ... The result is that the court is not restricted in its vision to the primary consignments of the goods in these cases to the neutral port of Copenhagen; but is entitled and bound to take a more extended outlook in order to ascertain whether this neutral destination was merely ostensible, and if so, what the real ultimate destination was.[88]

Any possibility that the British might abide by the Declaration of London was completely dispelled in July 1916, when, by Order in Council, the government declared 'that the Declaration of London Order in Council No. 2, 1914 [4 August 1914], and all Orders subsequent thereto amending the said Order are hereby withdrawn'[89] and 'The principle of continuous voyage or ultimate destination shall be applicable both in cases of contraband and of blockade'.[90]

That the British ultimately abandoned the constraints imposed by the unratified Declaration of London is understandable. The First World War was a desperate struggle for national survival, the likes of which had not been previously experienced.[91] Britain, more so than any other nation, was completely dependent on maritime shipping for its continued existence, and as she watched German U-boats deplete her merchant fleet by two vessels for each day that the war continued,[92] she disregarded the laws that restricted her scope of action at sea. Likewise, by the middle of 1917, Germany had abandoned all restraint by adhering to its policy of unrestricted submarine warfare. Adopting the principle of *tu quoque*, and characterizing their acts as reprisals[93] for each other's violations of the laws of naval warfare, the belligerents virtually discarded any pretext of lawfulness, choosing instead to dismiss centuries of legal evolution in favour of pragmatism and military expediency.

The signing of the armistice on 11 November 1918 brought the disastrous land war in Europe to a close; but it did not bring the blockade of Germany to an end. On the contrary, in a strategy aimed at forcing the conditions of the Versailles Treaty upon the German government, the allies tightened the food blockade on Germany with the intent of starving the country into submission.[94] The Hunger Blockade, as it has come to be known, lasted from November 1918 until the signing of the Treaty

---

[88] Ibid.

[89] George R.I., Order in Council of 7 July 1916, (1916) London Gazette 29657, 6821.

[90] Ibid, 6822.

[91] Few nations emerged from the war with their governments or borders unchanged.

[92] Nigel Hawkins, *The Starvation Blockades* (Pen and Sword Books Ltd, 2002) 232 (hereafter Hawkins, *The Starvation Blockades*).

[93] A reprisal between belligerents is an act, otherwise unlawful, that is exceptionally permitted to a belligerent as a reaction against a previous violation of law by an enemy. See Tucker, *Neutrality* (n 34) 31.

[94] Hawkins, *The Starvation Blockades* (n 92) 241.

of Versailles in July 1919, during which time Germany and her allies were subjected to the worst famine since the Thirty Years War.

Second World War (1939–45)

Twenty years after the signing of the Treaty of Versailles, Europe was once again on the precipice of war. With the battle lines drawn very similarly to what they had been during the First World War, the main tasks for the belligerent navies were to isolate their foes and deny them access to sea-lanes of communication. In anticipation of the coming conflict, Germany, under the leadership of Hitler, had taken significant measures to ensure that it would not be seriously affected by a naval blockade. In addition to identifying sources of raw material that did not require goods to be shipped by sea, the government built a vast network of railways, and as the Nazis invaded countries, expanded the system in tandem. 'The idea behind this transcontinental service was that a single train would transport as much as a freighter.'[95] Although Germany had taken measures to reduce its reliance on maritime trade, both it and England remained vulnerable to the interdiction of their sea lines of communication. While the first months following England's declaration of war against Germany have been characterized as a 'phoney war' due to the lack of action by air and ground forces, the plans and preparations for naval warfare between Germany and Great Britain were proceeding at full steam.[96]

As was the case in the First World War, the conflict between the belligerent naval forces began very early, but in the case of the Second World War, it escalated much more quickly than it had in the First, with initial naval skirmishes between the United Kingdom and Germany commencing in September 1939. By Order in Council on 4 September 1939,[97] the British government published its contraband list, which included foodstuffs as conditional contraband. Redolent of its strategy in the Great War, the German Navy immediately commenced submarine warfare operations, sinking the passenger vessel *SS Athenia* on 3 September 1939,[98] the aircraft carrier *HMS Courageous*, on 17 September,[99] and attacking the British fleet in its home ports.[100] In response to 'German forces indiscriminately and without notification'[101] sinking merchant vessels, 'in contravention of the obligations of humanity and the provisions of the Hague Convention No. VIII of 1907',[102] Britain tightened its restrictions on German maritime commerce by implementing

---

[95] Albert Speer, *Inside the Third Reich* (The Macmillan Company, 1970) 301.

[96] Nick Smart, *British Strategy and Politics During the Phony War: Before the Balloon Went Up* (Praeger 2003) 74.

[97] George R.I., Order in Council of 4 September 1939 (1939) London Gazette 34667, 6051.

[98] Francis M. Carroll, *Athenia Torpedoed: The U-Boat Attack that Ignited the Battle of the Atlantic* (Naval Institute Press, 2012) 26.

[99] Raymond A. Burt, *British Battleships: 1919–1939* (Arms and Armour Press, 1993) 286.

[100] Karl Döenitz, *Memoirs: Ten Years and Twenty Days*, English translation by R.H. Stevens (Da Capo Press 1959) 67–9.

[101] Ibid.   [102] Ibid.

an Order in Council[103] that brought into effect the doctrine of continuous voyage and combined it with the doctrine distance blockade.[104]

As it had done in the First World War, Britain announced that it would mine the entire North Sea approaches between Holland and Norway.[105] Germany's response was predictable. Announcing that 'the unsuccessful British attempt to starve German women and children, through a hunger blockade, [would be] answered by Germany with the complete blockade of the British Isles',[106] Germany warned neutrals that maritime trade with Britain must 'henceforth be avoided by all who do not wish to come in contact with the horrors of war'.[107]

As was the case in the First World War, the major naval blockade actions of the Second War departed significantly from the model that was created in the Declaration of London. As Robert Tucker points out, there are two principal theories regarding the continued authority of the traditional law of blockade at the conclusion of the world wars:

[The first is that] whatever judgment is made concerning the legitimacy of these measures, ... it cannot affect the continued validity of the law governing blockade. If this position is adopted it would appear that the traditional law remains on the whole— unchanged, ... At the same time, acceptance of this view entails at least the admission that in the circumstances characterizing recent naval hostilities the traditional blockade, and therefore a number of the rules governing its operation, have become largely irrelevant. If, however, recent belligerent practice is looked upon as a thinly veiled endeavor to replace the traditional law through the instrument of reprisals, and this would seem to represent the more realistic view, then the question of legal change must be squarely faced.[108]

Two major lessons in the practical application of blockade can be drawn from the world wars. First, the danger posed by land-based weapons systems, submarines, and mines have made it necessary for blockading forces to avoid coastal areas that are under the control of a modern, sophisticated, and well-equipped adversary. The result is that article 1 of the Declaration of London[109] has been rendered completely obsolete. Secondly, because of the capacity of modern land-based transportation

---

[103] George R.I., Order in Council (27 November 1939) London Gazette 34742, 7959 (hereafter OIC 34742):

   1. Every merchant vessel which sailed from any enemy port, including any port in territory under enemy occupation or control, after the 4th day of December, 1939, may be required to discharge in a British or Allied port any goods on board laden in such enemy port.
   2. Every merchant vessel which sailed from a port other than an enemy port after the 4th day of December, 1939, having on board goods which are of enemy origin or are enemy property may be required to discharge such goods in a British or Allied port.

[104] As had been the case in the First World War, England did not call its action a blockade. Instead it described its actions as reprisals against the unlawful and inhuman tactics of its German foe.

[105] OIC 34742 (n 103).

[106] German 'Blockade' Announcement (New York Times, 18 August 1940) in *U.S. Naval War College, International Law Documents: 1940* (US Government Printing Office 1942) 49.

[107] Ibid, 52.   [108] Tucker, *Neutrality* (n 34) 316.

[109] Declaration of London (n 3). Article 1 stated that, 'A blockade must not extend beyond the ports and coasts belonging to or occupied by the enemy'.

systems, any blockade that does not incorporate the doctrine of continuous voyage can, in most cases, be easily rendered virtually ineffective.[110]

Korean War (1950–53)

Five years after the end of the Second World War, the world was once again embroiled in a major multinational armed conflict. In a surprise attack on its southern neighbour on 25 June 1950, North Korea invaded the Republic of Korea, overwhelming the forces of the South and their United States allies. With a United Nations Security Council mandate to defend South Korea,[111] the United States and other participating states' forces scrambled to contain the North Korean advance through the summer. In an attempt to prevent North Korea from being resupplied and equipped by sea, one of the first strategic decisions that the allies made was to establish a maritime blockade against North Korea's coastlines. In ordering the blockade on 1 July 1950, the US government instructed the Commander in Chief (Far East), to 'deny unauthorized ingress and egress from the Korean coast ... [and] suppress seaborne traffic to and from North Korea and to prevent movement by sea of forces and supplies for use in operations against South Korea'.[112]

The North Korean Navy was miniscule in comparison to the combined naval forces of the United Nations force, allowing the UN to establish and maintain naval superiority throughout the war. The lack of North Korean naval power, combined with very limited capabilities in ground based anti-ship weaponry, meant that throughout the war the UN blockade was able to be conducted at relatively close range with minimal interference by communist forces.

Because of their superiority the UN naval forces were able to maintain and enforce the blockade in nearly full accordance with the provisions of the London Declaration.[113] The blockade was unquestionably effective; in 1950 UN vessels sank some 213 junks and sampans and damaged 147 more, while capturing nine.[114] The vessels that did manage to evade the blockaders were generally small coastal vessels that moved very small cargoes under the cover of darkness. Evidence of the effectiveness of the blockade is found in the heavy reliance that the north placed on road and rail traffic, which became the only means by which the communist forces could

---

[110] It is acknowledged that a blockade against a location that does not have access to alternative modes of transportation (eg a mountainous peninsula or an island) can be effectively blockaded without resort to continuous voyage.

[111] UNSC Res 83 (27 June 1950) UN Doc S/RES/83 (1950) (hereafter S/RES/83 (1950)).

[112] US Joint Chiefs of Staff message JCS 84808, 011528Z June 1950. In accordance with the guidance in this message, notice to mariners was to be issued from Washington.

[113] Wolff Heintschel von Heinegg, 'Naval Blockade' [2000] 75 International Law Studies 203, 211 (hereafter Heintschel von Heinegg, 'Blockade').

[114] George Politakis, *Modern Aspects of the Laws of Naval Warfare and Maritime Neutrality* (Keegan Paul International, 1998) 66 (hereafter Politakis, *Modern Aspects*). As Professor Politakis notes, the immediate sinking of merchant vessels and fishing vessels was 'an extension beyond previous economic warfare practices'. Indeed, the UN forces' actions were carried out in clear contradiction to historical and customary practice, as evidenced in art 48 of the Declaration of London, which required that: 'A neutral vessel which has been captured may not be destroyed by the captor; she must be taken into such port as is proper for the determination there of all questions concerning the validity of the capture'.

move material from north to south.[115] The blockade was properly announced and did not interfere with any neutral ports, and was applied impartially against all commercial vessels.

The blockade ordered by President Truman was established and conducted under the auspices of a United Nations Security Council Resolution,[116] thus invoking the operation of article 103 of the United Nations Charter. Because of the interplay of article 103[117] it is uncertain whether the departures from, or indeed the compliance with any provision of the Declaration of London or other customary international law during the Korean War blockade is significant in the development of the law of maritime blockade.

Vietnam (1972)

One of the more controversial blockade-type actions of the post-World War period occurred in Vietnam in May 1972.[118] Towards the end of the Vietnam War (1956–75), and after several years of deliberation, the United States implemented a mining action against Haiphong harbour with the goal of shutting the harbour off from all inward and outward traffic. While considered by some to have been a blockade, because of the fact that the action was notified, effective, and impartial,[119] in reality the action bore little resemblance to any pre-existing concept of blockade. As was addressed by the authors of the San Remo Manual in their commentary on blockade, the fact that there was not a naval force present to capture vessels in breach of the blockade, or to permit vessels in distress to enter, was a clear departure from the traditional law and practice of blockade.[120]

That the mining action was not to be considered a blockade accords with the intent of Secretary of State, Henry Kissinger, when he proposed the idea of mining Haiphong to President Nixon. In his memoir, *The White House Years*, Kissinger recalls discussing the matter with the President:

---

[115] In some ways, the blockade during the Korean War was a throwback to the days of siege with the primary purpose of the Korean blockade being not so much to stem the flow of trade but, to interdict military supplies and traffic along the coast. Additionally, the fact that blockading vessels regularly engaged trains and vehicle convoys with naval gunfire, and often exchanged fire with land based artillery, points to an operation that was more akin to a siege than it was to modern blockade. For a discussion on this campaign see Malcolm Muir Jr, 'Air and Sea Power in Korea' in Bruce Elleman and S.C.M. Paine (eds), *Naval Blockades and Seapower: Strategies and Counter-strategies 1805–2005* (Routledge, Taylor and Francis Group, 2006).

[116] S/RES/83 (1950) (n 111).

[117] Charter of the United Nations (adopted 24 October 1945), 1 UNTS XVI, preamble (hereafter UN Charter) art 103.

[118] The mention of the mining of Haiphong is made in this chapter with the sole purpose of addressing the fact that there are some who have stated that the mining action was a blockade, and that their position is not widely supported.

[119] See, for example, Frank B. Swayze, 'Traditional Principles of Blockade in Modern Practice: United States Mining of Internal and Territorial Waters of North Vietnam' (1977) 29 JAG Journal 143.

[120] Louise Doswald-Beck (ed), *San Remo Manual on International Law Applicable to Armed Conflicts at Sea* (Cambridge University Press, 1995) (hereafter SRM) 97.

Why was mining preferable to a blockade, [the President] wanted to know. I replied that its chief advantage was that it required only one decision; after the mines had been seeded, that was that, until they turned themselves off, usually after four months. A blockade, in contrast, would produce daily confrontations with the Soviets. Every time a ship was stopped we would see a repetition of the drama of the Cuban missile crisis ... The danger of some slip or of a pretext for serious incident would be too great.[121]

While the question of whether or not the mining of Haiphong qualified as a blockade has persisted, and continues to be advocated by some, an examination of the opinions of the leading experts on blockade, including statements in the San Remo Manual,[122] reveals the general consensus that a blockade cannot be enforced by weapons systems alone. Unfortunately, there were a number of commentators who supported the notion that a simple mining operation could be considered to be a blockade, and mention of the mining operation as a form of blockade was included in the influential *Annotated Supplement to the Commander's Handbook on the Law of Naval Operations.*[123]

The contention that a mere mining operation could be considered a blockade did little to advance the law of blockade, and accomplished little other than to sow confusion in an area of law that is in desperate need of sound direction. It is, and continues to be the case that there must be a human decision maker who can make judgments regarding interception and seizure of vessels, and 'allow ships entry into and egress from the blockaded coastline in certain circumstances'.[124]

Israel and Gaza (2009–present)

Established by Israel following the creation of a Hamas-based government in Gaza in February 2006, the Gaza blockade is arguably the closest that any blockade has ever come to adhering to the rules on blockade as set out in the Declaration of London. In response to increased rocket attacks originating from within Gaza, Israel, which controls Gaza's eastern and northern borders, placed tight restrictions on the movement of all goods into and out of Gaza by land, including food, electricity, fuel, and building materials. Additionally, the Israeli government established a seaward blockade of Gaza, effectively cutting the region off from all outside commerce.[125]

The blockade against Gaza was properly announced by way of a notice to mariners, which continues to be in effect.[126] There is no question as to whether the

---

[121] Henry Kissinger, *White House Years* (Little, Brown and Company, 1979) 1179. For a full discussion of the mining of North Vietnamese harbours see ibid, 1165–201.

[122] SRM (n 120) 178.

[123] United States Naval War College, *Annotated Supplement to the Commanders Handbook on the Law of Naval Operations* (Naval Publication Library, 2007) 7.7.5 (hereafter *Commanders Handbook*).

[124] Ibid.

[125] See Louise Charbonneau, 'Collective Punishment for Gaza is Wrong: UN' (18 January 2008) Reuters <http://www.reuters.com/article/2008/01/18/idUSN18343083> accessed 13 May 2017.

[126] Notice to Mariners 1/2009. Online: Israel Ministry of Transport http://asp.mot.gov.il/en/shipping/notice2mariners/547-no12009> accessed 9 October 2017. Note, however, that the Notice to Mariners did not provide a period of time for neutral vessels to vacate Gazan ports, nor did it provide a length of time for which the blockade will be effective.

blockade is effective and impartial; Israel has continuously maintained a very tight, impartial blockade that is enforced against all vessels.[127] Other than the fact that Israel has applied the doctrine of continuous voyage to the Gaza blockade,[128] the blockade appears to be in compliance with the requirements of the Declaration of London.

In spite of general adherence to the provisions of the Declaration of London, there is significant controversy regarding the legality of Israel's blockade. The issue was brought to the forefront by the botched Israeli boarding of the MV Mavi Marmara, which was attempting to run the blockade on 31 May 2010, during which Israeli forces killed nine passengers on the vessel. In response to the calamitous operation, four different commissions[129] were set up to review the boarding and the blockade. Operating from the same basic facts, one commission concluded that the blockade was legal (Turkel Report),[130] two found the blockade illegal (Turkish Report,[131] Hudson-Phillips Report)[132] and one determined that the blockade was legal, but that the use of force by the Israelis was excessive (Palmer Report).[133]

In May 2013 the Office of the Prosecutor of the International Criminal Court received a referral from the Union of Comoros, asking it to investigate the incidents that occurred on the MV *Mavi Marmara* during the Israeli boarding operation that was conducted on 31 May 2010. Although the prosecutor determined that 'there [was] a reasonable basis to believe some IDF troops committed war crimes during and after boarding the *Mavi Marmara*', she also determined that 'any potential case would be inadmissible before [the] Court due to its lack of gravity'.[134,135]

The prosecutor went on to note that she had 'further determined, conditionally, that there [was] a reasonable basis to believe that the forcible boarding of the

---

[127] Israel, *The Public Commission to Examine the Maritime Incident of 31 May 2010, The Türkel Report* (23 January 2011) para 61 (hereafter Turkel Report).

[128] On 5 March 2014 Israel announced that it had seized a cargo of M-302 surface to surface missiles that were shipped from Iran and were to be transhipped through Sudan into Gaza. See BBC, 'Israel Halts Weapons Shipment from Iran' <http://www.bbc.com/news/world-middle-east-26451421> accessed 13 May 2017.

[129] Turkel Report (n 127); Turkey, 'Turkish National Commission of Inquiry: Interim Report On The Israeli Attack on The Humanitarian Aid Convoy To Gaza on 31 May 2010.' Turkish Ministry of Foreign Affairs <http://www.mfa.gov.tr/data/Turkish%20Interim%20Report.pdf> accessed 9 October 2017 (hereafter Turkish Report); United Nations, *Report of the Secretary-General's Panel of Inquiry on the 31 May 2010 Flotilla Incident July 2011*. UN, http://www.un.org/News/dh/infocus/middle_east/Gaza_Flotilla_Panel_Report.pdf accessed 9 October 2017 (hereafter Palmer Report); United Nations Human Rights Council, *Report of the International Fact-Finding Mission to Investigate Violations of International Law, Including International Humanitarian and Human Rights Law, Resulting from the Israeli Attacks on the Flotilla of Ships Carrying Humanitarian Assistance* (27 September 2010), online: <http://www2. ohchr.org/english/bodies/hrcouncil/docs/15session/A.HRC.15.21_en.pdf> accessed 9 October 2017 (hereafter Hudson-Phillips Report).

[130] Turkel Report (n 127), 61–3.   [131] Turkish Report (n 129) 66–83.

[132] Hudson-Phillips Report (n 129).   [133] Palmer Report (n 129) 73–5.

[134] Situation on Registered Vessels of Comoros, Greece and Cambodia: [2015] ICC-01/13 Date: 30 March 2015, Public Redacted Version of Prosecution Response to the Application for Review of its Determination under article 53(1)(b) of the Rome Statute, para 2. online, ICC <https://www.icc-cpi.int/CourtRecords/CR2015_03604.PDF> accessed 9 October 2017 (hereafter Prosecutor's Response).

[135] Situation on Registered Vessels of Comoros, Greece and Cambodia ICC-01/13-51 dated 06 November 2015 (Appeals Chamber Decision). In its decision, the Appeals Chamber requested that the prosecutor reconsider her decision not to investigate further.

Mavi Marmara ... would have constituted unlawful attacks on civilian objects if the blockade imposed by the IDF had been unlawful. The Prosecution refrained, however, from determining the legality of the blockade, a matter of international dispute.'[136] The fact that after four separate investigations there is still no consensus on the legality of the Israeli blockade,[137] provides strong indications that one century after the creation of the treaty that was supposed to have codified the law of blockade, 'the scope of the contemporary laws of blockade is not settled'.[138]

Blockade Under the Charter of the United Nations

> Should the Security Council consider that measures provided for in Article 41 would be inadequate or have proved to be inadequate, it may take such action by air, sea, or land forces as may be necessary to maintain or restore international peace and security. Such action may include demonstrations, blockade, and other operations by air, sea, or land forces of Members of the United Nations.[139]

The United Nations Charter specifically provides that, in order to maintain or restore international peace and security, the United Nations Security Council (UNSC) may employ blockades as coercive measures against non-compliant states. As stated in article 42, the Security Council may decide to used armed force to resolve an issue if 'measures provided for in Article 41 would be inadequate or have proved to be inadequate'.[140] The construction of article 42, therefore, implies that an action such as a blockade is a measure of last resort, to be used as part of a measured response to a threat to international peace and security. The effect of Security Council Resolutions is bolstered by the operation of article 103, which states that:

> In the event of a conflict between the obligations of the Members of the United Nations under the present Charter and their obligations under any other international agreement, their obligations under the present Charter shall prevail.[141]

In essence, article 103 is an overriding provision that provides the Security Council with the power to create rules and procedures that will not be encumbered by existing law or treaties. As a result of the operation of article 103, and the fact that there is no authoritative guidance on the law of blockade, no two embargoes or blockades that have been imposed by the UN have been same. Although a cause of consternation amongst those who decry the 'long but erratic history of embargo and blockade',[142] the UN's varied approach to the implementation of interdiction measures

---

[136] Prosecutor's Response (n 134) para 3.

[137] See '*Situation on Registered Vessels of Comoros, Greece and Cambodia; Article 53(1) Report, 6 November 2014* para 18. International Criminal Court <http://www.icc-cpi.int/iccdocs/otp/OTP-COM-Article_53(1)-Report-06Nov2014Eng.pdf>. accessed 9 October 2017.

[138] Martin Fink, 'Contemporary Views on the Lawfulness of Naval Blockades' (2011) 1 Aegean Review of the Law of the Sea 191, 212 (hereafter Fink, 'Contemporary Views').

[139] UN Charter (n 117) art 42.   [140] Fink, 'Contemporary Views' (n 138) 212.

[141] UN Charter (n 117) art 103.   [142] Fink, 'Contemporary Views' (n 138) 250.

can be seen not as a lack of consistency, but as a reflection of the inherent flexibility of the system established under Chapter VII. As Professor Rob McLaughlin notes, in order to understand the sometimes ambiguous nature of UNSC imposed maritime interdiction measures, it is 'essential that we understand how articles 40, 41 and 42 interact, because it is this interaction which defines the spectrum within which UN mandated interdiction operations can take place',[143] and how, in concert with article 103, the practice and rules surrounding blockade may be effected.

This inherent flexibility of the Security Council Resolution regime has permitted the UN's policies towards blockade and embargo to evolve, with lessons being learned along the way. Through an examination of three crises that involved UNSC-authorized blockade-type actions; Iraq (1990), Bosnia (1992), and Libya (2011), the evolution of UN practice and policy will be considered.

Iraq—UNSCR 665 (1990)

The implementation of UNSCR 665 on 25 August 1990 marked the first time that the United Nations adopted a comprehensive maritime sanctions regime against a country.[144] The measures found in UNSCR 665 were imposed as part of the response to the Iraqi invasion of Kuwait on 2 August 1990, following on the heels of UNSCR 661 (1990) which had enacted wide ranging sanctions that prohibited states from engaging in the 'sale or supply ... of any commodities or products, including weapons or any other military equipment, ... but not including supplies intended strictly for medical purposes, and, in humanitarian circumstances, food-stuffs, to any person or body in Iraq or Kuwait'.[145]

In UNSCR 665, the Security Council called upon states cooperating in the coalition against Iraq to, 'use such measures commensurate to the specific circumstances as may be necessary ...to halt all inward and outward maritime shipping in order to ... ensure strict implementation of the provisions related to such shipping laid down in UNSCR 661 (1990))'.[146] Insofar as UNSCR 665 included the authority to use force to prohibit both imports and exports, it created a blockade in all but name.[147] In keeping with the generally accepted principles of blockade, notice of

---

[143] R McLaughlin, 'United Nations Mandated Naval Interdiction Operations in the Territorial Sea?' (2002) 51:2 ICLQ 249, 253.

[144] It is acknowledged that the UN authorized the Korean blockade; however, the authorization to establish the blockade and administer it was given to the force commander, and the blockade was declared by the government of the United States. Although there was a naval interdiction authorized to prevent transhipment of oil to Rhodesia (UNSCR 221 (1966)), this was a limited action that authorized only one nation (Britain) to use force to stop vessels from offloading oil in Beira, Mozambique. Although characterized by some as a blockade, the action under UNSCR 221 is more akin to an embargo for which a limited amount of force was authorized.

[145] UN Security Council, *Resolution 661 (1990)* 6 August 1990, UN Docs S/RES/661 (1990) (hereafter S/RES/661).

[146] UN Security Council, *Resolution 665 (1990)* 25 August 1990, UN Docs S/RES/665 (1990).

[147] See, for example, James Goldrick, 'Maritime Sanctions Enforcement Against Iraq, 1990–2003' in Bruce Elleman and S.C.M. Paine (eds), *Naval Blockades and Seapower: Strategies and Counter-strategies 1805–2005* (Routledge, Taylor and Francis Group, 2006). See also James Kraska and Raul Pedrozo, *International Maritime Security Law* (Martinus Nijhoff, 2013) 908.

the interdiction action was broadcast and published, it was impartially applied, and it was effective.

While the naval interdiction operations conducted under the umbrella of UNSCR 665 resembled a blockade in almost all respects, it departed from the traditional rules of blockade, in that it did not impose an absolute ban on the provision of foodstuffs to the Iraqi population. With the inclusion of the phrase 'but not including supplies intended strictly for medical purposes, and, in humanitarian circumstances, foodstuffs',[148] the Resolution allowed for the potential of humanitarian assistance in extenuating circumstances. In spite of apparent intentions to avert a humanitarian crisis, the provisions that were incorporated into the resolution did little to soften the effects of the blockade against Iraq, primarily because the Security Council 'did not specify who was responsible for evaluating the humanitarian needs in Iraq and Kuwait, and according to what criteria they were [to be evaluated]'.[149] Within months of the commencement of the blockade, Iraq was experiencing severe food shortages.[150] In an attempt to ameliorate the conditions, the Security Council established a sanctions committee to oversee the humanitarian consequences of the action,[151] and decided to end the embargo on foodstuffs.[152] However, the effects of the initial food embargo, Iraq's continuous attempts to frustrate weapons inspectors, and the lack of funds with which Iraq could purchase food (a direct result of the continuing blockade under UNSCR 687), ultimately combined to create a humanitarian disaster.[153]

By failing to provide unconditional humanitarian assistance to the people of Iraq, and by permitting the principal coalition powers to determine the threshold for 'humanitarian circumstances',[154] the Security Council created the conditions for a humanitarian catastrophe. While the Council did eventually take steps to mitigate the harm caused to the civilian population, significant irreparable damage was done in the early months of the embargo.[155]

While there is little doubt that the embargo met its goals of reducing Iraq's capacity to fight and to ultimately rebuild its military, the naval interdiction operation against Iraq is generally remembered for its devastating effects on the civilian population. The primary lesson that was learned from the Iraq embargo was that when a state is reliant on food imports to meet the nutritional requirements of

---

[148] S/RES/661 (1990) (n 145).

[149] Rene Provost, 'Starvation as a Weapon: Legal Implications of the United Nations Food Blockade Against Iraq and Kuwait' (1992) 30 Colum J Transnat'l L 577, 613.

[150] United Nations Security Council Document S/22366 dated 20 March 1991. Report to the Secretary-General on Humanitarian Needs in Kuwait and Iraq in the Immediate Post-Crisis Environment by a Mission to the Area led By Mr. Marti Ahtisaari, Under-Secretary-General for Administration and Management, dated 20 March 1991.

[151] UN Security Council, *Resolution 666 (1990)* 13 September 1990, UN Docs S/RES/666 (1990).

[152] UN Security Council, *Resolution 687 (1991)* 3 April 1991, UN Docs S/RES/687 (1991).

[153] See House of Lords Select Committee on Economic Affairs, 2nd Report of Session 2006–07, *The Impact of Economic Sanctions*, vol 1 (The Stationery Office Limited, 2007).

[154] S/RES/661 (1990) (n 145).

[155] Ala'din Alwan, 'Health in Iraq: The Current Situation, Our Vision for the Future and Areas of Work', 2nd edn, December 2004 (Iraq Ministry of Health) 21–2.

its population, it should never be subjected to blockade that does not permit the passage of foodstuffs, and access to humanitarian relief should never be made conditional upon a term that is as loosely defined as 'humanitarian circumstances'.[156]

Bosnia—UNSCR 787 (1992)

The disintegration of the Socialist Republic of Yugoslavia in 1991 led to the bloodiest civil war that Europe has experienced since the period immediately following the Second World War.[157] Struggling to contain the civil war, and bring an end to the ethnic violence that was gripping the region, the UN undertook several actions under both Chapters VI and VII of the Charter. When lesser measures proved fruitless, the Security Council established a peacekeeping force in February 1992[158] and imposed strict sanctions[159] against the Federal Republic of Yugoslavia in November of the same year.

The blockade-type action authorized under UNSCR 787, which called for states to halt all inward and outward maritime shipping in order to inspect and verify their cargoes and destinations, represented a significant departure from the model that had been used in the case of Iraq. Unlike UNSCRs 661 and 665, UNSCR 787 specifically exempted 'supplies intended strictly for medical purposes and foodstuffs'[160] from the reach of the blockade.

The fact that foodstuffs were excluded from the ambit of the blockade measures against Bosnia demonstrated that the Security Council had acknowledged that interdicting the flow of food, particularly to vulnerable populations, can result in unnecessary suffering and death. As a result of the Iraq experience, subsequent 'sanctions regimes imposed by the Security Council, as well as the European Union, were narrower and more refined, and ... recommendations for monitoring and preliminary assessments were implemented'.[161]

Libya—UNSCR 1973 (2011)

Responding to the violence of the civil war in Libya in the spring of 2011, the Security Council passed a series of resolutions aimed at protecting Libyan civilians against attacks from the Libyan military. Included in the measures outlined in UNSCR 1970 (2011)[162] and 1973 (2011) were an arms embargo and an operation that resembled a blockade. The resolution called upon all states to

---

[156] S/RES/661 (1990) (n 145).

[157] For a discussion of civil war in Europe in the period 1945–47, see Keith Lowe, *Savage Continent: Europe in the Aftermath of World War Two* (Macmillan, 2012).

[158] UNSC Res 743 (21 February 1992) UN Docs S/RES/743.

[159] UNSC Res 787 (16 November 1992) UN Docs S/RES/787.

[160] UNSC Res 757 (30 May 1992) UN Docs S/RES/757, para 4.c (hereafter S/RES/757).

[161] Joy Gordon, 'Smart Sanctions Revisited' (Fall 2011) 25:3 Ethics & International Affairs 315, 318 (hereafter Gordon, 'Smart Sanctions').

[162] UNSC Res 1970 (26 February 2011) UN Docs S/RES/1970 (hereafter S/RES/1970).

'take the necessary measures to prevent the direct or indirect supply, sale or transfer to the Libyan Arab Jamahiriya, from or through their territories or by their nationals, or using their flag vessels or aircraft, of arms and related materiel of all types, including weapons and ammunition, military vehicles and equipment, paramilitary equipment, and spare parts for the aforementioned, and technical assistance, training, financial or other assistance, related to military activities or the provision, maintenance or use of any arms and related materiel, including the provision of armed mercenary personnel'[163] ... and 'to inspect ... on the high seas, vessels and aircraft bound to or from the Libyan Arab Jamahiriya ... [and] to use all measures commensurate to the specific circumstances to carry out such inspections'.[164]

As was the case with the action against the Federal Republic of Yugoslavia, the regime emplaced for Libya specifically 'Call[ed] upon all Member states, working together and acting in cooperation with the Secretary General, to facilitate and support the return of humanitarian agencies and make available humanitarian and related assistance in the Libyan Arab Jamahiriya'.[165] By specifically requesting states to furnish humanitarian assistance, the Security Council took purposeful measures to mitigate harm in this nation that is reliant on food imports. Additionally, through the immediate creation of a sanctions monitoring committee,[166] the Council provided itself with the means of determining the effects of the naval interdiction operations conducted against Libya. In this manner, the UN not only recognized the potential for civilian harm, but took positive steps to ensure that a humanitarian crisis would not result from the naval interdiction actions.

The period stretching from the end of the Second World War until the early 1990s saw few comprehensive sanction regimes imposed against countries, and virtually no substantive blockades.[167] The few sanctions regimes that were imposed, such as those against Rhodesia[168] and the South African apartheid regime, were largely seen as effective means of influencing national policies,[169] without the resort to armed conflict or the infliction of serious harm on the civilian populations of the countries.[170] For these reasons, it is understandable that when the world imposed the sanctions regime against Iraq, many of the historical lessons learned regarding humanitarian concerns had been forgotten, and the notion that the sanctions regime would cause a humanitarian crisis was likely not given serious consideration.

While it is apparent through the most recent Security Council-sponsored embargoes[171] that the UN Security Council has recognized and implemented the requirement to address humanitarian concerns as part of the planning process for its blockade-like operations, it is unclear whether the UN's actions have affected the status of the customary law surrounding blockade. Israeli practices in the ongoing

---

[163] Ibid, para 9.   [164] UNSC Res 1973 (17 March 2011) UN Docs S/RES/1973.

[165] S/RES/1970 (n 162) para 26.   [166] Ibid, para 23.

[167] Gordon, 'Smart Sanctions' (n 161) 315.

[168] William Minter and Elizabeth Schmidt, 'When Sanctions Worked: The Case of Rhodesia Reexamined' (1988) 87:347 African Affairs 207, 233–4.

[169] 'President Ends Economic Sanctions Against South Africa' (1991) 2:1 Foreign Policy Bulletin 52–3.

[170] Gordon, 'Smart Sanctions' (n 161) 315.

[171] S/RES/1970 (n 162), S/RES/757 (n 163).

blockade against Gaza, which was established in accordance with the long-standing principles for creating a blockade, provides little reassurance that a requirement for positive action on the question of the protection of civilians has been incorporated into the contemporary vernacular of blockade law. Notwithstanding, humanitarian access and assistance has been, and will remain, an issue that should not be overlooked in the planning phases of such operations. As history has shown, the failure to protect civilians from the insidious nature of blockade can have devastating consequences, whether intended or not.

5

Blockade Law

The practice of maritime blockade is based almost exclusively in the domain of customary international law.[1] In order to understand how blockade law has developed over the centuries it is thus necessary to comprehend the mechanisms by which customary law is created, and equally important, how it may or may not become binding on states.

Customary International Law

Identified in article 38 of the Statute of the International Court of Justice as one of the four sources to which one can look to find evidence of international law, 'customary international law is made up of rules that come from "a general practice accepted as law," and that exist independent of treaty law.'[2] As is evidenced by the statement, 'a general practice accepted as law', for a rule to be established as customary international law (CIL) two requirements must be satisfied: first, there must be evidence of *opinio juris*, which is the belief by states that they are obligated to behave in a certain manner, and, secondly, there must be uniform, or virtually uniform practice of states conforming to the proposed rule.[3]

Evidence of CIL is found in 'widespread, but not necessarily unanimous state practice',[4] and, in some cases, acknowledgements by states that they consider a certain practice to have attained the status of customary law.[5] 'State practice ... should

---

[1] The notable exception is found in the Paris Declaration Respecting Maritime Law—1856 (adopted 16 April 1856), Martens, Nouveau Receuil Général 1st ser, vol XV, UK, HC, c. in *Sessional Papers* vol 66 (1856) note 61 (hereafter Paris Declaration) which states that, 'Blockades, in order to be binding, must be effective, that is to say, maintained by a force sufficient really to prevent access to the coast of the enemy'.

[2] ICRC, 'Customary International Humanitarian Law' <http://www.icrc.org/eng/war-and-law/treaties-customary-law/customary-law/> accessed 9 October 2017.

[3] *North Sea Continental Shelf*, Judgment, [1969] ICJ Rep 3, para 77 (hereafter North Sea Cases).

[4] UK Ministry of Defence, *The Manual of the Law of Armed Conflict* (Oxford University Press, 2004) 1.12.2 (hereafter *UK Manual*).

[5] In their article, 'A US Government Response to the International Committee of the Red Cross Study Customary International Humanitarian Law', John B. Bellinger and William J. Haynes cautioned readers against accepting mere statements or non-official manuals as evidence of customary law. Particularly, they stated that, 'The initial U.S. review of the state practice volumes suggests that the Study places too much emphasis on written materials, such as military manuals and other guidelines published by states, as opposed to actual operational practice by states during armed conflict. Although manuals may provide important indications of state behaviour and *opinio juris*, they cannot be a replacement

---

[be] both extensive and virtually uniform in the sense of the provision invoked; and should moreover ... [occur] in such a way as to show a general recognition that a rule of law or legal obligation is involved.'[6] Generally, the actions of states will be indicative of both state practice and the individual state's sense of obligation towards the rule in question. The International Court of Justice points out, however, that in order to constitute *opinio juris*, acts must:

> Not only ... amount to a settled practice, but they must also be such, or be carried out in such a way, as to be evidence of a belief that this practice is rendered obligatory by the existence of a rule of law requiring it. The need for such a belief ... is implicit in the very notion of the *opinio juris sive necessitatis*. The states concerned must therefore feel that they are conforming to what amounts to a legal obligation. The frequency, or even habitual character of the acts is not in itself enough.[7]

It follows, therefore, that 'if there is significantly differing conduct on the matter among states, this will prevent the emergence of such a rule'.[8]

The provisions of CIL normally bind all states, whereas treaties bind only the states that are party to them. In this respect, customary law can represent a significant infringement of the sovereign right of a state to be subjected only to obligations to which it has agreed. For this reason, the questions of whether or not a practice has crystallized into customary law, or whether it is binding on all states, can be contentious.

While customary law usually applies equally to all states, it has historically been accepted that if a state persistently objects to a practice while the law is in the process of development, then that state will not be bound by the emerging rule, even after the rule matures.[9] The persistent objector rule was developed in acknowledgement of states' sovereign rights to be held only to standards to which they have agreed.[10] While in the period leading up to the Second World War, states were permitted 'to derogate *inter se* from customary international law',[11] it is now generally accepted that the ability of states to avoid the obligations of CIL is limited. As is indicated by Professor Cassese and the American Restatement, the international community has, since the creation of the United Nations, undergone a fundamental shift whereby

---

for a meaningful assessment of operational state practice in connection with actual military operations. The United States also is troubled by the extent to which the Study relies on nonbinding resolutions of the General Assembly, given that states may lend their support to a particular resolution, or determine not to break consensus in regard to such a resolution, for reasons having nothing to do with a belief that the propositions in it reflect customary international law.' See John B. Bellinger and William J. Haynes, 'A US Government Response to the International Committee of the Red Cross Study Customary International Humanitarian Law' (2007) 89 Int'l Rev Red Cross 866, 443,445. (hereafter US Response to CIL Study).

[6] North Sea Cases (n 3) para 74.   [7] Ibid, para 77.

[8] William Boothby, *Weapons and the Law of Armed Conflict* (Oxford University Press, 2009) 24.

[9] The American Law Institute, *Restatement of the law, The foreign relations law of the United States/ as adopted and promulgated by The American Law Institute, Washington, D.C., May 14, 1986* (American Law Institute Publishers, 1987) 26 (hereafter American Restatement).

[10] See, for example, *US Response to International Committee of the Red Cross, Customary International Law Study* (Cambridge University Press, 2009).

[11] Antonio Cassese, *International Law* (Oxford University Press, 2001) 154.

individualistic and anarchic behaviours have been supplanted by general principles of nations as set out in the Charter and other international documents of significant importance. This holds especially true with respect to peremptory norms of international law; no state can avoid the application of rules that are considered *jus cogens*.[12]

Customary International Humanitarian Law

Customary international law plays a critical role in the law of armed conflict. Although derived from the same basic principles as general customary international law, the development and interpretation of customary international humanitarian law (IHL) differs significantly from general CIL in that the laws of war are based not on pragmatism, but rather in a 'motivation for restraint [that] stemmed from notions of what was considered to be honourable and ...what was perceived as civilized'.[13] This natural law approach to the creation of IHL is based in the philosophies of humanity and chivalry, which provide a moral and principled foundation upon which the law of armed conflict is anchored. Although these principles can be traced through the history of warfare, the culmination of the ideal was expressed in 1899 in the Martens Clause, which is found in the preamble to the 1899 Hague Convention II:

Until a more complete code of the laws of war is issued, the High Contracting Parties think it right to declare that in cases not included in the Regulations adopted by them, populations and belligerents remain under the protection and empire of the principles of international law, as they result from the usages established between civilized nations, from the laws of humanity and the requirements of the public conscience.[14]

The very construction of the Martens Clause allows for it to be interpreted in several ways. The first interpretation, which is based on a narrow reading of the clause, considers it to have limited importance, other than providing a 'recognition of the continued validity of customary rules that have not been altered by treaty, and of custom as a potential source of new rules'.[15] This interpretation, which is advocated by larger powers, regards the Martens Clause to be little more than an acknowledgement that in cases where treaty law is incomplete, customary law can be employed to fill the gaps.

---

[12] Ibid, 155.

[13] Louise Doswald-Beck and Sylvain Vité, 'International Humanitarian Law and Human Rights Law' (1993) 293 International Review of the Red Cross, online: ICRC <http://www.icrc.org/eng/resources/documents/misc/57jmrt.htm> accessed 13 May 2017.

[14] Hague Convention (II) with Respect to the Laws and Customs of War on Land and its annex: Regulations concerning the Laws and Customs of War on Land (29 July 1899) Preamble.

[15] Burrus M. Carnahan, *Customary Rules of International Humanitarian Law: Report on the Practice of the United States of America*. Online: Google Books <http://Customary_Rules_of_International_Humanit.html?id=bumRSwAACAAJ&redir_esc=y> accessed 13 May 2017.

At the other end of the spectrum, there exists a belief that the dictates of public conscience, as provided in the Martens Clause and the several iterations through which it has gone since 1899, are a source of customary IHL:

[T]he Martens Clause provided its own self-sufficient and conclusive authority for the proposition that there were already in existence principles of international law under which considerations of humanity could themselves exert legal force to govern military conduct in cases in which no relevant rule was provided by conventional law. Accordingly, it was not necessary to locate elsewhere the independent existence of such principles of international law; the source of the principles lay in the Clause itself.[16]

While there is disagreement between states as to how the Martens Clause should be interpreted,[17] and thus which principles can influence the creation of customary IHL,[18] most commentators acknowledge[19] that Judge Antonio Cassese's opinion in the *Kupreskic* case at the International Criminal Tribunal for Yugoslavia represents a commonly held understanding of the role that the Martens Clause plays in the development of customary IHL:

True, [the Martens Clause] may not be taken to mean that the 'principles of humanity' and the 'dictates of public conscience' have been elevated to the rank of independent sources of international law, for this conclusion is belied by international practice. However, this Clause enjoins, as a minimum, reference to those principles and dictates any time a rule of international humanitarian law is not sufficiently rigorous or precise: in those instances the scope and purport of the rule must be defined with reference to those principles and dictates.[20]

Customary Law and Blockade

Other than the few matters that were covered in the provisions of the Declaration of Paris, there has been no serious effort made to codify of the Law of Maritime Blockade since its inception into modern warfare in the sixteenth century. While the Declaration of London provided an historic opportunity for the law to be established by convention, its ultimate failure left the world with a body of law that has remained largely unsettled. In spite of the statement made in respect to 'generally recognized rules of international law' in the preamble to the London Declaration, consensus on a number of issues fragmented when the treaty failed. While some

---

[16] *Legality of the Threat of Use of Nuclear Weapons Opinion*, Advisory Opinion [1996] ICJ Rep 226, 408 (hereafter *Nuclear Weapons Case*).

[17] See, for example, Theodore Meron, 'The Humanization of Humanitarian Law' (2000) 94:2 AJIL 239, 250.

[18] Generally, the states that demand a narrow interpretation of the Martens Clause are those that are militarily powerful. Thus Russia (which considers the Martens Clause to be of no effect since the development of AP1), the United States, and Britain insist that the clause only informs the interpretation of *opinio juris* and state practice. Smaller and middle powers, such as Australia, consider the clause to have a much broader scope.

[19] Theodor Meron, 'The Martens Clause, Principles of Humanity, and Dictates of Public Conscience' (2000) 94:1 AJIL 78.

[20] *Prosecutor v Kupreskic et al.* IT-95-16-A, Judgement on Appeal (23 October 2001) International Criminal Tribunal for the former Yugoslavia (Appeals Chamber) para 525.

aspects of the Declaration were readily accepted as customary law, some of the most contentious issues were not. Consequently most matters of blockade law, beyond the basic elements of establishment (notice, effectiveness, impartial application, respect for neutral rights) have remained unsettled.[21] While some states have resisted any attempts to expand the scope of blockade law beyond the basic elements, others have embraced attempts to import humanitarian principles, such as those found in the San Remo Manual.[22]

As the various reports and assessments surrounding the Israeli blockade of Gaza have clearly demonstrated, there is confusion and disagreement as to what the duties and obligations of a blockading power are. The resultant confusion leaves states with no clear concept of maritime blockade law, or the rights and obligations of the various parties that are affected when a blockade is established.

Contentious Issues in Blockade Law

One of the primary goals of the participants at the London Conference was to reach consensus on the perennial issues of effectiveness, distance blockade, and the doctrine of continuous voyage. In creating a maritime court to adjudicate issue related to blockade, the delegates to the Conference anticipated that these issues would finally be resolved. When the Declaration failed to be ratified the idea of an international maritime court died on the table, as did the hope that blockade's most contentious issues would ultimately be settled.

Although a number of important issues regarding blockade are still not resolved, there are several points on which there is general agreement. First, in contemporary practice it is settled that in order to be lawful a blockade must be properly established.[23] The rules governing establishment of a blockade are relatively straightforward and uncontroversial. The decision and authority to establish a blockade rests with the government of the blockading state.[24] In accordance with the provisions that were laid out in article 9 of the Declaration of London, the blockading state, or naval authorities acting on its behalf, may make the declaration of blockade. Any declaration of blockade must include the following information:

(1) the date when the blockade begins;

(2) the geographical limits of the coastline under blockade;[25] and

---

[21] For example, blockade operations during the two world wars were characterized as reprisals. This characterization arose not only from the discomfort that some were feeling regarding the lawfulness of the actions, but also as a result of confusion as to what the law entailed. From this perspective it was far easier to acknowledge that the operation was not being conducted within the parameters of the law than it was to try to explain or defend the actions through reference to a legal standard.

[22] Louise Doswald-Beck (ed), *San Remo Manual on International Law Applicable to Armed Conflicts at Sea* (Cambridge University Press, 1995) arts 102–4 (hereafter SRM).

[23] Ibid, art 93.

[24] Robert W. Tucker, *The Law of War and Neutrality at Sea* (United States Government Printing Office, 1957) 287 (hereafter Tucker, *Neutrality*).

[25] In practice, the geographic limits of a blockade are expressed in map coordinates. See, for example, Israeli Notification of Blockade of Gaza, Notice to Mariners No 1/2009, dated 6 January 2009,

(3) the period within which neutral vessels may come out.[26]

As with the requirements for establishment, the criteria for blockade notification is universally acknowledged, with the accepted corollary that if a vessel has not received actual or presumptive notification of a blockade, then it may not be held or condemned for breach thereof.[27] The traditional protocols for notification are specified in article 11 of the Declaration of London, which required notification through diplomatic channels:

(1) To neutral Powers, by the blockading Power, by means of a communication addressed to the Governments direct, or to their representatives accredited to it; and,

(2) To the local authorities, by the officer commanding the blockading force. The local authorities will, in turn, inform the foreign consular officers at the port or on the coastline under blockade as soon as possible.[28]

Contemporarily, a variety of means of notification are used to ensure that masters of vessels are aware of blockade operations. As has been the case in the Israeli blockade of Gaza, official notification has been transmitted to regional governments, notice of the blockade is regularly broadcast on marine radio as notices to mariners, and the Israeli Ministry of Transport provides notice and details of the blockade on its website.[29]

The Principle of Effectiveness

[A] declaration unsupported by fact will not be sufficient to establish it.[30]

Few issues highlight the tension between neutral and belligerent rights more than does the principle of effectiveness. Although widely acknowledged as the most fundamental principle of blockade,[31] the principle has historically been preached far better than it has been practised.

One of the main goals of a blockade is to prevent maritime trade from being conducted in the blockaded area. In the eyes of neutrals, blockade has such far reaching economic consequences that if a belligerent wishes to establish a blockade, it must dedicate the resources necessary to accomplish the task of making it dangerous for

---

online: Ministry of Transport <http://asp.mot.gov.il/en/shipping/notice2mariners/547-no1200> accessed 13 May 2017.

[26] London Declaration Concerning the Laws of Naval War (1909) 208 Consol TS 338 (not entered into force), (hereafter Declaration of London) art 9.

[27] Ibid, art 14.   [28] Ibid, art 11.

[29] See discussion by Elizabeth Spelman, 'The Legality of the Israeli Blockade of the Gaza Strip' (2013) 19:1 Web JCLI. See also Israel MTO, 'Notice to Mariners 1/2009: Blockade of Gaza Strip' <http://asp.mot.gov.il/en/shipping/notice2mariners/547-no12009> accessed 13 May 2017.

[30] *The Mercurius*, 1 C Rob Adm 80, 83.

[31] The issue of effectiveness and paper blockades was one of the primary issues dealt with in the Declaration of Paris.

vessels to attempt to ingress or egress the area that is declared to be under blockade. Consequently, it has long been agreed that blockades must exist in fact, and that they must be effective. The corollary to this is that if a blockading force does not or cannot dedicate sufficient resources to enforce its action, then that force has no right to declare a maritime blockade.

While on its face the concept of effectiveness might seem to be quite clear, the interpretation of 'effective' has plagued modern blockade since the Dutch initiated the practice of modern blockade in 1584. In order to appreciate the challenges faced by those who have been tasked with adjudicating on the issue, it is necessary to recall the evolution of blockade, and to understand that a lack of consistency in interpretation and practice has hindered the development of a universal comprehension of the term.

As has been noted, the concept of blockade was born in siege operations, with the earliest blockades always being conducted as the seaward element of an investment against a port city. In the case of siege against port cities, it was essential to ensure that there could be no escape or resupply by sea. Thus, the accepted rule of the time, reflecting the reality that warships could not manoeuvre in the absence of wind, was that vessels conducting a blockade were required to be close enough to each other to have interlocking fires.[32] It was only in this manner that a blockading force could be assured of intercepting or sinking all vessels that attempted to reach the besieged locality.

The Dutch blockade of Spanish ports in 1584 was a watershed in the development of naval blockade. This new form of blockade, which barred access to areas rather than besieged localities, made the practice of ensuring interlocking fire impractical. While it was no longer necessary for ships be stationed off the beams of one another, it did require that a blockading force be of sufficient strength to pose a 'manifest danger [to all vessels] entering the blockaded area'.[33]

In spite of pronounced intentions to establish and maintain effective blockades, the general practice of the naval powers during the seventeenth and eighteenth centuries was to declare blockades over vast areas that they could not possibly control; one result of which was the creation of the League of Armed Neutrality of 1780. While at first the efforts of the League of Armed Neutrality were met with British derision, the movement towards incorporating effectiveness as a requirement in blockades was nonetheless initiated.[34]

Although during the Napoleonic Wars (1803–15) both the British and the French declared vast areas of ocean to be under blockade,[35] reality dictated that for the most part, the blockades were far from effective. The paper blockades pronounced by the major warring powers drew the ire of neutrals, not the least of which was the United

---

[32] John Westlake, *The Collected Papers of John Westlake on Public International Law* (Cambridge University Press, 1914) 343 (hereafter Westlake, *Collected Papers*).

[33] Ibid, 340.

[34] Michael Schmitt, *Essays on Law and War: The Fault Lines* (Asser Press, 2012) 222 (hereafter Schmitt, *Fault Lines*).

[35] François Crouzet, 'Wars, Blockade, and Economic Change in Europe, 1792–1815' (1964) 24:4 The Journal of Economic History 567, 574.

States, which, at the dawn of the nineteenth century, was emerging as a substantial power, both militarily and economically.[36]

While the Royal Navy paid little heed to the protests of the neutrals, the Admiralty courts[37] of the early 1800s began to signal their shift towards recognition of effectiveness as an essential element of blockade. The first evidence of the judicial shift towards compelling effectiveness can be found in the statement of noted jurist, Sir William Scott, in the 1799 case of *The Mercurius*, a ship that sailed out of Hamburg, carrying a cargo owned by a citizen of the United States. In finding that the vessel should be condemned for attempting to enter the blockaded port of Amsterdam, Sir William stated:

The powers who formed the armed neutrality in the last war, understood blockade in this sense; and Russia, who was the principal party in that confederacy, described a place to be in a state of blockade, when it is dangerous to attempt to enter into it.[38]

Similarly, in the prize case of *The Frederick Molke*, the Admiralty Court, in condemning the Danish vessel for a breach of the blockade of Havre, found that 'nothing farther is necessary to constitute blockade, than that there should be a force stationed to prevent communication, 'and a due notice, or prohibition given to the party'.[39]

While *The Mercuris* and *The Frederick Molke* provided judicial recognition of the requirement for effectiveness, the Admiralty case of *The Nancy*,[40] decided in 1809, was the first major case to examine the meaning of the term. *The Nancy* was an American vessel that was transporting a cargo from New York to Martinique, which was under British blockade. After unloading in Martinique and then taking on a new cargo, *The Nancy* was seized by the Royal Navy and taken to Halifax. In the Halifax prize court the master testified that he was not aware of the blockade over Martinique, and that during the period that *The Nancy* was alongside, he did not at any time see a blockading ship. In ordering that the vessel be restored to its owners, the court elaborated on the scope of effectiveness as follows:

[I]t was the duty of the blockaders to maintain such a force as would be of itself sufficient to enforce the blockade. This could only be effected [sic] by keeping a number of vessels on the different stations, so communicating with each other as to be able to intercept all vessels attempting to enter the ports of the island.[41]

In reaching its decision, the prize court accepted the testimony that the British had left one fifty-gun vessel on station to maintain the blockade of Martinique; a task that had previously been undertaken by a large number of ships. In finding that one vessel was not sufficient to blockade the area, the Court determined that, 'The

---

[36] Note that there are some commentators who blame Britain's blockade policy for the American decision to invade Canada in 1812.

[37] The Admiralty courts are generally considered as being the most authoritative voices on the laws of blockade and contraband in the seventeenth through nineteenth centuries. The reason for this lies in the fact that it is the domestic courts of the prize taker that determine prize cases. Insofar as Britain was by far the most active navy and had the busiest prize courts, the majority of jurisprudence for this timeframe arises from the United Kingdom.

[38] *The Mercurius* (n 30) 86.   [39] *The Frederick Molke* (1799) 1 C Rob 86,87.
[40] *The Nancy* (1809) 1 Act 57.   [41] Ibid, 59.

periodical appearance of a vessel of war in the offing could not be supposed a continuation of a blockade'.[42]

The Nancy was a turning point from which the Admiralty courts would not look back. While earlier cases had held that the fact that a vessel had been captured was sufficient proof of the effectiveness, *The Nancy* demonstrated that in order to prove effectiveness the blockading force would have to show that it had continuously maintained the capability 'to intercept all vessels attempting to enter [blockaded] ports'.[43]

Further examination of the issue of effectiveness was made in the case of *The Franciska*, a Danish vessel captured by the Royal Navy during its blockade of Riga in 1854. In *The Franciska*, the claimant challenged the legal existence of the blockade by suggesting that the Royal Navy had not deployed a sufficient number of ships to ensure effectiveness. Directly addressing the issue how many vessels it might take to ensure that a blockade was effective, the Court concluded:

The maintenance of a blockade must always be a question of degree—of the degree of danger attending ships going into, or leaving a blockaded port.... Nothing is further from my intention, nor indeed more opposed to my notions of the law of nations, than any relaxation of the rule, that a blockade must be efficiently maintained, ... It is most difficult to judge from numbers alone. Hence I believe (I have made search to ascertain the fact) that in every case the inquiry has been whether the force was competent and present, and if so, the performance of the duty was presumed ...; and most certainly, if the fact could be established, that from incompetency, or neglect of duty that force was not present in its proper place at times, and seasons, when there was no legal exception to justify its absence, the validity of this blockade would be greatly in danger.[44]

It is of little surprise that the jurisprudence of the prize courts of the nineteenth century began to emphasize the requirement for effectiveness. The growth of international commerce in Europe, spurred by the industrial revolution and its insatiable appetite for raw materials from the new world, had resulted in a massive expansion of maritime trade. As one of the catalysts that was sustaining their exponential economic growth, neutral powers regarded their trading rights as being inviolable;[45]

---

[42] Ibid.   [43] Ibid.

[44] James Parker Deane, *The Law of Blockade: As Contained in the Report of Eight Cases Argued and Determined in the High Court of Admiralty on the Blockade of the Coast of Courland, 1854* (Butterworths, 1855) 102.

[45] In 1861, the United States, which had been a long-time leading advocate of neutral rights, and thus an outspoken opponent of Britain's paper blockades, engaged in what is perhaps the most controversial blockade (in terms of effectiveness) in history when its Union Navy announced that it would blockade Confederate ports. When the blockade was proclaimed in April 1861, the Union Navy had only several vessels that were capable of engaging in blockade operations along the 5600km of coastline of the South. 'The blockade of 1861 was indeed very leaky. Estimates suggest that only one in ten ships attempting to trade with the South was captured in the first year of the war. However, as the war progressed and the Union navy increased in size, the blockade became increasingly effective. By 1864 one in three ships were being captured, although even that ratio still left a good chance of profit for the owner of a blockade runner.' In spite of the fact that, at its most effective, the Union Navy was capable of stopping less than 40 per cent of vessels that attempted to breach the blockade, there are some commentators who contend that the Union blockade was effective because of the devastating effect that it had on the South's economy, the fact that regular shipping into the South had declined significantly, and that exports of cotton during the war had declined by some 75 per cent. See, for example, Andrew

and the establishment of fake blockades was considered to be one of the most offensive forms of interference. As a result, the attention of publicists, legislators, and jurists alike was drawn to the issue.

Amongst those who examined the requirements for blockade in the nineteenth century was Theodore Ortolan, who stated in 1845:

A blockade does not exist simply because it is called a blockade. In order for a blockade to exist it must be effective, that is, constantly maintained by naval forces more or less numerous, according to the Nature of the places, and sufficiently close to render the approach of these places dangerous.[46]

Whether or not Ortolan's statement as to effectiveness influenced the decision in *The Franciska* is not clear; however, cases subsequent to it followed the precedent that 'the question of effectiveness must necessarily depend on the circumstances . . . [and] if a single modern cruiser blockading a port renders it in fact dangerous for other craft to enter the port, that is sufficient, since thereby the blockade is made practically effective'.[47] In other words, the question of whether or not a blockade was effective was a question of fact that could be determined only upon examination of the particular case.

The statements and observations made by the naval powers in preparation for the London Conference illustrate an apparent consensus on the issue of effectiveness.[48] On close examination, however, there is a subtle, yet significant difference between the statements of most of the European powers and those of the United States and Great Britain. Whereas the requirement for effectiveness was universally accepted, the question of where blockading vessels must be stationed remained unanswered. At the centre of the issue was the query as to whether a vessel could only be seized for crossing a certain line on the sea (the Continental view), or whether it could be seized for sailing towards a coast with the intent of reaching it (Anglo–American view). In other words there was a divergence as to whether blockading vessels were required to be stationed 'sufficiently close as to render attempted passage dangerous',[49] or whether the issue of distance from the blockaded area was immaterial.

While the General Report to the Conference of London acknowledged the difficulties in defining the meaning of 'effective', it also expressed optimism that the establishment of the international prize court as an absolutely impartial international tribunal would provide a mechanism by which to settle a number of the

---

F. Smith, *Starving the South: How the North Won the Civil War* (St. Martin's Press, 2011) and David G. Surdam, 'The Union Navy's Blockade Reconsidered' (1998) 51:4 Naval War College Review 85. As many commentators note, British recognition of the blockade should not be taken as an indication that Britain considered the blockade to be effective. Rather, it should be recognized as Britain's desire to remain neutral and not become entangled in yet another war in the Americas.

[46] Théodore Ortolan, *Règles internationales et diplomatie de la mer*, vol 2 (Paris: Cosse et Delemotte, 1845) 323 (author's translation) (hereafter Ortolan, *Règles*).

[47] *The Olinde Rodriguez* (1899) 174 US 510, 518.

[48] James Brown Scott, *The Declaration of London February 26, 1909: A Collection of Official Papers and Documents Relating to the International Naval Conference Held in London December 1908–February 1909* (Oxford University Press, 1919) 51–7 (hereafter Scott, *Declaration of London*).

[49] Ortolan, *Règles* (n 46) 323.

outstanding issues that had hitherto remained unresolved.[50] As history has borne out, however, the international prize court never became a reality; with the result that differences in the interpretations of effectiveness and other operational aspects of blockade have yet to be resolved.

Distance Blockade

Directly related to the issue of proximity, and a practice that has regularly drawn the ire of neutrals is the stratagem of distance blockade. Under the concept of distance blockade, a vessel that sets sail towards a blockaded port is liable to be seized and condemned for breach of blockade 'from the moment she appears on the high seas'.[51] Under this doctrine the Master's intention to violate the blockade is the element that creates the breach, not the actual entry or attempted entry into a blockaded area per se.

This genesis of distance blockade is found in the theory and practice of the Dutch *placaat* of 9 July 1630, which announced that the whole of the Flanders coast was blockaded, and that neutral ships found at any distance from Flanders and intending to call at blockaded ports would be seized.[52] In this respect, distance blockade represented the convergence of two previously distinct naval operations; the naval siege, and the belligerent right to intercept contraband destined for enemy ports at any point in its voyage.

At the time of the Dutch *placaat*, seagoing vessels were wholly dependent upon sail power. Although some naval vessels were fast under sail, many could not match the speed of small, manoeuvrable merchantmen. Consequently, in order to ensure interception of blockade runners, it was generally necessary to station naval ships so that they had interlocking fires from their main guns. As technology advanced, and naval ships became faster and less reliant upon sails, their ability to chase down blockade-runners improved. Concomitant with naval forces' improvements in speed and manoeuvre was the demise of the requirement to station blockading vessels in close proximity to each other. Rather, it was determined that blockades could be much more efficiently enforced by placing blockading vessels at choke points, or on station locations from which they could pursue evading ships. Thus began a new strategy under which vessels enforcing blockades were stationed further and further away from the enemy coasts.

The practice of distance blockade has long been associated with Britain. As the dominant naval power in post-seventeenth-century Europe, the Royal Navy embraced the doctrine of distance blockade with fervour,[53] regularly intercepting

---

[50] Scott, *Declaration of London* (n 48) 136.   [51] Ibid.

[52] Westlake, *Collected Papers* (n 32) 327.

[53] The British policy in the eighteenth century found opposition not only amongst the continental powers but also with the newly emerging naval power of the United States whose economy was heavily dependent on trans-Atlantic commerce, much of which was with France and her colonies. The British, who regularly used visit and search under the guise of blockade as a means of impressing American sailors into naval service, thus found themselves at odds not only with her traditional continental enemies, but with the world's fastest growing naval power as well. The American perspective on the issue is

vessels hundreds, if not thousands of miles from their destination ports.[54] The issue of distance was brought before the Admiralty Court in the case of *The Franciska* in which the claimant challenged the legality of the British blockade of Riga, claiming that a vessels stationed several hundred kilometres from a blockaded place could not be considered to be effectively conducting the operation. Addressing the issue directly, and acknowledging that it Europe the law might be different, Dr Lushington, writing for the prize court found:

> To me it is abundantly manifest the true criterion whereby the legality of a blockade shall be established is, not the place where the blockading force is stationed, nor its distance from the place blockaded, but the capability of the force, wherever stationed, adequately to maintain the blockade.[55] I am satisfied, both on principle and authority, that the requisites to a blockade are only two: 1st, that the ports blockaded shall be hostile territory; 2nd, that the blockading force could act as efficiently to maintain it ... therefore I say that the blockade of Riga was legitimate.[56]

Amongst the European powers, France, which had historically been England's greatest rival, was the most outspoken opponent to the practice of distance blockade. Taking the position that 'The blockade is an action of war, inseparable from the places where it is exercised, and whose violation cannot be enforced except in these very places',[57] the French restricted the area of seizure to a 'rayon d'action', outside of which neutral vessels were not to be harassed. In accordance with the French interpretation, blockading forces were permitted to intercept vessels only when they entered into a blockade zone, which was relatively close to the shoreline of the blockaded place. This divergence in practice and understanding, which underlay some of the significant tensions between the major maritime powers at the beginning of the twentieth century, represented a significant challenge for the plenipotentiaries to the London Naval Conference.

As hosts to the 1908 Naval Conference, the British were motivated to ensure that the conference would be a success. The desire of the British to reach settlement on

---

well illustrated in a letter from Secretary of State James Madison to US Ambassador to Britain, James Monroe in 1804 in which Madison expressed his indignation by stating, 'British Cruisers [were] seizing every Vessel bound to such Ports, whatever distance from them, and the British prize Courts [were] pronouncing condemnations wherever of the proclamation,the time of sailing could be presumed, altho' it might afterwards be known that no real blockade existed. The whole scene was a perfect mockery, in which fact was sacrificed to forms, and right to power and plunder.' 'Letter from James Madison to James Monroe, 5 January 1804' online: National Archives http://founders.archives. gov/documents/Madison/02-06-02-0264 accessed 9 October 2017.

[54] In fairness to the British, the Royal Navy has consistently practised and advocated distance blockade. While European powers have been consistent in their criticism of the practice, they have habitually practised distance blockade whenever they have been placed in the position of the blockading power. Spain, France, and the Netherlands have all, at one time or another practised distance blockade. Similarly, the United States, which historically condemned the practice, readily adopted it whenever it was convenient to do so.

[55] *The Franciska* (1855) Spinks, Ecclesiastical and Admiralty Reports II, 128.

[56] Ibid, 129.

[57] M. Fusinato, the second Hague Conference, as quoted in Georges Kaeckenbeeck 'Divergences between British and Other Views on International Law' (1918) 4 Transactions of the Grotius Society, Problems of the War: Papers Read Before the Society in the Year 1918, 213fn (m) (author's translation).

major naval issues was evidenced in Foreign Secretary Sir Edward Grey's instructions to the British delegates to the conference, particularly with respect to the issue of distance blockade. In noting that he could find no case in which British prize courts had 'condemned [a vessel] for breach of blockade except when actually close to, or directly approaching the blockaded port or coast',[58] Sir Edward suggested that in practical application, there was in reality little substantial difference between continental and British practices. Directing Lord Desart to abandon strict adherence to the concept of distance blockade, he stated:

If the *rayon d'action* may be defined as the area of operation of the blockading force, His Majesty's government would be disposed to accept a rule to the above effect as fairly representing the actual practice of both the rival systems, and therefore being capable of being described as of general application.[59]

Compromise on the issue was achieved through the inclusion of article 17 into the Declaration of London wherein it was agreed that neutral vessels could only be subjected to capture if they were in the 'area of operations' of the blockading force.[60] By adopting the language of the article, the delegates were able to satisfy both the Anglo–American and the Continental camps; the English accepted that they could not stop a vessel for breaching blockade wherever they saw fit, and the continental powers conceded that interceptions could occur in areas not immediately proximate to blockaded shores. As was the case with most of the contentious issues that had been resolved during the London Conference, when the Declaration of London failed, the agreement on distance blockade fell by the wayside. Absent the obligation of a binding treaty, states reverted to their past doctrine and practice. In the cases of the United States and Great Britain, the concept of distance blockade was re-born with intensity.[61]

The Doctrine of Continuous Voyage

[T]he landing of goods and payment of duties does not interrupt the continuity of the voyage of the cargo, unless there be an honest intention to bring them into the common stock of the country. If there be an intention, either formed

[58] 'Instructions Addressed to the British Delegates by Sir Edward Grey' in Scott, *Declaration of London* (n 48) 221.

[59] Ibid, 222. The American delegation to the conference also supported the notion of a 'rayon d'action' along terms similar to those laid down by Sir Edward Grey. The American position differed from the British in that the United States advocated for a maximum radius of action of 1000nm for a blockade.

[60] Declaration of London (n 27). Article 17 provided: 'Neutral vessels may not be captured for breach of blockade except within the area of operations of the warships detailed to render the blockade effective.'

[61] The United States Naval Instructions of 1917 illustrated a complete rebuke of art 17 of the Declaration of London. At para 31 the manual stated, 'The liability of a blockade runner to capture and condemnation begins and terminates with her voyage.' *Instructions for the Navy of the United States Governing Maritime Warfare: June 1917* (Government Printing Office, 1917) para 31 (hereafter 1917 Naval Instructions).

at the time of original shipment, or afterwards, to send the goods forward to an unlawful destination, the continuity of the voyage will not be broken, as to the cargo, by any transactions at the intermediate port.[62]

There are two ways that a maritime blockade can be breached by neutrals; by trading directly with the blockaded belligerent, or by using a neutral third country through which the goods can be trans-shipped. The latter method is referred to as 'ultimate destination', or more commonly, as 'continuous voyage'.[63] Under the doctrine of continuous voyage a vessel that attempts to circumvent a blockade by delivering its cargo to a neutral port through which the cargo will flow to an enemy destination, risks interception and condemnation by the blockading force.

The origin of the doctrine of continuous voyage can be traced to the eighteenth century, at which time neutral traders were attempting to frustrate British blockades against French colonial interests. At that time, colonial powers had a complete monopoly over trade from their colonies, to the extent that they forbade all others, including neutrals, from trading with them.[64] When, during the Seven Years War, the French were unable to conduct trade with their colonies due to Britain's dominance of the seas, they enlisted Dutch and other neutral vessels to conduct trade on France's behalf, moving goods between colonial ports as well as between the colonies and France. Using the rationale that the neutrals had been co-opted into French service and had aligned themselves with France's interests and purposes, the British government instructed the Royal Navy to seize neutral vessels conducting trade with and among the French colonies. The British policy, which has become known as 'The Rule of the War of 1756', was based on two general principles:

1. Neutrals have no right to carry on in time of war a commerce which is not permitted them in time of peace; and,
2. A ship, trading on account of the enemy has forfeited the immunity of its flag, and cannot be considered neutral.[65]

In order to circumvent the Rule of the War of 1756, neutral vessels carrying goods between the colonies and France began the practice of calling at neutral ports where they would sell and/or offload a cargo, immediately buy it back, and transport it to its ultimate destination. British prize courts proved unsympathetic to the neutrals' attempts to frustrate the Rule. Under the leadership of Sir William Scott, prize

---

[62] *The William* (1806) C. Rob, 399; 1 Kent's Commentaries, 84 (hereafter *The William*).

[63] The same principle applies for contraband. Recall that contraband means 'goods, [under neutral cartage], which are ultimately destined for territory under the control of the enemy and which may be susceptible for use in armed conflict'.

[64] At that time, the three principle reasons for which capture of neutral vessels could be permitted were: breach of blockade, carriage of contraband, and conducting trade that absent a war would not be permitted. See Lieutenant A.G. Leech, 'The Doctrine of Continuous Voyage: Its Origin and Development from the Seven Years' War (1756) to the Boer War' (1902) 46:298 Royal United Services Institution Journal 1524 (hereafter Leech, 'Continuous Voyage').

[65] D.I. Katchenovsky, 'Prize Law' as quoted in James W. Gantenbein, *The Doctrine of Continuous Voyage Particularly as Applied to Contraband and Blockade* (Keystone Press, 1929) 7 (fn 6).

courts created the 'doctrine of continuous voyage', the essence of which was that if the 'neutral seeks to evade the law by the mere trick of introducing a neutral port as a false and merely colourable destination, ... then the ... right of capture ought clearly to be upheld'.[66]

Neutral shippers, who considered that goods of any type that were being shipped to a neutral country could not be considered as contraband and could therefore not be subject to seizure, regardless of ultimate destination, despised the doctrine of continuous voyage.[67] In spite of the opposition of neutrals, the doctrine was embraced by the prevailing naval powers of the time, particularly Britain and the United States, in whose courts most prize law respecting continuous voyage was being decided. Such was the case with *The William*,[68] an American vessel that was captured running between Spanish colonies and Spain. In this case, the vessel attempted to evade the blockade against Spain by offloading its cargo at the neutral port of Marble Head, Massachusetts, while the ship underwent repairs. The apparent intent of the owners in this case was to change the status of the cargo from 'enemy' to 'neutral' by interjecting a neutral party into the transaction. Following the completion of the repairs, the cargo was reloaded. Shortly after setting sail, *The William* was captured by the Royal Navy and taken to Halifax for adjudication by the prize court. In condemning the vessel, Sir William Grant stated:

The act of shifting the cargo from the ship to the shore and from the shore back again to the ship does not necessarily amount to the termination of one voyage and the commencement of another. It may be wholly unconnected with any purpose of importation into the place where it is done.... The truth may not always be discernible, but when it is discovered, it is according to the truth and not according to fiction that we are to give the transaction its character and denomination. If the voyage from the place of lading be not really ended, it matters not by what acts the party may have evinced his desire of making it appear to have ended.[69]

The policies of both the United Kingdom and the United States in the closing years of the nineteenth century are summed up quite succinctly in the words of Sir Travis Twiss:

[I]t has remained for the [United States], under her extraordinary difficulties, to initiate the doctrine of a prospective intention, on the part of a neutral merchant, to violate a blockade, and to subject him to the confiscation of his property not upon the evidence of any present voyage of the ship and cargo, in which the ship and cargo have been intercepted, but, upon the presumption of a future voyage of the cargo alone to a blockaded port, after it had been landed from the ship at a neutral port.[70]

The doctrine of continuous voyage was one of the issues most likely to lead to an impasse when the participants arrived for the London Conference in December

---

[66] Leech, 'Continuous Voyage' (n 64) 1529.

[67] See discussion of Germany's position with respect to '*The Bundesrath*' in James W. Gantenbein, *The Doctrine of Continuous Voyage Particularly as Applied to Contraband and Blockade* (Keystone Press, 1929) 90–1.

[68] *The William* (n 62) 349.   [69] Ibid, 387.

[70] Travis Twiss, 'Continuous Voyage,' 3 Law Mag. & Rev. 4th series, 1.

1908. The continental powers of Germany and Austria–Hungary were the most outspoken opponents of the doctrine, sharing the position that, 'the doctrine of continuous voyage has no legitimate application to goods to be discharged in intermediate neutral ports',[71] and that the 'so-called "theory of continuous voyage" applied by the prize courts of some powers, is rejected almost unanimously by continental authors'.[72]

On the eve of the commencement of the London Conference, only the United Kingdom and the United States were inclined to support the application of continuous voyage to maritime blockade. Knowing that any attempt to uphold the doctrine as being applicable to blockade would face significant opposition, and might perhaps be a deal breaker, both nations' delegates were instructed to compromise on the issue. The resulting agreement, as outlined in the articles below, left no doubt that the doctrine of continuous voyage would have no place in blockade:

Art. 17. Neutral vessels may not be captured for breach of blockade except within the area of operations of the warships detailed to render the blockade effective.

Art. 18. The blockading forces must not bar access to neutral ports or coasts.

Art. 19. Whatever may be the ulterior destination of a vessel or of her cargo, she cannot be captured for breach of blockade, if, at the moment, she is on her way to a non-blockaded port.[73]

The inclusion of article 19 in the Declaration of London in 1909 reflected the continental powers' notion that if a vessel is heading to a neutral port with a cargo ultimately destined for a blockaded port, it commits no breach so long as it does not cross into the blockaded area. This position illustrates the idea that the essential aspect of blockade lies in the complete interdiction of maritime traffic into and out of the blockaded area. In accordance with this theory, the nature of the cargo on vessels is irrelevant; rather the prohibition of all maritime traffic into a specified area is the defining characteristic of blockade operations.

Although the British delegation to the London Conference made a pragmatic concession by agreeing to the provisions of article 19, the United Kingdom's true interpretation respecting continuous voyage were soon revealed when, during the First World War, the Royal Navy ardently incorporated the doctrine of continuous voyage (in combination with distance blockade) as a significant aspect of the blockade of Germany. In essence, the United Kingdom's near-immediate reversion to pre-London practice demonstrated Britain's historical tenet that the primary focus of a blockade is cargo. In that respect, the United Kingdom contended that 'a belligerent did not violate any "fundamental principle of international law" by applying a blockade in such a way as to cut off the enemy's commerce with foreign countries through neutral ports if the circumstances render such an application of the principles of blockade the only means of making it effective'.[74]

---

[71] Scott, *The Declaration of London* (n48) 73.   [72] Ibid, 74.
[73] Declaration of London (n 27) 89.   [74] Tucker, *Neutrality* (n 24) 309.

As was the case in the First World War, early in the Second World War the British invoked the doctrine of continuous voyage as an aspect of their blockade against Germany when, in July 1940, the British issued an Order in Council that declared that:

Goods consigned to any port or place from which they might reach enemy territory or the enemy armed forces, ... shall, until the contrary is established, be deemed to have an enemy destination.[75]

Although some commentators have opined that the United Kingdom's departure from the Declaration of London's framework regarding continuous voyage did not affect the status of the law of blockade because of the fact that the actions were warranted as reprisals against Germany's policy of unlimited maritime warfare, others advocate that the United Kingdom's wartime policies constituted a rejection of a regime that was outdated and no longer valid in the context of modern warfare and technology.

Continuous Voyage in the Twenty-first Century

It is evident that the views on the principle involved in the doctrine of continuous voyage have been divergent for more than two hundred and fifty years.[76]

In spite of the opinion by some that practice of blockade was 'entirely archaic ... [and] the traditional rules for formal blockade were in complete desuetude',[77] the authors of the San Remo Manual made a deliberate decision to address the subject of maritime blockade when they met in 1992. Although the authors dealt with many of the issues of blockade law, they assiduously avoided making any reference to the still-contentious doctrine of continuous voyage. Given the broad representation of the working groups, the limited time that they had to complete their tasks, and that the contributors were focusing on finding areas of agreement with respect to the content of customary law, the fact that the issue was not addressed at San Remo is not surprising.

While it is clear that it was followed by the victorious powers during the two world wars, that it is maintained as a valid doctrine, and has been consistently practised by the navies of the United States, Great Britain, some nations of the British Commonwealth, and more recently Israel,[78] it is difficult to conclude that the

---

[75] George VI, R.I., Order in Council, (31 July 1940) London Gazette 34195, 4800.

[76] Thomas Baty, 'The History of Continuous Voyage' (1941) 90: 2 University of Pennsylvania Law Review and American Law Register 127,136.

[77] Louise Doswald-Beck, 'Background—Development of the San Remo Manual and its Intended Purpose—Content of the San Remo Manual' International Review of the Red Cross, No 309. ICRC <http://www.icrc.org/eng/resources/documents/misc/57jmst.htm> accessed 13 May 2017.

[78] On 5 March 2014 Israel announced that it had seized a cargo of M-302 surface to surface missiles that were shipped from Iran and were to be transhipped through Sudan into Gaza. See BBC, 'Israel Halts Weapons Shipment from Iran' <http://www.bbc.com/news/world-middle-east-26451421> accessed 13 May 2017.

doctrine has crystallized into customary international law. Evidence of the enduring opposition to continuous voyage can be found in the German Navy's Commander's Handbook, which states the Continental position quite clearly:

There is no reason to presume a breach or an attempted breach of blockade if the [vessel] is not en route to the blockaded area. This applies even if vessel or cargo are destined for the blockaded area later on. The principle of the continuous voyage does not apply.[79]

The fact that the issue of continuous voyage remains unsettled in the twenty-first century provides an interesting insight into some of the various approaches to the development of CIL. Whereas some may look to the doctrine of continuous voyage and consider that it makes sense in light of the extraordinary advances made in ground transportation since the nineteenth century, others hold steadfastly to the notion that cargo bound for a neutral port must not be interfered with, irrespective of its ultimate destination. Of interest in the situation of blockade is the fact that those states that object to the practice of continuous voyage in blockade have rarely, if ever, engaged in blockade operations since the commencement of the twentieth century. On the other hand, the countries that have employed blockades over the past 100 years have advocated for the use of continuous voyage, and have generally practised the doctrine when and as necessary. Thus, the issue of continuous voyage brings to a head the question of whether the subjective component (*opinio juris*) or the objective component (state practice) is the determinative element in the formation of CIL. Insofar as there is little guidance from international tribunals in cases where parties have directly opposing views and practice, the doctrine of continuous voyage is one of the elements of blockade law that is likely to remain contentious for the foreseeable future.

---

[79] *Unbehau, Kommandanten-Handbuch—Rechtsgrundlagen für den Einsatz von Seestreitkräften* (Bundessprachenamt—Referat, 2002) 157 (hereafter German Handbook).

6

Blockade and the Civilian Population

It is predictable that sanctions which inflict high economic costs on a country ... are likely to result in severe suffering among the general population ...[1]

One of the goals of a maritime blockades is to inflict 'the maximum degree of economic strangulation of an opposing belligerent that can be achieved'.[2] In this manner, blockades have the potential to wreak havoc not only on the economies of targeted states, but on the civilian populations that rely on the effective functioning of those economies for their very survival.

While the process of industrialization over the past two and a half centuries has contributed significantly to the ability of states to raise large militaries and conduct lengthy wars,[3] the massive shift of populations to urban centres has made those populations heavily dependent on intensive agricultural production and imports of foodstuffs for their sustenance.[4] Consequently, and as will be demonstrated through an examination of the blockade of Germany during the First World War, the maritime interdiction operations against Iraq in the 1990s, and the ongoing blockade of Gaza, in cases where states are either wholly or substantially reliant on imports food to feed their citizenry, or agricultural goods or implements to sustain their agricultural sector, the imposition of a lengthy and effective maritime blockade can cause widespread hunger, malnutrition, and ultimately starvation.

The Blockade of Germany 1914–1919

Described as the 'great seminal catastrophe of the [twentieth] century',[5] the First World War is most commonly remembered for its sheer brutality and the

---

[1] UK, HL, *The Impact of Economic Sanctions 2nd Report*, session 1 (2007), vol 1 No 96-I, 20 (9 May 2007).

[2] Thomas David Jones, 'The International Law of Blockade—A Measure of Naval Economic Interdiction' (1983) 26 Howard LJ 759, 767.

[3] J.M. Bourne, *Britain and the Great War, 1914–1918* (Edward Arnold, 1983) 12 (hereafter Bourne, *Great War*).

[4] Tammy Proctor, *Civilians in a World at War, 1914–1918* (New York University Press, 2010) 84–7 (hereafter Proctor, *Civilians*).

[5] George F. Kennan, *The Decline of Bismarck's European Order: Franco–Prussian Relations, 1875–1890* (Princeton University Press, 1979) 3.

The Law of Maritime Blockade: Past, Present, and Future. Phillip Drew. © Phillip Drew 2017. Published 2017 by Oxford University Press.

decimation of a generation of young men on the battlefields of Europe.[6] What is often lost in the popular narrative, however, is the fact that the enormity of the conflict brought about a complete transformation of the economies and societies of the states involved, including fundamental changes in the relationship between the state and its people in times of armed conflict. Locked in a struggle for national survival, with their armies consuming materials and supplies at such a rate that the sustainment of the war effort became their principal focus, states were forced to completely incorporate their national economies and civilian populations into the war effort in a paradigm that is contemporarily described as total war.[7]

Because the economies were a key instrument of the war effort, belligerents began to consider their enemies' economies to be 'not only as important as the war front but also inseparable from it'.[8] Consequently, the warring nations adopted the attitude that 'in a war for existence, the will of the enemy nation, not merely the bodies of their soldiers, [became] the ultimate target'.[9] Those who worked in the factories, farms, and other sectors supporting the war effort seen as an instrumental part of each state's military machinery.[10]

While the first direct attacks against civilians were carried out by aerial bombardment of British population centres by Zeppelin airships beginning in January 1915,[11] the nascent technology of aerial warfare in the First World War did not readily permit either the Triple Entente or the Axis Powers to conduct regular and effective direct attacks against each other's industrial centres. On the other hand, their naval forces did have the capacity to inflict severe damage on one another's economies through the implementation of blockades and by the interdiction of neutral shipping bound for enemy ports.[12] Understanding that each other's industrialized economies were highly reliant on imported commodities, control of the seas and of maritime trade assumed an unprecedented level of strategic importance for the belligerents.[13]

As the world's largest and most powerful naval force at the outbreak of the First World War, the Royal Navy was in a particularly strong position to influence the outcome of the war.[14] Its dominance of the sea would prove effective; both as a method for debilitating the German economy, and undermining the nation's resolve to continue fighting by cutting off its access to maritime trade through the imposition of a crushing blockade.[15]

Liddell Hart has proffered that, 'No historian would underrate the direct effect of the semi starvation of the German people in causing the final collapse of the "home front"',[16] and that the 'intangible all-pervading factor of the blockade intrudes into every consideration of the military situation'.[17] To understand the

---

[6] J.M. Winter, 'Britain's "Lost Generation" of the First World War' (1977) 31:3 Population Studies 449, 451–2.

[7] Proctor, *Civilians* (n 4) 40–4.   [8] Bourne, *Great War* (n 3) 199.

[9] Liddell Hart, *History of the First World War* (Pan Books Ltd, 1982) 76 (hereafter Hart, *First World War*).

[10] Roger Chickering and Stig Förstner (eds), *Great War, Total War: Combat and Mobilization on the Western Front 1914–1918* (Cambridge University Press, 2000) 5.

[11] Hart, *First World War* (n 9) 76.   [12] Ibid, 72.   [13] Ibid, 460.

[14] Bourne, *Great War* (n 3) 31.

[15] Hart, *First World War* (n 9) 461.   [16] Ibid, 460.   [17] Ibid, 461.

significance of Hart's statement it is necessary to acknowledge that in the years prior to the war, Germany was a thriving and modern economic power that had become heavily reliant on international trade to sustain its population. A snapshot of the pre-war German economy shows that the country depended on foreign suppliers for a third of its food,[18] and that virtually all of its nitrogenous and phosphatic fertilizers for agricultural use were imported.[19] This heavy reliance on foreign supply as a central aspect of its economic power made the country highly susceptible to economic warfare, such as that which was about to be visited on it by the Royal Navy's blockade.

While at the advent of the war some authorities in the German government warned of the potential for food shortages should the conflict become protracted,[20] at the commencement of the war Germany's main efforts were focused on producing military materiel and sustaining its forces in the field. It is quite evident that when the war commenced in August, many of Europe's military and political elite 'thought in terms of a single great campaign across the summer countryside ... , of Berlin taken before Christmas or Paris entered between harvest time and frost'.[21] Consequently the warnings about food supplies that were proffered by a small number of officials at the commencement of the armed conflict went unheeded.

As is the case in most forms of economic warfare, 'the full impact of blockade on Germany [was] progressive and slow'.[22] In spite of the gradual nature of its increasing effects, the civilian population of Germany began to feel the influence of the blockade relatively early in the war.[23] By 1915, German imports had fallen by 55 per cent from pre-war levels and bread rationing commenced.[24]

As is the case in virtually all conflicts, the overall well-being of the civilian population was subordinated to the requirements of maintaining a healthy and combat capable military. Germany was no exception to this general rule; 'soldiers ... [were given] priority when distributing food; they were vital to the defence of the nation. Those who came lowest down the food-chain were those who contributed the least to the war effort: the old, the young, the deranged, the physically unfit. These ... were the principal victims of the economic war.'[25] By the winter of 1916 staple foodstuffs such as grain, potatoes, meat, and dairy products had become so scarce that much of

---

[18] C. Paul Vincent, *The Politics of Hunger* (Ohio University Press 1985) 20 (hereafter Vincent, *The Politics of Hunger*).

[19] Ibid.

[20] Shulamit Volkov, *Walther Rathenau: Weimar's Fallen Statesman* (Yale University Press, 2012) 121–4.

[21] D.J. Goodspeed, *The Road Past Vimy: The Canadian Corps 1914–1918* (MacMillan of Canada 1969) 8. See also David Welch, *Germany, Propaganda and Total War, 1914–1918* (Rutgers University Press, 2000) 58; and Hart, *First World War* (n 9) 41.

[22] Hew Strachan, *The First World War* (Oxford University Press 2001) 401.

[23] Proctor, *Civilians* (n 4) 84–95.

[24] National Archives of the United Kingdom, *Spotlights on History: The Blockade of Germany*, The National Archives <http://www.nationalarchives.gov.uk/pathways/firstworldwar/spotlights/blockade.htm> accessed 9 October 2017 (hereafter Spotlights).

[25] Hew Strachan, 'Strategic Bombing and the Question of Civilian Casualties up to 1945' in Paul Addison and Jeremy A. Crang (eds), *Firestorm: The Bombing of Dresden, 1945* (Random House 2006) 5.

the German population was surviving on a meagre diet of ersatz bread and turnips.[26] By the end of the war in November 1918, the average daily diet of 1,000 calories was insufficient even for small children. Disorders related to malnutrition—scurvy, rickets, tuberculosis, and dysentery—were common.[27]

The winter of 1918–19 was particularly deadly for the population of Germany. In spite of the armistice having been signed on 11 November 1918, the blockade was continued, both as a tactic by the allies to force the Central powers to agree to the terms of a lasting peace, and as an assurance that 'the period of the Armistice [w]ould not be utilised to reequip Germany for a renewal of the War'.[28] Weakened by hunger and malnutrition as a result of the ongoing blockade, the people of Germany were particularly susceptible to the Spanish Flu pandemic as it swept through Europe.[29] Conservative estimates are that approximately 250,000 German civilians died of starvation during the winter of 1918–19,[30] with many more thousands succumbing to influenza, the effects of which were exacerbated by severe malnutrition.[31]

While historians continue to debate the over-all humanitarian toll of the blockade, the British government has estimated that approximately 763,000 wartime deaths in Germany can be attributed to starvation caused by the five-year economic strangulation of the country.[32] As compared to the combat losses of Germany, estimated at approximately 1.74 million persons,[33] the effects of the blockade are clearly remarkable. Put in perspective, the 1915–19 blockade of Germany was responsible for the deaths of more German civilians than was the allied strategic bombing campaign of the Second World War.[34]

The United Nations Sanctions Against Iraq: 1990–2003

The scale of economic sanctions against Iraq is probably unprecedented in recent history. The imposition of sanctions can be regarded as a macroeconomic shock of massive proportions. Although the sanctions regime has allowed for an

---

[26] Vincent, *The Politics of Hunger* (n 18) 21.   [27] Spotlights (n 24) 434.

[28] David Lloyd George, *Memoirs of Lloyd George: 1918* (Little Brown and Company, 1937) 249.

[29] Vincent, *The Politics of Hunger* (n 18) 124–56. Although influenza killed a significant number of German citizens in 1918–19, the most alarming mortality figures are found in the incidence of tuberculosis, the virility of which has a strong relationship to nutrition levels. While tuberculosis was generally on the rise amongst civilians in Europe during the war, mortality rates among women in Germany increased 72 per cent, while in the United Kingdom the increase was 28 per cent. By 1919 the mortality rate from tuberculosis in young children in Germany increased 100 per cent over the 1913 rate. For those children who did survive disease, many were afflicted with rickets.

[30] N.P. Howard, 'The Social and Political Consequences of the Allied Food Blockade of Germany 1918–1919' (1993) 11 German History 161.

[31] Spotlights (n 24) 434.   [32] Ibid.

[33] 'Casualty and Death Tables: World War One' online: PBS <http://www.pbs.org/greatwar/resources/casdeath_pop.html>accessed 9 October 2017.

[34] John Keegan, *The Second World War* (Viking, 1990). Historian John Keegan places the civilian death toll from the allied strategic bombing campaign at approximately 593,000.

easing of the restrictions on the importation of foodstuffs and medical supplies, the availability of these essential supplies, among other things, continues to fall far short of the requirements of the civilian population.[35]

The invasion of Kuwait by Iraq in August 1990 was the catalyst for the longest blockade action in modern history. Passed unanimously by the United Nations Security Council on 6 August 1990, UNSCR 661 authorized the banning of all imports and exports of goods to and from Iraq, with the exception of 'supplies intended strictly for medical purposes, and, in humanitarian circumstances, foodstuffs'.[36]

At the completion of the Gulf War in March 1991, the Security Council, in resolution 687 (1991) authorized the continuation of the embargo and sanctions against Iraq, with the same humanitarian caveats that were contained in resolution 661.[37] The embargo against Iraq was strictly and effectively enforced, with the navies of many nations policing maritime traffic in the Arabian Gulf region, and stopping all maritime traffic into and out of Iraq. The provisions of UNSCR remained in place until the completion of the Second Gulf War in 2003.

With its infrastructure decimated by the Gulf War, and an economy that depended on oil revenues for its main source of income, Iraq was particularly vulnerable to the effects of the sanctions regime. Reporting on the UN-imposed sanctions in 1999, the United Nations Economic and Social Council stated, 'The sanctions against Iraq are the most comprehensive, total sanctions that have ever been imposed on a country.'[38]

Much of Iraq is non-arable desert.[39] As was the case with Germany in the First World War, Iraq's ability to feed its population was dependent not only on the importation of foodstuffs, but on the external supply of fertilizers and farm machinery as well. When the UN blockade was imposed, virtually all imports of food were halted. With these items subjected to the embargo, Iraq was faced with an immediate and significant food crisis. While immediate government rationing helped to fend off mass starvation, the meagre diet imposed on the majority of Iraq's citizenry was barely sufficient to keep them alive.[40]

Although the provisions of UNSC Resolution 687, established a sanctions committee that had the authority to permit Iraq to export petroleum in order to pay

[35] Peter Boone, Haris Gazdar, and Athar Hussain, 'Sanctions Against Iraq: The Cost of Failure' (1997), a report prepared for the Center for Economic and Social Rights (formerly the Harvard Study Team) on the impact of United Nations-imposed economic sanctions on the economic well-being of the civilian population of Iraq. CESR http://www.cesr.org/downloads/Sanctions% 20Against% 20Iraq%20 Costs% 20of%20Failure %201997.pdf accessed 13 May 2017 (hereafter Boone, 'Sanctions').

[36] UN Security Council, *Resolution 661 (1990)*, 6 August 1990, S/RES/661 (1990) (hereafter S/RES/661) 3.

[37] The term blockade refers to a belligerent act, thus indicating that it is a *jus in bello* concept. In the case of Iraq, while the extension of the sanctions were part of the ceasefire provisions as contained in UNSCR 687, the sanctions were effectively tighter after the war than they were prior to it. Insofar as the sanctions were imposed under Chapter VII, and the resulting naval action resembled a blockade in every manner, the term blockade has regularly been used to describe the action.

[38] *The Adverse Consequences of Economic Sanctions on The Enjoyment Of Human Rights*, UN ESCOR, UN Docs E/CN4/Sub 2/2000/33 (2000) 15.

[39] Boone, 'Sanctions' (n 35).

[40] Ibid.

for imports of foodstuffs, medicines, and essential civilian supplies, the committee included the United States, which was Iraq's foremost protagonist. The committee was given the power and discretion to determine whether the humanitarian circumstances necessitated the temporary lifting of the sanctions to permit food imports. Working under the banner of secrecy, each member of the sanctions committee could exercise a veto. Under this arrangement, any transaction or thing that could be seen as having the potential to support Iraq's military was disallowed. Consequently the importation of goods ranging from computers, tractors, and building materials through to food and clothing was blocked. Recognizing that Iraq was in a situation wherein it was unable to afford medicines and other humanitarian items for its population, the Security Council passed UNSC Resolution 986[41] in 1995, permitting Iraq to export small amounts of oil in what has become known as the 'Oil for Food Program'. Although the programme alleviated some of the shortages, it was seen as a measure that was too little and too late. By the time the programme began operating in December 1996, much of the population was suffering the effects of prolonged malnutrition and starvation.

In 1998, the Parliament of the United Kingdom was advised that '[s]ince the imposition of economic sanctions on Iraq in 1990, the humanitarian situation in Iraq has deteriorated significantly ... and that there are some 960,000 chronically malnourished children in Iraq, representing a rise of 72% since 1991'.[42] The following year, the United Nations Children Emergency Fund reported that 'under-5 mortality more than doubled from 56 deaths per 1000 live births (1984–1989) to 131 deaths per 1000 live births (1994–1999). Likewise infant mortality—defined as the death of children in their first year—increased from 47 per 1000 live births to 108 per 1000 live births within the same time frame.'[43] In the same report, the executive director of UNICEF, Ms. Carol Bellamy, noted 'that if the substantial reduction in child mortality throughout Iraq during the 1980s had continued through the 1990s, there would have been half a million fewer deaths of children under-five in the country as a whole during the eight year period 1991 to 1998'.[44]

Upon review of the resolutions that established the Iraq sanctions regime (UNSCRs 661 and 687), it is abundantly clear that by allowing the provision of food aid to be conditional on a demonstrated humanitarian requirement and linked to the policies and practices of the government of Iraq, including its implementation and compliance with all relevant resolutions of the Council[45] the Security Council placed far more emphasis on its military goals than it did on humanitarian concerns.[46] Under such a system it was virtually inevitable that the civilian population of Iraq would bear the brunt of the sanctions.

---

[41] UN Security Council, *Resolution 986 (1990)*, 14 April 1995, UN Docs S/RES/985 (1990).
[42] 'United Kingdom House of Commons Research Paper 98/28' HC Deb 21 January 1998, c990 [House of Commons 98/28].
[43] UNICEF, 'Iraq surveys show "humanitarian emergency"' http://www.unicef.org/newsline/99pr29.htm accessed 13 May 2017.
[44] Ibid.
[45] UN Security Council, *Resolution 687 (1991)*, 3 April 1991, UN Docs S/RES/687 (1991) para 21.
[46] Boone, 'Sanctions' (n 35) 34.

The Israeli Blockade of Gaza: 2009–Present

> The idea is to put the Palestinians on a diet, but not to make them die of hunger.[47]

Few, if any, conflicts are more politically charged than the interminable conflict between Israel and its Palestinian neighbours, particularly those in Gaza. Described by many as an ongoing occupation,[48] by others as active international or non-international armed conflict,[49] and by some as a situation that can only 'be considered an armed conflict on an irregular and sporadic basis',[50] the very basic question of the classification of Israel's struggle with Gaza has been highly politicized. The undeniable fact arising from this conflict, however, is that irrespective of what the conflict is called, Palestinian civilians are caught in the middle, and it is those civilians who are being most adversely affected by it.[51]

With stated goals of preventing weapons from being imported into Gaza, keeping the 'Gazan economy on the brink of collapse without quite pushing it over the edge',[52] and 'encourag[ing] the people of Gaza to force Hamas to change its attitude towards Israel',[53] Israel has maintained an effective and impartial blockade against Gaza since 2009.

While it is indisputable that Israel has the right under international law to defend itself and its citizens from attacks originating from within Gaza, the method with which it has chosen to respond at the strategic level to the attacks are highly contentious.[54] One of the most controversial aspects of the blockade has been the

---

[47] Duv Weisglas, senior advisor to Israeli Prime Minister Ehud Olmert as quoted in Conal Urquhart, 'Gaza On Brink Of Implosion As Aid Cut-Off Starts To Bite' *The Guardian* (16 April 2006) Guardian http://www.guardian.co.uk/world/2006/apr/16/israel accessed 13 May 2017 (hereafter Urquhart, 'Gaza').

[48] See Legal Consequences of the Construction of a Wall in the Occupied Palestinian Territory (Advisory Opinion) [2004] ICJ Rep 136, para 101 (hereafter *Wall Opinion*).

[49] Israel, *The Public Commission to Examine the Maritime Incident of 31 May 2010, The Türkel Report* (23 January 2011) paras 45–53 (hereafter Turkel Report).

[50] Douglas Guilfoyle, 'The Mavi Marmara Incident and Blockade in Armed Conflict (2011) 81:1 BYIL 171, 189.

[51] Because of the highly politicized nature of the Gaza conflict, and the polarization of the international community regarding the Israeli policies towards the Gaza Strip, it is very difficult to objectively determine the exact effects of the Gaza blockade. For the purposes of this chapter, statistics used will be derived from United Nations bodies and the ICRC. While these statistics might not be completely accurate, they do reflect a middle range between the extremes as offered by Israel and its detractors. As such the statistics from these organizations are considered to be the least objectionable.

[52] Jeffrey Heller, 'Israel Said Would Keep Gaza Near Collapse: Wikileaks' (5 January 2011) Reuters <http://www.reuters.com/article/2011/01/05/us-palestinians-israel-wikileaks-idUSTRE7041GH20110105> accessed 13 May 2017.

[53] Urquhart, 'Gaza' (n 47).

[54] See, for example, CNN, 'Clinton: Gaza Situation Unacceptable' online <http://www.cnn.com/video/#/video/us/2010/06/01/sot.hillary.flotilla.attack.cnn> and Australian Broadcasting Corporation, 'Statement by Australian Prime Minister Kevin Rudd, condemning the use of violence' <http://www.abc.net.au/news/2010-06-01/rudd-condemns-aid-flotilla-violence/849712> both accessed 13 May 2017.

implementation of a ban that prohibits Gazan fishing vessels from fishing more than three miles offshore, a policy that is contrary to the provisions of Hague XI, which states that, 'Vessels used exclusively for fishing, along the coast or small boats employed in local trade are exempt from capture, as well as their appliances, rigging, tackle, and cargo'.[55] The essence of this article is that so long as fishing vessels do not engage in military type acts or other forms of hostile activity, they should be permitted to go about their activities unmolested. By the language of the treaty, it is apparent that the onus is on the accusing party to show that the fishing vessel is engaging in hostile activity. The assumption in Hague XI therefore, is that fishing vessels are to be permitted to conduct their regular business. A blanket prohibition against fishing appears to be a contravention of the letter and spirit of the law.

Although the Israelis claim that the restriction is designed to keep fishermen from importing weapons and terrorists, the primary effect of this restriction is to deny Palestinian fishermen access to their most productive fishing grounds. As the United Nations Office for the Coordination of Humanitarian Affairs noted in its special report of August 2009,[56]

Since the beginning of 'Cast Lead' [in January 2008], the IDF has prohibited Palestinians from fishing beyond three nautical miles (nm) from the shore, undermining the volume of fishing catch, the bulk of which is located in deeper waters than 3 nm. This prohibition followed a previous reduction of the fishing zone in October 2006 from 12 to 6 nm ... The total fishing catch in April 2009 amounted to 79mt, which represents one third of the amount of fish available in the market place in April 2007.[57]

In April 2010, the UNOCHA reported that, 'The deterioration of living conditions in the Gaza Strip, mainly as a result of the Israeli blockade continued to be of concern'.[58] Furthermore, a poverty survey conducted by the United Nations Relief and Works Agency (UNRWA) 'showed that the number of Palestine refugees completely unable to secure access to food and lacking the means to purchase even the most basic items, such as soap, school stationary and safe drinking water ("abject poverty") has tripled since the imposition of the blockade'.[59] While Israel did ease some of the restrictions against Gaza following its raid on the Turkish vessel MS *Mavi Marmara* on 31 May 2010, most of the fundamental aspects of Israel's blockade

---

[55] Hague Conventions; 18 October 1907, 205 Cons TS 395 (entered into force 26 January 1910) Hague XI, art 3. Although Israel is not Party to the Hague Convention, the provision regarding fishing activities is considered to be customary international law.

[56] UN Office for the Coordination of Humanitarian Affairs (OCHA), *Locked in: The Humanitarian Impact of Two Years of Blockade on the Gaza Strip*, (August 2009) online UNOCHA, <http://www.unhcr.org/refworld/docid/4a8a5d272.html> (hereafter 'Locked In').

[57] UN Office for the Coordination of Humanitarian Affairs (OCHA), 'Farming Without Land, Fishing Without Water: Gaza Agriculture Sector Struggles to Survive' (May 2010) online: UNOCHA <http://www.ochaopt.org/documents/gaza_agriculture	_25_05_2010_fact_sheet_english.pdf> accessed 9 October 2017. Of note, the fishing limits were increased to six miles in 2012, and then reduced to three miles on 6 July 2014.

[58] UN Office for the Coordination of Humanitarian Affairs (OCHA), *The Humanitarian Monitor* (April 2010) online: UNOCHA <http://www.ochaopt.org/documents/ocha_opt_the_ humanitarian_ monitor_2010_04_english.pdf> 2, accessed 13 May 2017.

[59] Ibid.

remained in place. As of the end of 2010, 'one third of the Palestinian population, or 1.43 million people, continued to be food insecure, i.e. lacking secure access to sufficient amounts of safe and nutritious food for normal growth and development and an active and healthy life.'[60] Furthermore, the high unemployment rate caused by the isolation of Gaza's economy, combined with scarce supplies of fish has led to 'a gradual shift in the diet of Gazans from high-cost and protein-rich foods such as fruit, vegetables and animal products, to low-cost and high carbohydrate foods such as cereals, sugar, and oil, which can lead to micro-nutrient deficiencies, particularly among children and pregnant women.'[61]

History has shown that a protracted blockade conducted without due consideration for the protection of civilians can create a humanitarian disaster, particularly in states that are not self-sufficient in food production. While there is ample evidence to show that it is possible to engage in a blockade without causing serious harm to the civilian population of a blockaded area,[62] the fact remains that the slow and progressive nature of the effects of a blockade are often not realized until significant and irreversible damage has been done. As has been the case since the beginning of the industrial revolution, many modern states are heavily dependent on international trade to feed their populations and/or sustain the intensive agricultural practices required to feed them. Thus, when a blockade is being contemplated it is important to remember that its relatively benign façade hides its potentially devastating and deadly character.

---

[60] Ibid.   [61] 'Locked In' (n 56) 3.
[62] For example, the blockade against Lebanon in 2006 and the blockade against North Korea during the Korean War had negligible effects on food supplies.

7

International Humanitarian Law and Blockade

At the heart of contemporary analysis of blockade law is the issue of whether and to what extent the law of blockade must encompass requirements for humanitarian assistance and the protection of the civilian population. Whereas the rules regarding the establishment of blockade were once considered to be the totality of blockade law, the absence of any provisions relating to the humanitarianeffects of maritime blockades can lead one to the conclusion that the current law 'is it so far out of step that it needs to be set to true time'.[1]

Largely as a result of the UN embargo against Iraq, and the ongoing Israeli blockade of Gaza, blockade is now being examined through the lens of contemporary humanitarian law, and from that perspective it has been found wanting.[2] Whilst some commentators and organizations have advocated for modernization that would require a blockading party to permit essential goods to pass through to the civilian population of a blockaded area, recent practice indicates that countries that engage in blockades are reluctant to permit any loosening of their stranglehold on a country, even in the face of significant suffering amongst the civilian population.[3]

As can be discerned through a basic examination of early IHL conventions, the original laws of war were focused on means and methods of warfare and the protection of the hors de combat. Although the very earliest of these IHL conventions acknowledged that 'the only legitimate object which states should endeavour to accomplish during war is to weaken the military forces of the enemy',[4] it was not until the aftermath of the Second World War, in which tens of millions of civilians

---

[1] James F. McNulty, 'Blockade: Evolution and Expectation' (1991) 62 Int'l L Stud 172, 185.

[2] Empirical evidence of the concerns for humanitarian issues is found in the large number of reports and scholarly articles written on the issue. It should be noted as well that the authors of the San Remo Manual struggled with the issue of blockade and ultimately chose to adopt Additional Protocol 1 requirements for the provision of humanitarian assistance in some circumstances. See discussion in Louise Doswald-Beck, 'Background—Development of the San Remo Manual and its Intended Purpose—Content of the San Remo Manual' online: ICRC <https://www.icrc.org/eng/resources/documents/article/other/57jmst.htm> accessed 13 May 2017.

[3] The example of Iraq stands out as a particularly devastating contemporary action. Although it is acknowledged that the sanction regime against Iraq (1991–2003) was not an official blockade, it was enforced with the same vigour. As was discussed in Chapter 6, the humanitarian consequences of the Iraq sanctions were severe.

[4] Declaration of St. Petersburg Renouncing the Use, in Time of War, of Explosive Projectiles Under 400 grammes Weight (11 December 1868).

The Law of Maritime Blockade: Past, Present, and Future. Phillip Drew. © Phillip Drew 2017. Published 2017 by Oxford University Press.

were killed as a result of direct military action, that the international community agreed upon explicit protections for civilians under the laws of armed conflict.[5]

As IHL evolved through the latter half of the twentieth century, and the protection of civilians became a central aspect of the laws of war, four fundamental principles of humanitarian law emerged; distinction, military necessity, humanity, and proportionality.[6] The essence of the principles is to acknowledge that violence and destruction are the inherent characteristics of armed conflict, but that there must be limits with respect to how and against whom violence can be directed. The spirit and meaning of the principles of humanitarian law is exemplified in the Martens Clause,[7] which states that, 'the inhabitants and the belligerents remain under the protection and the rule of the principles of the law of nations, as they result from the usages established among civilized peoples, from the laws of humanity, and the dictates of the public conscience'.[8]

The Principle of Distinction

> [T]he civilian population and civilian objects must be respected and protected in armed conflict, and for this purpose they must be distinguished from combatants and military objectives.[9]

Considered to be the 'Basic Rule' of modern international humanitarian law, the principle of distinction, found in article 48 of Additional Protocol I, requires parties to a conflict, at all times, to 'distinguish between the civilian population and combatants and between civilian objects and military objectives, and accordingly ... direct their operations only against military objectives'.[10] As is noted in the commentaries, 'The basic rule of protection and distinction is confirmed in this article. It is the foundation on which the codification of the laws and customs of war rests: the civilian population and civilian objects must be respected and protected in armed conflict, and for this purpose they must be distinguished from

---

[5] The Geneva Convention Relative to the Protection of Civilian Persons in Time of War Of August 12, 1949, 75 UNTS 287 (hereafter GC IV). See also International Committee of the Red Cross (ICRC), Protocol Additional to the Geneva Conventions of 12 August 1949, and relating to the Protection of Victims of International Armed Conflicts (Protocol I) (8 June 1977) 1125 UNTS 3.

[6] UK Ministry of Defence, *The Manual of the Law of Armed Conflict* (Oxford University Press, 2004) 21 (hereafter, UK Manual).

[7] ICRC, 'The Martens Clause and the Laws of Armed Conflict' <http://www.icrc.org/eng/resources/documents/misc/57jnhy.htm> accessed 13 May 2017.

[8] Of note, the Martens Clause stands in stark contrast to the regular rule of construction in international law, as outlined in the *Lotus* case. *The Case of The S.S. Lotus (France V. Turkey)* (1927) PCIJ (Ser.A) No 10 stands for the principle that 'under international law, anything that is not prohibited is permitted'.

[9] Yves Sandoz, Christophe Swinarski, and Bruno Zimmermann (eds), *Commentary on the Additional Protocols of 8 June 1977 to the Geneva Conventions of 12 August 1949* (International Committee of the Red Cross & Martinus Nijhoff Publishers 1987) art 48. (hereafter Sandoz, Commentaries).

[10] International Committee of the Red Cross (ICRC), Protocol Additional to the Geneva Conventions of 12 August 1949, and relating to the Protection of Victims of International Armed Conflicts (Protocol I) (8 June 1977) 1125 UNTS 3, art 48 (hereafter AP1).

combatants and military objectives. The entire system established in The Hague in 1899 and 1907 (1) and in Geneva from 1864 to 1977 (2) is founded on this rule of customary law.'[11]

The explicit requirement for militaries to refrain from directly attacking civilians, and to refrain as far as possible from harming their property,[12] is a relatively recent development of the law of armed conflict. The concept of distinction was first introduced in written form in 1863, as part of the United States Army's *Lieber Code*, which stated that:

22. ... the unarmed citizen is to be spared in person, property, and honor as much as the exigencies of war will admit;

23. Private citizens are no longer murdered, enslaved, or carried off to distant parts, and the inoffensive individual is as little disturbed in his private relations as the commander of the hostile troops can afford to grant in the overruling demands of a vigorous war; and,

25. ... protection of the inoffensive citizen of the hostile country is the rule; privation and disturbance of private relations are the exceptions.[13]

The *Lieber Code*, although not binding on any forces other than the Union Army, was a foundational document in the laws of armed conflict. Widely recognized for its innovativeness, it provided a foundation for the principle of distinction that would be used in the creation of humanitarian law in the ensuing decades.[14] The principle was first implicitly incorporated into treaty in the first multi-national convention aimed at regulating means and methods of warfare, the St. Petersburg Declaration of 1868. In the preamble of the Declaration, the parties to the convention affirmed that, 'the only legitimate object which states should endeavour to accomplish during war is to weaken the military forces of the enemy'.[15]

In spite of having been introduced into conventional law in 1868, no specific attempts were made to enshrine specific protections for civilians into humanitarian law until 1923, with the drafting of *The Rules Concerning the Control of Wireless Telegraphy in Time of War and Air Warfare* ('Draft Air Rules of 1923'). Recognizing the potential of emerging technologies, particularly in the field of aerial warfare, the authors of the Draft Air Rules created article 22, which provided that, 'Aerial bombardment for the purpose of terrorizing civilian population, of destroying or damaging private property not of military character, or of injuring non-combatants

---

[11] Sandoz, Commentaries (n 9) art 48.   [12] AP1 (n10) art 51.

[13] General Orders No 100, Instructions for the Government of Armies of the United States in the Field (24 April 1863) arts 22, 23, 25 (hereafter Lieber Code).

[14] Theodore Meron, 'The Humanization of Humanitarian Law' (2000) 94:2 AJIL 239, 243.

[15] Declaration Renouncing the Use, in Time of War, of Explosive Projectiles Under 400 Grammes Weight (1868) (hereafter St. Petersburg Declaration). Note also, that the Lieber Code (n 13) provided that: 'as civilization has advanced during the last centuries, so has likewise steadily advanced, especially in war on land, the distinction between the private individual belonging to a hostile country and the hostile country itself, with its men in arms. The principle has been more and more acknowledged that the unarmed citizen is to be spared in person, property, and honor as much as the exigencies of war will admit.'

is prohibited'.[16] While Draft Air Rules symbolized a noteworthy attempt to codify the principle of distinction the initiative was rejected, partly because of the belief that such rules would interfere with states' abilities to pursue their goals in war.[17]

In 1938, with the possibility of a European war looming, and the destruction caused by aerial bombardment during the Spanish Civil War fresh in their minds, the member states of the League of Nations attempted to establish rules to protect civilians from aerial bombardment by declaring the following principles as a necessary basis for any subsequent regulations:

1. The intentional bombing of civilian populations is illegal;

2. Objectives aimed at from the air must be legitimate military objectives and must be identifiable;

3. Any attack on legitimate military objectives must be carried out in such a way that civilian populations in the neighbourhood are not bombed through negligence.[18]

Although the League of Nations passed the resolution unanimously, it was of symbolic value only; because Germany, Italy, and Japan had withdrawn their membership from the League several years earlier, the resolution was not binding on them. As a result, on the eve of the Second World War, while there were fairly robust international rules in place for regulating warfare between combatants, there were no universally accepted protections in place to safeguard civilians from the effects of armed conflict. The principle of distinction, to the extent that it existed in either conventional or customary law, was largely ignored during the Second World War.[19] From the early days of the conflict, all of the major protagonists engaged in aerial bombardment against cities with the intent of 'undermining of the morale of the . . . people to the point where their capacity for armed resistance [was] fatally weakened'.[20] Cloaked under the terminology of reprisals, area bombing that employed indiscriminate means and methods of warfare in order to cause mass destruction also became a retaliatory measure in response to the bombing of each other's cities.[21]

In spite of, and perhaps because of, the virtual rejection of the principle of distinction during the war, there was a renewed emphasis following the Second World War to create safeguards for civilians in the modern laws of war. The first serious

---

[16] ICRC, *The Rules Concerning the Control of Wireless Telegraphy in Time of War and Air Warfare. Drafted by a Commission of Jurists at the Hague, December 1922—February 1923* http://www.icrc.org/ihl.nsf/FULL/275?OpenDocument accessed 13 May 2017 (hereafter *Draft Air Rules*).

[17] Ibid. Although the rules were rejected, many of the provisions were recognized as universal principles. Completely ignored in the Second World War, the principles were eventually revived and now form the basis of rules for the protection of civilian populations as outlined in Part IV of Additional Protocol 1.

[18] 'Protection of Civilian Populations Against Bombing From The Air In Case Of War' Unanimous resolution of the League of Nations Assembly, 30 September 1938.

[19] *United States Strategic Bombing Survey 1946* (reprinted) (Air University Press, 1987) (hereafter USSBS).

[20] Ibid, 14.

[21] Brett Holman,' 'Bomb Back, and Bomb Hard': Debating Reprisals during the Blitz' (2012) 58 Australian Journal of Politics & History 394, 398.

post-war attempt to create new rules got its foothold at the nineteenth International Conference of the Red Cross in 1956. At that meeting, *Draft Rules for the Limitation of Dangers Incurred by the Civilian Population in Times of War*[22] were created, and the implementation of measures designed to provide true protection for civilians became an international priority. The efforts to enshrine protection of civilians into humanitarian law were finally realized in the adoption of Additional Protocol 1 in 1977, a milestone which has been described as the 'crowning achievement . . . and the most significant victory achieved in IHL since the adoption of the Fourth Geneva Convention in 1949'.[23]

The introduction of the Additional Protocols into conventional law was a watershed in IHL. For the first time, specific protections were formulated that obligated belligerents to distinguish between combatants and civilians, to protect civilians from the effects of military operations, and to balance the requirements of military necessity against those of humanity. Of particular importance were the thirty-one articles of Part IV of Additional Protocol 1 that are dedicated to the protection of civilians, all of which are predicated on the rule as set out in article 48, which states that:

In order to ensure respect for and protection of the civilian population and civilian objects, the Parties to the conflict shall at all times distinguish between the civilian population and combatants and between civilian objects and military objectives and accordingly shall direct their operations only against military objectives.[24]

Distinction and Maritime Blockade

Although it is widely agreed that the principle of distinction applies to military operations that result in harm, there is some disagreement as to whether or not the principle applies when an operation does not cause direct harm through the use of violence. As a type of warfare that typically does not employ kinetic force or directly affect people on land, it is argued by some that the requirement for distinction does not apply to blockade.[25]

In order to appreciate the arguments of those who contend that maritime blockade operations do not fall under the umbrella of article 48, it is necessary to examine the intent of the drafters when they were contemplating the term 'shall direct their operations'.[26] Evidence of their intentions is found by analysing the records of the

---

[22] *Draft Rules for the Limitation of Dangers Incurred by the Civilian Population in Times of War* (International Committee for the Red Cross, 1956).

[23] Sandoz, Commentaries (n 9) para 1816.

[24] AP1 (n 10) contains the following major parts: Part I—General Provisions; Part II—Wounded Sick and Shipwrecked; Part III—Methods and Means of Warfare, Combatant and Prisoner of War Status; Part IV—Civilian Population; Part V—Execution of the Conventions and of the Protocol; and Part VI—Final Provisions.

[25] AP1 (n 10) art 49.3.

[26] When one considers the wide variety of operations in which contemporary militaries participate, such as aerial reconnaissance, psychological operations, and humanitarian operations, it is evident that some military operations might not cause deleterious effects against the civilian population, while some

working group that developed Part IV of the Protocol (Protection of Civilians). As can be found in volume 15 of the *Official Records of the Diplomatic Conference on the Reaffirmation and Development of International Humanitarian Law Applicable in Armed Conflicts, Geneva (1974–1977)*:

[T]he Working Group was unanimously of the view that Protocol I should at least cover military operations on land and military operations from the sea and air against persons and objects on land (notably in the form of bombardment) which affect civilians on land. Beyond that there was disagreement. Delegations were of differing views whether the Section should be applicable to operations at sea (e.g. blockade, sinking of merchant ships, etc.) which affect civilians at sea (such as crews and passengers of ships) or on land.[27]

The fact that there was disagreement on the scope of 'distinction' at the working group level has resulted in ongoing disagreement as to whether or not the provisions of civilian protection apply to maritime blockade. Insofar as blockade law is grounded in customary international law, the lack of universal consensus on this fundamental point makes it impossible to positively establish the obligations of blockading forces vis a vis affected civilian populations.

The Meaning of 'Attack'

Comprehending the scope of Part IV and its relationship to the distinction principle requires an appreciation that in the context of the Protocol, the meaning of 'operations' is analogous to the meaning of 'attack'. Understanding this to be the case, it becomes necessary to consider the interpretation of the latter term. An analysis of the meaning of the term 'attack' begins with an examination of article 49, which states the following:

1. 'Attacks' means acts of violence against the adversary, whether in offence or in defence.
2. The provisions of this Protocol with respect to attacks apply to all attacks in whatever territory conducted, including the national territory belonging to a Party to the conflict but under the control of an adverse Party.
3. The provisions of this section apply to any land, air or sea warfare which may affect the civilian population, individual civilians or civilian objects on land. They further apply to all attacks from the sea or from the air against objectives on land *but do not*

---

might very well have a beneficial effect, depending on the circumstances. For example, a psychological operations campaign aimed at encouraging a civilian population to leave an area before it is attacked can significantly reduce civilian casualties in an impending attack. Thus, because a psychological operations campaign of this type would not be dangerous to the civilian population, such an operation would not fall under the prohibition in art 51.1.

[27] Diplomatic Conference on the Reaffirmation and Development of International Humanitarian Law Applicable in Armed Conflicts (Geneva, 1974–1977) Committee Three Records, Official Records Volume III, 255 (hereafter CDDH/III/67).

otherwise affect the rules of international law applicable in armed conflict at sea or in the air ...[28]

As is noted in the commentaries to Additional Protocol 1, article 49.3 clearly establishes that any naval bombardment of a shoreline would invoke the attack provisions as set out in Part IV.[29] The construction of the last portion of article 49.3, however, has been the catalyst for significant disagreement as to the applicability of Part IV in the case of blockade, particularly if the blockading forces do not engage in any forms of bombardment of targets on land.[30]

In order to appreciate whether or not the term 'attack' applies to maritime blockade, it is necessary to understand the fact that contemporary blockades rarely, if ever, involve any sort of bombardment of the shoreline; instead, blockading forces generally remain far enough out to sea that they cannot be engaged by the enemy's shore defence systems. For some, the inclusion of the phrase 'do not otherwise affect the rules of international law applicable in armed conflict at sea', indicates that if the action does not directly harm civilians or their property on land, then it is not an attack.

In the years following the coming into force of Additional Protocol 1, the term 'attack' was generally understood to mean 'the use of physical force'. Under this interpretation, military operations such as psychological operations, the dissemination of propaganda, embargoes, or other non-physical means of psychological, political, or economic warfare were not considered to be attacks.[31] Understanding, however, that it has been four decades since the Additional Protocols were negotiated, it must be asked whether or not the traditional interpretation of 'attacks' remains valid in the context of twenty-first-century humanitarian law.

Professor Mike Schmitt has scrutinized the meaning of attack. Adopting the position that the concept of 'attack' must be modernized, he suggests that 'attack' is:

a term of prescriptive shorthand intended to address specific consequences. It is clear that what the relevant provisions hope to accomplish is shielding protected individuals from injury or death and protected objects from damage or destruction. To the extent that the term 'violence' is explicative, it must be considered in the sense of violent *consequences* rather than violent *acts*. Significant human physical or mental suffering is logically included in the concept of injury. ....[32]

Schmitt's analysis contemplates and reflects advancements in both means and methods of warfare and humanitarian principles. Through the use of a purposive approach to legal analysis, Schmitt contends that means and methods of warfare that cause significant non-kinetic harm, such as cyber attacks, constitute attacks and that they should therefore fall under the umbrella of protections afforded in the Protocol.[33]

---

[28] AP1 (n 10) art 49. Author's emphasis.　　[29] Sandoz, Commentaries (n 9) para 1898.

[30] Ibid.　　[31] CDDH/III/67 (n 27) 289.

[32] Michael Schmitt, 'Wired Warfare: Computer Network Attack and Jus in Bello' (2002) 84:846 IRRC 365, 377.

[33] A review of legal literature and military doctrine manuals indicates a broad acceptance of Professor Schmitt's conclusions that non-kinetic actions which cause physical damage and suffering constitute attacks for the purposes of determining the application of the attack provisions of AP1.

By adopting this consequence-based interpretation of 'attacks' Schmitt acknowledges that the continuing evolution of civilian protection necessitates a broader and more expansive interpretation of the term than has traditionally been the case.

Schmitt is not alone in this approach.[34] In its discussion of 'attacks', the Tallinn Manual states that, 'The crux of the notion lies in the effects that are caused... Restated, the consequences of an operation, not its nature, are what generally determine the scope of the term "attack"'.[35] In keeping with this approach, the International Criminal Court has held that, 'In characterizing a certain conduct as an "attack", what matters is the consequences of the act, and particularly whether injury, death, damage or destruction are intended or foreseeable consequences thereof'.[36] Similarly, Knut Dörmann, writing in support of Schmitt's analysis, offers that 'CNA through viruses, worms, logic bombs etc. that result in physical damage to persons, or damage to objects that goes beyond the computer program or data attacked can be qualified as 'acts of violence' and thus as an attack in the sense of IHL'.[37] Of note, while Dörmann agrees that there is no requirement for the form of the attack to be kinetic, he qualifies his interpretation of 'attack' by noting that in order to qualify as an 'attack' the action in question must cause physical damage to persons or objects. In essence, Dörmann concludes that unless an act meets the threshold of causing some form of damage, it does not qualify as an 'attack'. This approach makes complete sense, in that it recognizes that some military operations directed at civilians, such as psychological and propaganda operations, may have no deleterious consequences for the civilian population. In this manner, Dörmann's approach allows for the evolution of the term, all the while respecting the original concept that an attack is an action that causes harm.

This acceptance of the consequence-based interpretation of 'attacks' not only opens the door to a the incorporation of new methods of warfare into IHL, but permits as well, a re-evaluation of existing means and methods of warfare to determine whether they constitute attacks, in spite of their outwardly benign appearance.

---

[34] See, for example, Louise Doswald-Beck, 'Some Thoughts on Computer Network Attack and the International Law of Armed Conflict', and Knutt Dörmann, 'Applicability of the Additional Protocols to Computer Network Attacks', both in Michael N. Schmitt and Brian T. O'Donnel (eds), *Computer Network Attack and International Law: War Studies*, vol 76 (US Naval War College, 2002); Paul A. Walker, 'Rethinking Computer Network Attack: Implications for Law and US Doctrine' (2010), SSRN <http://ssrn.com/abstract=1586504>; United States Joint Publication 3-13: *Information Operations* (2006) Joint Electronic Library <http://www.dtic.mil/doctrine/new_pubs/jp3_13.pdf> accessed 13 May 2017.

[35] Michael Schmitt (ed), *Tallinn Manual on the International Law Applicable to Cyber Warfare* (Cambridge University Press, 2013).

[36] *Prosecutor v Bosco Ntaganda* (Trial Chamber) [2014] ICC-01/04-02/06, para 46 (hereafter *Ntaganda*).

[37] Knutt Dörmann, 'Applicability of the Additional Protocols to Computer Network Attacks' in Michael N. Schmitt and Brian T. O'Donnel (eds), *Computer Network Attack and International Law: War Studies*, vol 76 (US Naval War College, 2002) 4.

Is a Blockade an Attack?

As has been illustrated in the examples of Germany, Iraq, and Gaza, the intentional destruction of an economy through blockade can cause hunger, disease, and starvation.[38] These effects are not direct; rather, they are secondary or tertiary. Accordingly, the utilization of a literal interpretation of the definition of attack, as found at article 49,[39] could lead one to conclude that because the effects of blockade are not immediate, they are too remote for this method of warfare to qualify as an attack. This interpretation is in keeping with the original understanding of the parameters of articles 49[40] and 51.[41]

In the face of the evolution of the consequence-based approach to interpreting the term 'attacks', as outlined in current scholarship, and as supported by the International Criminal Court,[42] it is apparent that 'attacks' now encompass actions that 'may affect the civilian population',[43] not just those that are 'acts of violence'.[44]

The expanded interpretation of 'attacks' also accords with the general trend towards the enhanced protection of civilians that has matured over the past several decades. As has been evidenced through contemporary writing, jurisprudence of international tribunals, and statements from international organizations,[45] the protection of the civilian population in times of war is becoming an increasingly important facet of IHL. In this environment, it would be difficult, if not disingenuous, for any party that causes harm to a civilian population to claim that the protections offered to civilians under Part IV of Additional Protocol 1 do not apply because the act does not qualify as an attack.

Is the Economy a Military Objective?

> [F]rom a military measure designed to permit belligerents to conduct effective siege by sea, ... blockade had become a measure whose significance was economic rather than military. As such it was questioned, if ... an enemy's economy could not of itself form a legitimate military objective ...[46]

Military objectives are those objects which by their nature, location, purpose, or use make an effective contribution to military action and whose total or partial destruction, capture, or neutralization, in the circumstances ruling at the time, offers a

---

[38] The author acknowledges that actions that cause mere inconvenience to a civilian population are to be expected and accepted in armed conflict. It is the responsibility of the targeted state to provide its citizenry with the necessities of life. While the author contends that a blockade qualifies as an attack, it is only in situations where the blockaded state can no longer provide for its civilian population that the protections from attack provisions as found in AP1 and in customary law should apply.

[39] AP1 (n 10) art 49.   [40] Ibid.   [41] Ibid, art 51.   [42] *Ntaganda* (n 36).

[43] AP1 (n 10) art 49.3.   [44] Ibid, art 49.1.

[45] See, for example, United Nations General Assembly Resolution 71/203 (19 December 2016) Situation of human rights in the Syrian Arab Republic.

[46] Robert W. Tucker, *The Law of War and Neutrality at Sea* (United States Government Printing Office 1957) 284 (hereafter Tucker, *Neutrality*).

definite military advantage.[47] In order to qualify as a military objective an object must satisfy three concurring conditions:

1. the object must have a military purpose or use;

2. the object must make an effective contribution to the military action of the user; and

3. its destruction, capture, or neutralization must offer the attacker a definite military advantage.

As Professor Schmitt puts it quite succinctly, 'a potential target either qualifies as a military objective because it makes an effective contribution to military action through nature, location, purpose or use) and destruction or neutralization will yield a definite military advantage ... or it does not'.[48]

The *Law of War Manual*, written by the United Kingdom's Ministry of Defence provides a comprehensive interpretation of the term 'military objective'.[49] As the British Manual notes, the definition of 'military objective' as found in article 52(2) requires some clarification. It goes on to explain the term as follows:

a. The second part of the definition limits the first. Both parts must apply before an object can be considered a military objective.

b. Attacks on military objectives that cause incidental loss or damage to civilians are not prohibited so long as the proportionality rule is complied with.

c. 'Nature' refers to the type of object, for example, military transports, command and control centres or communications stations.

d. 'Location' includes areas which are militarily important because they must be captured or denied to the enemy or because the enemy must be made to retreat from them. An area of land can, thus, be a military objective.

e. 'Purpose' means the future intended use of an object while 'use' means its present function.

f. The words 'nature, location, purpose or use' seem at first sight to allow a wide discretion, but they are subject to the qualifications later in the definition of 'effective contribution to military action' and the offering of 'a definite military advantage'. There does not have to be geographical proximity between 'effective contribution' and 'military advantage'. That means that attacks on military supply dumps in the rear or diversionary attacks, away from the area of actual military operations, can be launched.

g. 'Military action' means military action generally, not a limited or specific military operation.

h. The words 'in the circumstances ruling at the time' are important. If, for example, the enemy moved a divisional headquarters into a disused textile factory, an attack on that headquarters would be permissible (even though the factory might be destroyed in the process) because of the prevailing circumstances. Once the enemy moved their headquarters

---

[47] AP1 (n 10) art 52(2). See also Jean-Marie Henckaerts and Louise Doswald-Beck, *Customary International Humanitarian Law* (Cambridge University Press, 2009) Rule 8 (hereafter Henckaerts, *Customary Law Study*).

[48] Michael N. Schmitt, 'Fault Lines in the Law of Attack' in Susan C. Breau and Agnieszka Jachec-Neale (eds), *Testing the Boundaries of IHL* (The British Institute of International and Comparative Law, 2006) 285.

[49] UK Manual (n 6) para 5.4.4.

away, the circumstances would change again and the immunity of the factory would be restored.

i. 'Definite' means a concrete and perceptible military advantage rather than a hypothetical and speculative one.

j. 'Military advantage'. The military advantage anticipated from an attack refers to the advantage anticipated from the attack considered as a whole and not only from isolated or particular parts of the attack. The advantage need not be immediate.

A review of military manuals and much of the literature written since the coming into force of Additional Protocol 1 indicates that the discussion of 'military objectives' in the UK Manual is an accurate reflection of the conventional and customary understanding of the term.[50] Under the test for 'military objective' as outlined in the *UK Manual of the Law of Armed Conflict*, the economy as a whole cannot be a military objective; first, because the economies of most states are civilian objects; and, secondly, because the destruction of most states' economies would generally be considered too remote to offer a *direct* military advantage.

The United States, which is not a signatory to Additional Protocol 1, is one of the few nations that use a modified interpretation of 'military objective'. The difference between the US interpretation and that of the majority of states is evident in the United States Naval War College Commanders' Handbook, which defines military objectives as:

[C]ombatants, military equipment and facilities (except medical and religious equipment and facilities), and those objects which, by their nature, location, purpose, or use, *effectively contribute to the enemy's war-fighting or war-sustaining capability* and whose total or partial destruction, capture, or neutralization would constitute a definite military advantage to the attacker under the circumstances at the time of the attack.[51]

The use of the phrase 'effectively contribute to the enemy's war-fighting or war-sustaining capability' permits a very broad interpretation of 'military objective', with the result that 'Economic objects of the enemy that indirectly but effectively support and sustain the enemy's war-fighting capability may also be attacked'.[52] The effect of this departure from the standard meaning of the term means that the United States may consider objects, such as the economy, electricity generating stations, and other items to be military objectives, whereas most other states would not.

With the exception of the United States, and perhaps several other states that are not party to Additional Protocol 1, most countries agree that the entirety of an economy cannot be considered to be a 'military objective'. While attacks against the whole of the economy cannot generally be considered as attacks that are directed at military objectives, there is no doubt that attacks against portions of the economy can be conducted lawfully. For example, munitions factories and aircraft and

---

[50] Henckaerts, *Customary Law Study* (n 47) 29.

[51] *US Naval War College Commander's Handbook on the Law of Naval Operations* (US Naval War College 2007) para 8-2 (hereafter *Commander's Handbook*).

[52] Ibid, para 8-2-5. Of note, while the US Army's Operational Law Handbook (OP Law Handbook) uses the Protocol definition of 'military objective' it accepts a broader definition of the phrase definite advantage.

weapons manufacturing facilities can be considered to be military objectives and may be lawfully attacked. In the eyes of most nations, however, an attack or operation that has the primary goal of destroying a state's economy would be a violation of the principle of distinction. Thus, a blockade that has as one of its primary goals the disruption of the entire economy of a country could, and should, be considered to be an indiscriminate attack in accordance with the provisions of article 51(4).[53]

Starvation and Blockade

> We are enforcing the blockade with rigour. It is repugnant to the British nation to use this weapon of starvation which falls mainly on the women and children, upon the old and the weak and the poor [of Germany] ... one minute longer than is necessary.[54]

> Winston Churchill, 1919

The Emperor Napoleon Bonaparte is often credited for having stated that 'An army marches on its stomach'. Whether or not Napoleon actually uttered those words, the maxim's meaning is clear and obvious; in order to wage successful campaigns, either in the defence or offence, armies must be fed and watered. In the law of armed conflict, there is no prohibition against causing the starvation of enemy combatants. Indeed, in campaigns such as the Persian Gulf War of 1991, the denial of food and water to Iraq's frontline troops through the interdiction of their supply lines was a legitimate and incredibly effective strategy.

Whilst in armed conflict it is perfectly lawful to starve combatants into submission, the same does not hold true for civilians.[55] However, this has not always been the accepted rule. Prior to the latter half of the twentieth century little attention was paid to the plight of civilians who suffered from starvation as a result of military operations.[56] Protection against the deliberate starvation of civilians was introduced to the international community in 1949, by way of article 23 of the Fourth Geneva Convention (GC IV), which provided in part, that 'Each High Contracting Party shall allow the free passage of all consignments of medical and hospital stores and objects necessary for religious worship intended only for civilians of another High Contracting Party, even if the latter is its adversary. It shall likewise permit the free passage of all consignments of essential foodstuffs, clothing and tonics intended for children under fifteen, expectant mothers and maternity cases.'[57] A fundamental flaw in the starvation provisions of GC IV, however, lies in the fact that they apply only to those whose suffering

[53] AP1 (n 10) art 51.4.

[54] Winston Churchill, speech to Parliament 3 March 1919, as quoted in Nicholson Baker, *Human Smoke: The Beginnings of World War II, the End of Civilization* (Simon and Schuster, 2008) 6.

[55] AP1 (n 10) art 54.1.

[56] Adam Tooze, *The Wages of Destruction: The Making and Breaking of the Nazi Economy* (Allen Lane, 2006) 476–85.

[57] *The Geneva Convention Relative to the Protection of Civilian Persons in Time of War Of August 12, 1949*, 75 UNTS 287, art 23.

is caused in situations of occupation. Additionally, the provisions of article 23 are 'subject to the condition that [a] Party is satisfied that there are no serious reasons for fearing: (a) that the consignments may be diverted from their destination, (b) that the control may not be effective, or (c) that a definite advantage may accrue to the military efforts or economy of the enemy'.[58] This conditional construction provides an occupying army with a number of pretexts for refusing to permit food aid to flow, and provides no protection whatsoever to those civilians who are unfortunate enough to find themselves in an area in which active hostilities are occurring.

Recognizing that the provisions of GC IV were limited in application to situations of occupation, and acknowledging the problems inherent in article 23, the drafting committees for the Additional Protocols to the Geneva Conventions set about to tighten the rules respecting starvation of civilians. Their solution is found at article 54 of Additional Protocol 1, which provides in part:

1. Starvation of civilians as a method of warfare is prohibited; and
2. It is prohibited to attack, destroy, remove or render useless objects indispensable to the survival of the civilian population, such as food-stuffs, agricultural areas for the production of food-stuffs, crops, livestock, drinking water installations and supplies and irrigation works, for the specific purpose of denying them for their sustenance value to the civilian population or to the adverse Party, whatever the motive, whether in order to starve out civilians, to cause them to move away, or for any other motive.[59]

The fact that starvation of civilians is prohibited under article 54 does not necessarily infer that this method of warfare cannot be used against civilians in all cases. As has been discussed, during the negotiations of the Part IV to the Protocol, there was a specific intention to ensure that the provisions of article 54 would not apply to blockade. This is reflected in the statement of the Rapporteur of Committee III when he said that, 'The fact that the paragraph does not change the law of naval blockade is made clear by article [49].'[60] While the wording of article 49.3 has been the subject of numerous debates, it is notable that the authors of the Commentaries to the Geneva Conventions and their Protocols have remarked that the fact that the drafters of the Protocol intended to exempt blockade from the starvation provisions 'appears to be correct'.[61]

As has been noted, article 49.3 and applicability in maritime blockade has been the subject of continuing disagreement within the IHL community. Perhaps one of the best examples of this divergence of opinion is demonstrated in the differing interpretations that Professors Dinstein and Heintschel von Heinegg have on the matter.

Professor Dinstein, in several of his writings has reiterated his legal assessment that under the law of armed conflict, 'no ... obligations exist outside of occupied territories'[62] that require the free passage of foodstuffs for all civilians. Professor Heintschel von Heinegg, on the other hand, believes that Dinstein's interpretation

---

[58] Henckaerts, *Customary Law Study* (n 47) para 1138.   [59] AP1 (n 10) art 54.
[60] Sandoz, Commentaries (n 9) para 2092.   [61] Ibid.
[62] Yoram Dinstein, *The Conduct of Hostilities Under the Law of International Armed Conflict* (Cambridge University Press, 2008) 139. See also Yoram Dinstein, 'The Right to Humanitarian Assistance' (2000) 53:4 USNWC Rev 5.

of the law in this matter is untenable.[63] Instead, Heintschel von Heinegg advocates that the proper interpretation of article 49 is that it 'applies to naval blockades if they may affect the civilian population ... on land'. [64] He further argues that 'if the establishment of a blockade causes the civilian population to be inadequately provided with food and other objects essential for their survival, the blockading party must provide for free passage of such essential supplies'.[65]

The different viewpoints of Professors Dinstein and Heintschel von Heinegg regarding this matter are reflected in a number of military LOAC manuals. For example, nations such as New Zealand adhere to the notion that because of the operation of article 49.3 the provisions of Part IV of Additional Protocol 1 do not apply to blockade operations, 'so long as starvation is not the specific purpose' of the blockade.[66] In essence, this position reflects the notion that a blockade undertaken with the *sole purpose* of causing civilians to starve would constitute an indiscriminate attack. Having stated such, it is readily acknowledged that the 'sole purpose' test could only be invoked in the context of a blockade being waged against an undefended locality, since under virtually any other circumstances there could always be an attendant military purpose.

Between 1988–94, a group of legal experts from across the globe engaged in a project to 'provide a contemporary re-statement of international law applicable to armed conflict at sea'.[67] The product of their efforts was the *San Remo Manual on International Armed Conflict Applicable to Armed Conflict at Sea*, which is widely considered to be one of the best resources for those who study or apply the law of naval warfare.[68] Included in their project was a review of the customary law of blockade. With the intention of bringing the law of blockade into the modern sphere of IHL, the authors of the San Remo Manual incorporated protections for civilians into their provisions on blockade.[69]

A number of states, including Canada and Israel, have adopted the provisions of the San Remo Manual.[70] It represents a slightly different approach to the issue of starvation in blockade by providing that, 'The declaration or establishment of a blockade is prohibited if:

a. it has the sole purpose of starving the civilian population or denying it other objects essential for its survival; or

b. the damage to the civilian population is, or may be expected to be, excessive in relation to the concrete and direct military advantage anticipated from the blockade.'[71]

[63] Wolff Heintschel von Heinegg, 'The Law of Armed Conflict at Sea' in Deiter Fleck (ed), *The Handbook of International Humanitarian Law* (Oxford University Press, 2008) 555 (hereafter Heintschel von Heinegg, *IHL Handbook*).
   [64] Ibid.   [65] Ibid.
   [66] New Zealand Military Manual as quoted in Henckaerts, *Customary Law Study* (n 47) 190.
   [67] Louise Doswald-Beck (ed), *San Remo Manual on International Law Applicable to Armed Conflicts at Sea* (Cambridge University Press, 1995) 5 (hereafter SRM).
   [68] Heintschel von Heinegg, 'The Current State of the Law of Naval Warfare: A Fresh Look at the *San Remo Manual*' (2006) 82 ILS 269, 269.
   [69] SRM (n 67) 179.   [70] See discussion on the San Remo Manual below.
   [71] See US Naval War College, *Maritime Operational Zones* (US Naval War College 2006) 4–25.

As can be noted, both the sole purpose and San Remo Manual approaches ultimately permit the starvation of civilians, the central difference being that one requires that the proportionality test must be applied to the operation, while the other does not.[72]

A third approach to the issue of starvation and blockade is exemplified in the manuals of France and the United States,[73] which circumvent the issue of article 49.3 by adopting the language of article 70 which states in part:

1. If the civilian population of any territory under the control of a Party to the conflict, other than occupied territory, is not adequately provided with the supplies mentioned in Article 69, relief actions which are humanitarian and impartial in character and conducted without any adverse distinction shall be undertaken, subject to the agreement of the Parties concerned in such relief actions . . .[74]

While article 70 extends protection beyond those provided in GC IV article 23, it contains an inherent flaw that is found in the conditional nature of the provision; it is subject to the agreement of the Parties concerned in such relief actions. Ultimately, if the blockading force and its adversary cannot agree on a humanitarian relief plan, there is no requirement for the blockading force to allow any aid to pass through the blockade.

As was the case in attempting to apply article 54 to blockade, the reliance on article 70 also runs up squarely against the issue of the intention of the drafters of the Protocol. In its discussion of article 70, the Committee Three Report noted that there was significant opposition to the extension of article 70 to blockade, noting that, 'the paragraph does not change the law of naval blockade is made clear by Article [49.3]'.[75] Evidence of the continuing strong position that some parties have taken with respect to the operation of article 70 is found in the reservations that the United Kingdom and France have declared to Additional Protocol 1, declaring:

It is the understanding of the United Kingdom that this Article does not affect the existing rules of naval warfare regarding naval blockade, submarine warfare or mine warfare.[76]

and

Le gouvernement de la république française considère que l'article 70 relatif aux actions de secours n'a pas d'implication sur les règles existantes dans le domaine de la guerre navale en ce qui concerne le blocus maritime, la guerre sous-marine ou la guerre des mines.[77]

---

[72] See discussion in Henckaerts, *Customary Law Study* (n 47) Rule 53.

[73] *Commander's Handbook* (n 50) para 7–10: '[N]eutral vessels and aircraft engaged in the carriage of qualifying relief supplies for the civilian population and the sick and wounded should be authorized to pass through the blockade cordon, subject to the right of the blockading force to prescribe the technical arrangements.'

[74] AP1 (n 10) art 70.   [75] CDDH/III/67 (n 27).

[76] The United Kingdom of Great Britain and Northern Ireland, reservation declaration 2 July 2002. ICRC <http://www.icrc.org/ihl/NORM/0A9E03F0F2EE757CC1256402003FB6D2?OpenDocum ent> accessed 13 May 2017.

[77] France, Réserves et Déclarations 11 April 2001. Online: ICRC <http://www.icrc.org/applic/ihl/ ihl.nsf/Notification.xsp?action=openDocument&documentId=D8041036B40EBC44C1256A3400 4897B2>.

Of note, both the British and French law of armed conflict manuals have adopted a contradictory approach to their governments' official positions on the issue of article 49.3. Insofar as there exists a discrepancy between military writers and their governments on the issue of starvation in blockade, it must be acknowledged that any authority that the manuals may have is necessarily tentative. As Professor Garraway notes in his article 'The Use And Abuse Of Military Manuals', national manuals 'do not form law, as of themselves',[78] and over-reliance on them can lead to mistaken conclusions as to the state of customary law, particularly when the manuals contradict the law as interpreted and understood by their own state governments.

The Swedish IHL Manual, which does not take a position on the issue of starvation of civilians in blockade operations, sums up the fundamental problem faced by those who seek to determine the state of the law with regard to the issue by stating:

Certain states have maintained that the prohibition against starvation shall apply without exception which would also mean its application against blockade in naval warfare. Other states have claimed that this method of warfare is the province of the international law of naval warfare, which, according to Article 49:3, shall not be affected by the new rules of Additional Protocol I. There is thus no consensus that the prohibition of starvation shall be considered to include maritime blockade.[79]

Insofar as the law of blockade is based entirely on customary international law, the Swedish manual exposes the fact that because there exists such a wide variety of interpretations respecting the provisions on starvation, it is impossible to state categorically that there is definitive customary law on the issue. While it can certainly be conceded that those who share the viewpoint of Professor Heintschel von Heinegg are justifiably interpreting the starvation provisions in a broad, generous, and purposive manner in accordance with the spirit of the Martens Clause, it must also be acknowledged that those who agree with Dinstein understand that it was the express intention of some of the drafters of Additional Protocol 1 to ensure that the Protocol's provisions on starvation would not apply to blockade.

While the issue of starvation has been addressed by a number of scholars during the four decades since the adoption of Additional Protocol 1, there has been no concrete movement by states towards settling the question. Instead, states have generally left the matter in the hands of academicians and other writers, relying on 'soft law' initiatives to fill gaps or address contentious issues of international law. While such efforts can provide some guidance, they are generally not binding on states

---

[78] Charles Garraway, 'The Use And Abuse Of Military Manuals' (2004) 7 Yearbook of International Humanitarian Law 425.

[79] Government of Sweden, *IHL Manual* (Stockholm, 1991), Section 3.2.1.5, 59–60. Consider also Germany's Military Manual which, in a section on blockades, states that 'starvation of the civilian population as a method of warfare is prohibited'. New Zealand's Military Manual states that blockade is not prohibited 'even if it causes some collateral deprivation to the civilian population, so long as starvation is not the specific purpose'. The US Naval Handbook states that 'neutral vessels and aircraft engaged in the carriage of qualifying relief supplies for the civilian population ... should be authorized to pass through the blockade cordon'.

(unless accepted as customary law) and are not a satisfactory replacement for state action. The discrepancies found in the various manuals and opinions that address the issue of starvation in blockade demonstrate the requirement for states to resolve the question.

The Principle of Proportionality

The law of armed conflict implicitly recognizes that loss of civilian life, injury to civilians, or damage to civilian objects may occur when military force is used to attack military objectives. While the law does not prohibit such incidental damage, it does forbid military attacks that are expected to cause collateral damage that is excessive in relation to the anticipated concrete and direct military advantage of the attack.[80] This formulation is widely referred to as the IHL proportionality test.[81]

Prior to the introduction of the proportionality test in Additional Protocol 1 in 1977, civilians had virtually no protection from the consequential effects of warfare. Under the pre-1977 regime, once it was determined that it was militarily necessary to neutralize or destroy a military objective, the incidental damage that might be caused to civilians and their property was legally irrelevant; 'any unavoidable injury or damage caused to civilians or civilians was accepted'.[82]

Very closely aligned to the principle of distinction, the proportionality test requires military forces to assess the possibility of civilian casualties before conducting an attack, and to make the determination as to whether or not such damage will be acceptable in relation to the military advantage that is anticipated therefrom. If it is determined that such damage would be excessive, then an attack must be cancelled or suspended.[83] Any attack that violates the principle of proportionality is considered to be an indiscriminate attack and may constitute a grave breach of the law of armed conflict.[84]

Proportionality in the Context of Blockade

> The Protocol refers to expected injury to civilians and to anticipated military advantage. From this, one can deduce that what ultimately counts, in appraising whether an attack which engenders incidental loss of civilian life or damage to civilian objects is 'excessive', is not the actual outcome of the attack, but the initial expectation and anticipation.[85]

---

[80] AP1 (n 10) art 51.5(b).
[81] Kenneth Watkin, *Fighting at the Legal Boundaries: Controlling the Use of Force in Contemporary Conflict* (Oxford University Press, 2016) 245.
[82] Dinstein, *Hostilities* (n 63) 119.   [83] AP1 (n 10) art 57.2(b).
[84] Ibid, art 85.3(b).   [85] Dinstein, *Hostilities* (n 63) 121.

In 1992, the authors of the San Remo Manual proposed a solution to the issue of starvation in blockade by creating a rule that provided:

102. The declaration or establishment of a blockade is prohibited if:
(a) it has the sole purpose of starving the civilian population or denying it other objects essential for its survival; or
(b) the damage to the civilian population is, or may be expected to be, excessive in relation to the concrete and direct military advantage anticipated from the blockade.[86]

By importing the language from the proportionality test into blockade law, the Manual's drafting team attempted to utilize soft law to change the state of the existing customary law. While this effort was commendable, its very effectiveness hinges on the question of whether or not the proportionality test is a viable solution to the problem of starvation in blockade.

Applying the Proportionality Test to Blockade

> The main problem with the principle of proportionality is not whether or not it exists but what it means and how it is to be applied ...[87]

In the Final Report to the Prosecutor by the Committee Established to Review the NATO Bombing Campaign Against the Federal Republic of Yugoslavia, the committee noted that, 'It is much easier to formulate the principle of proportionality in general terms than it is to apply it to a particular set of circumstances'.[88] This holds true in the case of maritime blockade, where there exist three fundamental problems in applying the proportionality test.

First, the very nature of the proportionality test is that it is anticipatory; that is to say, operational planners must be able to estimate the expected damage to civilians and their property as the first step in the proportionality calculation. As Professor Francoise Hampson notes, 'commanders must first define the target ... Second, they must estimate the number of casualties and, third, the anticipated military advantage. The important element is that they cannot proceed to the second stage until they [can determine] the foreseeable civilian losses.'[89] Consequently, if the expected losses cannot be reasonably established, it is impossible to complete the proportionality test. In the ICTY case of *Kupreskic*, the trial chamber noted that when considering the application of the proportionality test, 'regard might be had to considerations such as the cumulative effect of attacks on military objectives causing incidental damage to civilians ... it might be warranted to conclude that the

---

[86] SRM (n 67) art 10.
[87] Final Report to the Prosecutor by the Committee Established to Review the NATO Bombing Campaign Against the Federal Republic of Yugoslavia para 48 (13 June 2000). Online: ICTY <http://www.icty.org/en/press/final-report-prosecutor-committee-established-review-nato-bombing-campaign-against-federal> accessed 9 October 2017..
[88] Ibid.
[89] Francoise Hampson, 'Means and Methods of Warfare in the Conflict in the Gulf' in P. Rowe (ed), *The Gulf War 1990–91 in International and English Law* (Routledge, 1993) 89, 92.

cumulative effect of such acts entails that they may not be in keeping with inter-national law. Indeed, this pattern of military conduct may turn out to jeopardise excessively the lives and assets of civilians, contrary to the demands of humanity.'[90]

While in a kinetic attack it is generally relatively easy to determine the damage that will likely be caused within a certain radius of a weapon's detonation point, there is truly no way to approximate the effects of an operation that may last several years, particularly in situations where the harm to civilians becomes exponentially worse with time.

The second challenge in applying the proportionality test for an operation such as blockade lies in the very nature and purpose of the test. On review of the Official Records of the Diplomatic Conference on the Reaffirmation and Development of International Humanitarian Law Applicable in Armed Conflicts,[91] it is readily apparent that when the provisions regarding proportionality were being discussed, the working groups were proceeding under the presumption that the test was being created to deal with individual targets and finite areas around military objectives, not an entire country. This is evident in the provisions for precautions in the attack, found in articles 57 and 58 of Additional Protocol 1, that call upon Parties to select a target 'which may be expected to cause the least danger to civilian lives and to civilian objects'[92] and to 'endeavor to remove the civilian population ... from the vicinity of military objectives'.[93] This language implies that a target is to be limited in its size and scope. In this light, Ken Watkin is correct to point out that the use of the test in a 'strategic analytical framework may raise concerns over an erosion of the principle of distinction, such as occurred during extensive bombing campaigns of World War II'.[94]

The third, and no less challenging, characteristic of the proportionality test is its inherent ambiguity. During the working group meetings of the Diplomatic Conference for Additional Protocol 1, the issue of proportionality was the subject of many frank deliberations.[95] Fully cognizant of the fact that they were required to construct a formula that would provide protection for civilians while permitting the military to conduct operations in their vicinity, the delegates strove to find a compromise between those who advocated a complete prohibition on attacks that would result in any civilian casualties and those who promoted the notion that the requirements of military necessity should prevail, irrespective of the collateral harm. The resultant clause, which incorporates the phrase, 'excessive in relation to the concrete and direct military advantage anticipated',[96] has proven problematic in its application and has evoked the ire of some who have described it as a concept that is 'void for vagueness',[97] and a 'rule of paramount importance that rests on comparing

---

[90] *Prosecutor v Kupreskic et al.* IT-95-16-T, Trial Judgement (14 January 2000) International Criminal Tribunal for the former Yugoslavia (Trial Chamber) para 526.

[91] CDDH/III/67 (n27) SR 41 and 42.   [92] AP1 (n 10) art 57.3.

[93] Ibid, art 58(a).

[94] Ken Watkin, 'Assessing Proportionality: Moral Complexity and Legal Rules' (2005) 8 Yearbook of International Humanitarian Law 3, 43.

[95] CDDH/III/67 (n 27).   [96] AP1 (n 10) art 51.5(b)

[97] Hays Park, 'Air War and the Law of War' (1990) 32:1 Air Force L Rev 1, 173.

two incomparable concepts, purports to subjectively quantify the basically unquantifiable notion of "military advantage" and defers all decision making to [military commanders]'.[98]

The wording of the proportionality test is imprecise. In this regard, there is no concrete standard and very little guidance for commanders and staff to follow when they are tasked with assessing proportionality during the planning stages of operations. For these people, the responsibility of determining how many civilian deaths will be 'excessive' in relation to the 'direct and concrete military advantage' that they believe will be gained form an attack is a formidably difficult moral and legal question.

Attempting to determine what 'excessive' might mean in the situation of a protracted maritime blockade would be an exceptionally difficult task. Even assuming that the potential injury to civilians and civilian objects could be accurately estimated prior to the initiation of a blockade, it must be asked if 'military necessity' could ever justify the death by starvation of potentially thousands of civilians. The reality of twenty-first-century warfare and the negative public reaction to civilian casualties would indicate that a blockade that could be expected to cause widespread suffering and mass starvation would not be politically or morally palatable, irrespective of the anticipated military advantage.

The drafters of the San Remo Manual should be commended for recognizing and addressing the issue of starvation in blockade. When the working group experts gathered in San Remo in 1992, the prevailing attitude in the international community was that blockade had been unaffected by the adoption of Additional Protocol 1. This left the drafters in a dilemma; they could either accept the status quo and concede that the starvation of civilians was a tolerable incidental consequence of blockade, or they could attempt to influence customary law by allowing for the protection of civilians subjected to blockades. The drafters signalled a desire to correct a wrong that had been done when the drafters of Additional Protocol 1 deliberately excluded blockade from the provisions protecting civilians from starvation.

The inclusion of articles 102 and 103 in the San Remo Manual in 1995 was a bold move that promised to invite significant backlash from legal positivists. However it was, in this writer's opinion, the correct action, demonstrating a principled, reasonable, and responsible approach that is in keeping with the intention of the Additional Protocols 'to reaffirm and develop the provisions protecting the victims of armed conflicts and to supplement measures intended to reinforce their application'.[99]

Although the intentions behind importing the proportionality test into the law of blockade are to be lauded, the difficulties inherent in calculating the humanitarian impact of a blockade before the operation commences, the design of the test as a tactical level tool, and the ambiguity of the wording of the test make it impractical for commanders and staff to use it in the context of maritime blockade. Consequently, a more definitive approach to the issue of starvation by maritime blockade is required.

---

[98] Jeffrey Walker, 'Strategic Targeting and International Law: The Ambiguity of Law Meets the Reality of a Single-Superpower World' (2006) 80 Int'l L Stud 121, 126.

[99] AP1 (n 10) preamble.

8

Blockade in Non-International Armed Conflict

[I]t is likely there will be a willingness on the part of courts and other bodies to recognize that the rules governing the imposition and enforcement of a naval blockade are applicable to non-international armed conflicts.[1]

The laws of naval warfare have evolved to regulate conflicts between entities that have the capacity to acquire, maintain, and operate warships (that is, generally states). Consequently, it is rare that the issue of the applicability of the law of naval warfare is discussed in relation to non-international armed conflict. In recognition of the increasing preponderance of internal armed conflicts over the last several decades, an examination of the applicability of the laws of naval warfare, and particularly maritime blockade, to non-international armed conflict is in order.

A survey of literature demonstrates that traditionally there has been general agreement towards the view that maritime blockade is a method of warfare that can be practised only in situations of international armed conflict.[2] Those who have asserted this position generally find support for their opinions in the historical practice of blockade, the exigencies of the laws of neutrality, substantial *opinio juris*, the doctrine of recognition of belligerency, and the plain meaning of various conventions.

Professor Heintschel von Heinegg examined the application of the laws of naval warfare in non-international armed conflict, and the extent to which parties to a non-international armed conflict may or may not be permitted to exercise belligerent rights at sea.[3] In conducting an analysis of the legal foundations for the existence of non-international armed conflict, he pointed to common article 3 of the Geneva Conventions, and to article 1(1) of Additional Protocol 2, noting that one of the key aspects of non-international armed conflicts is that they occur 'in the

---

[1] Israel, *The Public Commission to Examine the Maritime Incident of 31 May 2010, The Türkel Report* (23 January 2011) 49 (hereafter Turkel Report).

[2] While it is true that the majority of blockades have been conducted during international armed conflicts, it is equally true that blockade operations have been employed in several non-international armed conflicts including the United States blockade of Confederate ports during the US Civil War (1861–65), the British blockade of Russian ports during the Russian Civil War (1919), the blockade of Spanish ports by nationalist forces during the Spanish Civil War (1936–39), the Nationalist blockade of China (1949–58), and the Israeli blockade of Gaza (2009–present).

[3] Wolff Heintschel von Heinegg, 'Methods and Means of Naval Warfare in Non-International Armed Conflicts' (2012) 88 International Law Studies 211, 213 (hereafter Heintschel von Heinegg, 'Methods and Means').

The Law of Maritime Blockade: Past, Present, and Future. Phillip Drew. © Phillip Drew 2017. Published 2017 by Oxford University Press.

territory of one of the High Contracting Parties'.[4] Assessing the parameters of non-international armed conflict from a perspective of plain meaning, he proffered that the territorial component of these foundational documents dictates that parties to a non-international armed conflict must confine their operations to the territory of the affected state(s). Based on this analysis, Professor Heintschel von Heinegg suggested that belligerent parties to a civil war may lawfully conduct naval operations in the territorial sea, or perhaps even the contiguous zone of the state in which the conflict is occurring, but there is no right for either side to interfere with neutral shipping in international waters.[5] It follows, under Heintschel von Heinegg's interpretation, that insofar as the declaration of a maritime blockade invokes the right of the blockading party to intercept goods bound for a blockaded location, the lack of a legal basis upon which to intercept vessels in international waters implies that a blockade cannot exist in non-international armed conflict.

In support of this position, Professor Heintschel von Heinegg referred to the examples of the Spanish Civil War and the Sri Lankan Civil War, both during which regional states refused to acknowledge belligerency or concede to the various parties' efforts to establish blockades or otherwise interfere with neutral shipping. Writing with a similar approach, Professor Natalino Ronzitti has noted that other than in cases of recognized belligerency, there is no support for the notion that parties to a non-international armed conflict may lawfully interfere with neutral shipping, particularly in international waters.[6]

The Doctrine of Recognition of Belligerency

Not referred to in any convention, the doctrine of recognition of belligerency constitutes an acknowledgment in the sphere of international law that a non-state actor is involved in an armed conflict with its parent state. The theory behind recognition of belligerence is that once an organized armed group is recognized as a belligerent to an armed conflict, either by the conflict state or another affected state, the laws and customs of international armed conflict will apply to the armed conflict, with all of their inherent rights and privileges.[7] Under the doctrine, there are three ways that recognition of belligerency can be granted:[8] implicitly, through the conflict state establishing a blockade against the armed group; explicitly through the conflicted

---

[4] *The Geneva Convention Relative to the Protection of Civilian Persons in Time of War Of August 12, 1949*, 75 UNTS 287, art 3 (hereafter common article 3).

[5] Heintschel von Heinegg, 'Methods and Means' (n 3) 217.

[6] See also Natalino Ronzitti, 'The Crisis of the Traditional Law Regulating International Armed Conflicts at Sea and the Need for its Revision' in Natalino Ronzitti (ed), *The Law of Naval Warfare: A Collection of Agreements and Documents with Commentaries* (Martinus Nijhoff, 1988) 11–13.

[7] See discussion in Yair M. Lootsen, 'The Concept of Belligerency in International Law' (2000) 166 Mil Law Rev 109, 110.

[8] Wyndam L. Walker, 'Recognition of Belligerency and Grant of Belligerent Rights' in *Transactions of the Grotius Society, Vol. 23, Problems of Peace and War, Papers Read before the Society in the Year 1937* (Cambridge University Press, 1937) 177, 208 (hereafter Walker, 'Recognition').

state's formal recognition of belligerency; or, explicitly by a third state's declaration of neutrality vis a vis the parties to the non-international armed conflict. [9]

It is widely accepted that the doctrine of recognition of belligerence is a creation of the American Civil War.[10] The state of the law with respect to civil wars prior to that point was articulated by Emerich Vattel:

[W]hen the bands of the political society are broken, or at least suspended, between the sovereign and his people, the contending parties may then be considered as two distinct powers; ... It follows, then in virtue of the voluntary law of nations that the two parties may act as having an equal right, and behave to each other accordingly till the decision of the affair.[11]

While Vattel's enunciation may have been perfectly valid with respect to armed conflicts that occurred on land, there is no indication that there was any acceptance at the time that the same held true for the maritime domain. Certainly, in the months following President Lincoln's proclamation of the Union blockade of Confederate ports in April 1861,[12] European states expressed doubts about the legality of the proclamation, 'question[ing] the legality of the blockade, [and] echoing the concerns ... that Union action was an unlawful impairment of the right of all nations to exercise freedom of the seas during peacetime'.[13]

While there is evidence that points to the apprehension that European powers had towards the Union blockade at the commencement of the war, it is equally apparent that as the civil war continued, there was pragmatic, if not somewhat reluctant, acceptance of the Union's actions, and acknowledgement that a state of war existed between the Union and the Confederacy. When President Lincoln proclaimed the blockade, the Union was of the belief that the right to exercise the blockade would be a one-sided affair, bestowing the rights of warfare only on the government of the

---

[9] The classic example of recognition of belligerence is found in the American Civil War. In that war, the United Kingdom was found to have recognized the belligerent status of the Confederate states by the issuance of a Royal proclamation in 1861 by which it proclaimed its neutrality in the conflict. Abraham Lincoln: 'Proclamation 81—Declaring a Blockade of Ports in Rebellious states' 19 April 1861. Online: Gerhard Peters and John T. Woolley, *The American Presidency Project* <http://www.presidency>. ucsb.edu/ws/?pid=70101> accessed 9 October 2017, and Victoria R.I., Proclamation 14 May 1861, Proclamation of Neutrality (1861) London Gazette, 2046. See also *The Amy Warwick*, 67 US 635 (1862) 670.

[10] Walker, 'Recognition'(n 8) 190. See, however, *The Santissima Trinidad* (1822) 20 US 283 in which the US Supreme Court held:

The government of the United States has recognized the existence of a civil war between Spain and her colonies, and has avowed a determination to remain neutral between the parties, and to allow to each the same rights of asylum and hospitality and intercourse. Each party is therefore deemed by us a belligerent nation, having, so far as concerns us, the sovereign rights of war, and entitled to be respected in the exercise of those rights.

[11] Emerich Vattel, *The Law of Nations, or, Principles of the Law of Nature, Applied to the Conduct and Affairs of Nations and Sovereigns*, 1797 edn, translated by Joseph Chitty (T. & J. W. Johnson, 1853) para 56.

[12] The American Presidency Project, 'Proclamation 81—Declaring a Blockade of Ports in Rebellious States' <http://www.presidency.ucsb.edu/ws/?pid=70101> accessed 13 May 2017.

[13] James Kraska, 'Rule Selection in the Case of Israel's Naval Blockade of Gaza: Law of Naval Warfare or Law of the Sea?' (2010) 13 Yearbook of International Humanitarian Law 367, 388.

United States. European recognition of the blockade, however, came in a form that had not been contemplated by the Union when the blockade was announced: most European powers ultimately recognized both sides in the civil war and accorded them full rights.

The Union government was initially reluctant to extend recognition that the Confederate states could have standing under the law of nations. This position, however, was shattered by the United States Supreme Court in The Prize Cases.[14] In that decision, the Court, referring to actions taken by the United States government to maintain neutrality during the war between Spain and her colonies, noted that in 1822 the United States 'recognized the existence of a civil war between Spain and her colonies, and ... avowed a determination to remain neutral between the parties ... Each party [was], therefore, deemed ... a belligerent nation having ... the sovereign rights of war, and entitled to be respected in the exercise of those rights.'[15]

Determining that 'civil war exists',[16] the Supreme Court ruled that, 'a civil war such as that waged between the Northern and Southern states is properly conducted according to the humane regulations of public law as regards capture on the ocean'.[17] It was from this ruling that the doctrine of belligerent recognition evolved.

The rise of the doctrine of recognition of belligerency reflected a nineteenth-century acknowledgment that not all internal conflicts were equal. As Professor McLaughlin points out, there were three categories of internal conflict identified in the nineteenth century; rebellion, insurgency, and belligerency.[18] Under this system of classification, recognition of belligerency constituted an acknowledgement that a civil war had risen beyond mere unorganized insurrection, and had become so large as to seriously threaten the existence of the sovereign state. Recognizing the same, Professor Lauterpacht, writing in 1947, outlined the conditions under which the doctrine of belligerent recognition could be applied:

First, there must exist within a state an armed conflict of a general (as distinguished from a purely local) character; secondly, the insurgents must occupy and administer a substantial portion of national territory; thirdly, they must conduct the hostilities in accordance with the rules of war and through organized armed forces acting under a responsible authority; fourthly, there must exist circumstances which make it necessary for outside states to define their attitude by means of recognition of belligerency.[19]

During the nineteenth century, the recognition of belligerency was the only means by which non-state actors could be accorded rights and personality under international law. It was also the only manner by which insurgent groups could gain

---

[14] The Prize Cases (1863) 67 US 635 (hereafter Prize Cases).
[15] *Santissima Trinidad*, 7 Wheaton 283, 337.   [16] Prize Cases (n 14) 667–8.
[17] Ibid, 673.
[18] Rob McLaughlin, 'The Law Applicable to Naval Mine Warfare in a Non-International Armed Conflict' (2014) 90 Int'l L Stud 475, 482 (hereafter McLaughlin, 'NIAC').
[19] Hersch Lauterpacht, *Recognition in International Law* (Cambridge University Press 1948) 176 (hereafter Lauterpacht, *Recognition*). See also Charles Hyde, *International Law Chiefly as Interpreted and Applied by the United States*, 2nd rev edn, vol 1 (Little, Brown and Company, 1947) 200. See also Prize Cases (n 14) 674.

status vis a vis neutral states.[20] Thus, once belligerency was recognized, the non-state party could legally engage in acts of war and, as Professor McLaughlin notes, 'the full suite of maritime LOAC applicable in a state against state conflict ... was then applied as between the rebel group and the conflict state'.[21]

While McLaughlin's point certainly reflects the state of the law as it existed between the mid-nineteenth and mid-twentieth centuries, legal academics in the period between the two world wars began to question the contemporary thinking of the time, particularly whether or not recognition of belligerency was a valid concept in twentieth-century law. Much of the controversy during that period arose from the fact that Britain and other European states had refused to recognize belligerency in the Spanish Civil War, in spite of the size and complexity of the conflict.[22]

Speaking in 1937 in relation to the Spanish Civil War, Wyndham Leigh Walker challenged the existing framework, stating, 'War exists *in fact*—whatever we have to say about it or however inconvenient it may be to have our shipping interfered with—and is the fact of war not the fact of recognition that really carries with it war rights.'[23] He went on to state that:

To denounce as illegal a capture of a British ship on the high seas for a clear breach of an effective blockade or carriage of contraband appears to me to be incorrect. We have a right to object that the captor is in the service of a community which does not fulfil the requirements of belligerency at all-we have no right to object merely because we have not recognized actually existing belligerency ...[24]

Lauterpacht buttressed Walker's position with respect to the recognition of belligerency, noting that, 'the essence of [recognition of belligerence] is that recognition is not in the nature of a grant of a favour or a manner of unfettered political discretion, but a duty imposed by the facts of the situation'.[25] He went on to state that, 'To grant recognition of belligerency when these conditions are absent is to commit an international wrong as against the lawful government ... To refuse to recognize the insurgents as belligerents although these conditions are present is to act in a manner which finds no warrant in international law.'[26]

In 1949 the Geneva Conventions extended the application of the laws of war to 'armed conflict not of an international character' through the adoption of common article 3.[27] The implementation of common article 3 effectively opened a new chapter in the laws of war by extending the operation of IHL to internal armed conflict,

---

[20] Anthony Cullen, *The Concept of Non-International Armed Conflict in International Humanitarian Law* (Cambridge University Press, 2010) 20.

[21] McLaughlin, 'NIAC' (n 18) 482.

[22] During the Spanish Civil War both the Nationalist and Republican sides had large air forces and substantial naval fleets, including battleships, cruisers, and destroyers. International interference was significant, with Germany and Italy supporting the Nationalists while France and the USSR supported the Republicans. It is estimated that there were in excess of 500,000 casualties during the war. 'The Spanish Civil War' HistoryLearningSite.co.uk. <http://www.historylearningsite.co.uk/spanish_civil_war1.htm> accessed 13 May 2017.

[23] Walker 'Recognition' (n 8) 200.   [24] Ibid, 210.

[25] Lauterpacht, *Recognition* (n 19) 175.   [26] Ibid, 176.

[27] Common art 3 (n 4), in part: 'In the case of armed conflict not of an international character ...'.

the existence of which was to be determined by fact rather than through the specious and highly subjective concept of recognition of belligerency.[28]

The conventional recognition of the existence of non-international armed conflict in the 1949 Geneva Conventions has not put an end to the debate over the continuing applicability of the doctrine of recognition of belligerency. In the words of some, the doctrine has been rendered, 'for the most part, useless'[29] and that its continuing existence 'derail[s] intelligent commentators and statesmen from the more productive pursuit of a genuine consensus on minimal humanitarian principles applicable in such domestic settings'.[30] Others adopt a less categorical approach to the issue, preferring instead to acknowledge that while the customary rules of IHL can be applied in times of all civil wars, it is only in cases of recognized belligerency that the parties to a non-international armed conflict can interfere with neutral rights at sea. For such scholars, the requirement for belligerency has only been modified by the incorporation of the 1949 Geneva Conventions, and 'it is difficult to see why the pre-1949 scheme should be considered defunct ... [W]e are still left with the legal possibility that a subset of ... belligerency situations ... still persists'.[31] Finally, there remain those who continue to advocate that recognition of the traditional doctrine of recognition of belligerency remains valid, arguing that a 'non-state actor may not interfere with neutral shipping unless the neutral state has—either explicitly or implicitly—recognized it as a belligerent'.[32]

It is correct to state that blockade and the law of naval warfare cannot, and should not, be applied in all cases of internal armed conflicts.[33] Considering Professor McLaughlin's categorization of the types of civil wars, it is evident that there are some internal conflicts, such as rebellion and insurgency, to which the general rules applicable to naval warfare should not apply, simply because they have not reached a threshold that can permit interference with neutral trade. In such cases, insurgents who interfere with neutral rights in international waters can be characterized as pirates. The corollary to McLaughlin's classification is that there are some non-international armed conflicts which are of such size and complexity that the application of the laws of naval warfare may be justified; namely the type of internal armed conflict described in Additional Protocol 2 to the Geneva Conventions of 1949.[34] Similarly, Professor Guilfoyle has suggested that, 'On the basis of relevant state practice one can at most hazard a suggestion that irrespective of the precise classification of a conflict, states are likely to tolerate the assertion of a blockade only in cases

---

[28] Adam Roberts and Richard Guelff, *Documents on the Laws of War*, 3rd edn (Oxford Press, 2000) 12.

[29] Erik Castren, 'Recognition of Insurgency' (1965) 4 Indian J Int'l L 443, 454.

[30] Ibid.　　　[31] McLaughlin, 'NIAC' (n 18) 488–9.

[32] Heintschel von Heinegg, 'Methods and Means' (n 3) 213.

[33] See McLaughlin, 'NIAC' (n 18) 4–5. In comparing the traditional forms of conflicts to modern concepts, McLaughlin opines that rebellion would not meet the contemporary threshold for armed conflict and that only domestic law would apply. Insurrection, which is a step up in seriousness, might, depending on circumstances, trigger the LOAC and possibly have some effect in the maritime domain.

[34] International Committee of the Red Cross (ICRC), *Protocol Additional to the Geneva Conventions of 12 August 1949, and relating to the Protection of Victims of Non-International Armed Conflicts (Protocol II)*, 8 June 1977, 1125 UNTS 609 (hereafter AP2).

of higher-intensity conflicts on a par with the traditional understanding of war'.[35] This, in turn, aligns with the US Supreme Court's direction in Prize Cases in which the Court noted that it would be improper to confer status to a 'loose, unorganized insurrection, having no defined boundary or possession'.[36] In recognizing that there was an armed conflict to which the laws of nations should apply, the Court explicitly recognized that the South was controlled by a Confederate government that had raised a very large army, and which exercised effective control over its territory.[37]

A comparison of the criteria for belligerent recognition as set out by Professor Lauterpacht,[38] and the application requirements for Additional Protocol 2 demonstrates that the triggering provisions are incredibly similar:[39]

This Protocol ... shall apply to all armed conflicts ... [that] take place in the territory of a High Contracting Party between its armed forces and dissident armed forces or other organized armed groups which, under responsible command, exercise such control over a part of its territory as to enable them to carry out sustained and concerted military operations and to implement this Protocol.[40]

Insofar as the conditions for initiating the operation of Additional Protocol 2 are virtually identical to those for the recognition of belligerency, it may be that the traditional requirement for recognition of belligerence is no longer relevant, and that custom has changed to reflect the contemporary reality that status is conferred by the fact that a non-international armed conflict exists, rather than by the arbitrary declarations of states.[41]

Although the trigger for the application of IHL is the existence of an armed conflict, the term 'armed conflict' is not defined in any international convention. Rather, the definition was provided by the International Criminal Tribunal for the Former Yugoslav Republics (ICTY) in its 1995 ruling in the case of *Tadic*, wherein the Court found that:

an armed conflict exists whenever there is a resort to armed force between states or protracted armed violence between governmental authorities and organized armed groups or between such groups within a state. International humanitarian law applies from the initiation of such armed conflicts and extends beyond the cessation of hostilities until a general conclusion of peace is reached; or, in the case of internal conflicts, a peaceful settlement is achieved.[42]

A fundamental difference between the pre-1949 state of the law and modern humanitarian law lies in the recognition that declarations of war are no longer necessary for

---

[35] Douglas Guilfoyle, 'The Mavi Marmara Incident and Blockade in Armed Conflict' (2011) 81:1 BYIL 171, 194 (hereafter Guilfoyle, 'The Mavi Marmara Incident').
[36] Prize Cases (n 14) 673.   [37] Ibid, 674.   [38] Lauterpacht, *Recognition* (n 19).
[39] See Turkel Report (n 1) 49. It is acknowledged that the criteria of belligerency might have required organized armed groups to have somewhat more administrative and governance responsibilities over the local population than does the requirement under AP2. However, given that no state has recognized a state of belligerency since the end of the Second World War, it is difficult to discern whether or not the criteria of AP2 have supplanted the customary law aspects of belligerency. Although some commentators have classified the armed conflict between Israel and Gaza as 'international' due to belligerency, Israel categorically denies that belligerency is relevant to its current conflict with Hamas.
[40] AP2 (n 34) art 1.   [41] Most of the provisions of AP2 are considered customary law.
[42] AP2 (n 34) 70.

the laws of armed conflict to apply.[43] It is now well settled that humanitarian law will 'apply to all cases of declared war or of any other armed conflict which may arise between two ... Parties, *even if the state of war is not recognized by one of them*'.[44]

The extension of the application of IHL, primarily in customary form, 'to armed conflict not of an international character', was included in common article 3. The addition of common article 3 to the Geneva Conventions not only confirmed the existence of non-international armed conflict in conventional international law, but also imposed rights and obligations through the application of customary international law.[45] The case of *Tadic* instructs us that a non-international armed conflict exists when there is 'protracted armed violence between governmental authorities and organized armed groups or between such groups within a state.'[46] In this respect, the existence of an armed conflict is a matter of fact that is not subject to the discretionary recognition of any third party.[47] 'International humanitarian law applies from the initiation of such armed conflicts and extends ... [until] a peaceful settlement is achieved.'[48]

The grant of quasi-personality to organized armed groups was an important advancement in the law of armed conflict, one that ensured that all parties to an internal armed conflict would have rights and obligations under the laws of war. With this in mind, one must enquire as to whether there is a valid reason that either party in a substantive non-international armed conflict should or should not be legally permitted to interdict neutral shipping through the application of contraband or blockade law, or, for that matter, be entitled to exercise the full suite of the laws of armed conflict as they apply to maritime warfare.

---

[43] See '1952 Commentary—art 2, Chapter 1: General Provisions' ICRC.org <https://www.icrc.org/applic/ihl/ihl.nsf/Treaty.xsp?action=openDocument&documentId=4825657B0C7E6BF0C12563CD002D6B0B> accessed 13 May 2017. The commentary to Geneva Convention 1 states, 'Until recent times war was ordinarily preceded by a regular diplomatic ceremonial. Before there was any resort to arms, there was a declaration of war by one of the opposing parties, followed by the inauguration of a state of war by both belligerents with all the legal consequences which that entailed, both in relation to nationals and in relation to enemy nationals and enemy property.' Consequently, in those days, in theory, where war had not been declared, or the state of war had not been recognized by one of the parties for one reason or another (e.g. the non-recognition by one party of the Government of the other party), the applicability of the Convention might be contested.

[44] International Committee of the Red Cross (ICRC), Geneva Convention for the Amelioration of the Condition of the Wounded and Sick in Armed Forces in the Field. (First Geneva Convention), 12 August 1949, 75 UNTS 287, art 2 (author's emphasis).

[45] It is becoming increasingly common for IHL conventions to adopt language that expresses the intent for the treaties to apply to non-state parties in armed conflict. See, for example, Convention on Prohibitions or Restrictions on the Use of Certain Conventional Weapons Which May be Deemed to be Excessively Injurious or to Have Indiscriminate Effects (and Protocols) (As Amended on 21 December 2001), 10 October 1980, 1342 UNTS 137, art 1(3).

[46] *Prosecutor v Dusko Tadic a/k/a 'Dule'* IT-94-1-A, Decision on the Defence Motion for Interlocutory Appeal on Jurisdiction (2 October 1995) International Criminal Tribunal for the Former Yugoslavia (Appeals Chamber) para 70 (hereafter *Tadic*).

[47] See AP2 (n 34). It is recognized that there are often disagreements as to whether or not a conflict has reached the threshold for NIAC. It is also noted that while parties to a NIAC have status, that status is not equal to that of states. For example, insurgents are not generally granted combatant immunity in a NIAC whereas members of the state military do enjoy that privilege.

[48] *Tadic* (n 46) para 70.

It can be argued that non-state actors are prohibited from engaging in naval warfare because, 'Under the law of international armed conflict, only warships are entitled to exercise belligerent rights'.[49] The contemporary conventional definition of warship is found at article 29 of UNCLOS, and is reflected in the San Remo Manual, both which state:

'warship' means a ship belonging to the armed forces of a state bearing the external marks distinguishing such ships of its nationality, under the command of an officer duly commissioned by the government of the state and whose name appears in the appropriate service list or its equivalent, and manned by a crew which is under regular armed forces discipline.[50]

While the issue of 'belonging to the armed forces of a state' might first appear to be an insurmountable hurdle for organized armed, this is not necessarily the case. Insofar as the doctrine of recognition of belligerency has historically conferred warship status to vessels under the command of organized armed groups, it is apparent that in the correct circumstances, the definition of 'warship' can be extended to apply to non-state vessels.[51] As Professor McLaughlin notes, once an armed group was recognized under the doctrine of belligerency, 'the full suite of maritime LOAC applicable in a state against state conflict ... was then applied as between the [parties to the non-international armed conflict]'.[52] Thus, there should be no reason in law why under the modern laws of armed conflict the status of 'warship' cannot be conferred upon vessels belonging to organized armed groups that are engaged in armed conflict against a state, so long as the vessel meets the operational criteria as found in UNCLOS.[53] Similarly, so long as an armed group controls coastline from which it can engage in naval operations, demonstrates that it is capable of establishing and maintaining an effective blockade against its adversary, and can adjudicate prize law, there should be no reason why this de facto capacity should not be lawful.[54] This notion was supported by Professor Walker in 1937, who, in his comments aimed at England's refusal to recognize belligerency in the Spanish Civil War, stated:

We have a right to object if any belligerent, recognized or unrecognized, claims to establish an ineffective blockade or does other acts contrary to the usages of war; we have no legal right to claim to obstruct the naval operations of either side merely because they are parties to a civil war, to one side in which we have not accorded formal recognition.[55]

---

[49] Heintschel von Heinegg, 'Methods and Means' (n 3) 219.

[50] United Nations Convention on the Law of the Sea (adopted 10 December 1982) 3163 UNTS 94, art 29 (hereafter UNCLOS). Note that this definition, which derives from Hague VII (1907), is reflected in the San Remo Manual, Louise Doswald-Beck (ed), *San Remo Manual on International Law Applicable to Armed Conflicts at Sea* (Cambridge University Press, 1995) 9 (hereafter SRM).

[51] Note that in the Spanish Civil War both sides had significant naval forces, including battleships, destroyers, and cruisers. See, for example, 'The Navies of the Civil War' online: Civil War Trust <http://www.civilwar.org/education/history/warfare-and-logistics/warfare/navy.html> accessed 9 October 2017, and John M. Kersh, 'Influence of Naval Power on The Course of The Spanish Civil War, 1936–1939', online: USAWC Strategy Research Project <http://www.handle.dtic.mil/100.2/ADA389113> accessed 9 October 2017.

[52] McLaughlin, 'NIAC' (n 18) 489.   [53] UNCLOS (n 50).

[54] In this regard, at the minimum, a blockade would necessarily be effective, be properly notified, applied impartially to all vessels, and not block access to neutral ports.

[55] Walker, 'Recognition' (n 8) 210.

In order for a law or doctrine to remain relevant, it must evolve to meet the demands and realities of the society(/ies) to which it applies. In considering the lawfulness of the Israeli blockade of Gaza, the authors of the Turkel Report directly addressed the issue of the doctrine of recognition of belligerency. Specifically rejecting the doctrine, and adopting a functional approach to the determination of status, the members of the Commission stated that:

it should be noted that given the degree of de facto control that the Hamas exercises over the Gaza Strip; the significant security threat that it presents; and its attempts to import weapons, ammunition and other military supplies, inter alia, by sea; the Commission would have considered applying the rules governing the imposition and enforcement of a naval blockade even if the conflict between Israel and the Gaza Strip had been classified as a non-international armed conflict.[56]

In making the declaration that the doctrine of recognition of belligerency 'become less important, and today is almost irrelevant',[57] Israel, as the only state that has implemented a prolonged blockade since 1949, has provided strong evidence that the customary law surrounding belligerency has been supplanted by the application of common article 3 and the operational provisions of Additional Protocol 2.[58]

During the nineteenth century the doctrine of recognition of belligerency served an essential function by limiting the circumstances under which an armed group could be elevated to the status of having legal personality in armed conflict. By creating a threshold of control and responsibility, it ensured that mere rebels and brigands could not engage in acts of piracy and larceny under the guise of naval warfare. The doctrine's primary flaw, as was plainly evident in the case of the Spanish Civil War, was that rather than being based on objective criteria, its application was dependent upon the subjective discretion of third states' decisions to either grant or refuse to grant recognition.

The existence of an armed conflict, either international or non-international, is a question of fact; the case of *Tadic*[59] informs us that once an armed conflict is underway, the laws of armed conflict apply. While the rights of neutrals must be respected in any armed conflict, so too must the rights of the parties to it. Lauterpacht addressed this issue directly, noting that:

So long as there are good grounds for the refusal to recognize the belligerency of the insurgents [then refusal to grant belligerent status] is not open to objection. When recognition is refused notwithstanding the existence of the requirements of recognition of belligerency, it amounts, when coupled with discrimination against the insurgents, to intervention denying to a state what is the essence of its sovereignty and independence, namely, the right of political self-determination.[60]

While it is agreed that there should be no right for mere rebels to engage in maritime interdiction operations such as blockade, the same should not hold true in cases in which insurgent forces have met the objective threshold for the traditional doctrine

---

[56] Ibid, 50.   [57] Turkel Report (n 1) 46.
[58] It is acknowledged that Israel is not party to the Additional Protocols to the Geneva Conventions.
[59] *Tadic* (n 46).   [60] Lauterpacht, *Recognition* (n 19) 230.

of belligerent recognition, as is largely reflected in article 1 of Additional Protocol 2. Professor Guilfoyle offers that 'states are likely to tolerate the assertion of a blockade only in cases of higher intensity conflicts on a par with the traditional understanding of war'.[61] There should, accordingly, be no reason that once the threshold is met, that such groups should not be permitted to engage in blockade, or for that matter, any other lawful maritime operations. This could, and should be achieved, by rejecting the outmoded doctrine of recognition belligerence in favour of a modern theory that encompasses the operational threshold of belligerence with the factual existence of armed conflict. Once these criteria are met, the laws applicable to armed conflicts at sea should apply to the non-international armed conflict at issue.[62] The concern of neutrals wishing to trade with Parties to a non-international armed conflict should not be so much that one party or the other is engaged in naval interdiction, but whether or not, as Professor Walker stated, long ago, the parties are engaging in 'acts contrary to the usages of war'.[63]

---

[61] Guilfoyle, 'The Mavi Marmara Incident' (n 35) 194.

[62] SRM (n 50) 73. Of note, the San Remo Manual specifically states, 'although the provisions of this Manual are primarily meant to apply to international armed conflicts at Sea, this has intentionally not been expressly indicated in paragraph 1 in order not to dissuade the implementation of these rules in non-international armed conflicts involving naval operations'.

[63] Walker, 'Recognition' (n 8) 210.

9

International Human Rights Law and Blockade

The basic tenets of human rights can be traced to the very beginnings of human civilization.[1] From the development of the earliest religious codes,[2] through to the modern construct of international conventions, concepts of human rights have been a part of the cultural and political evolution of societies.[3] As these rights have matured, particularly in the period since the European Enlightenment, they have grown not only in scope, but in application as well.[4]

One of the most significant manifestations of the advancement in human rights was the rise of modern liberal democracies and their attendant ideals.[5] While these developments provided individuals with rights to life, property, freedom of religion, and other political, social, and economic rights, those rights existed only at the national level, as between the sovereign and its citizens.

The sanctity of the relationship between a government and its subjects has historically been considered as a sovereign right that is not subject to any form of oversight in international law. 'What a state did inside its borders in relations to its own nationals remained its own affair, an element of its autonomy . . .'.[6]

The creation and adoption of international human rights conventions in the wake of the Second World War marked a paradigm shift in the relationship between the international community, states, and their citizens. Beginning with the adoption of the Universal Declaration of Human Rights in 1948,[7] and with the creation of successive international and regional human rights conventions, 'the large majority of states have become part of a body of international law the scope, breadth, and general significance of which would have been impossible to predict'[8] prior to the war. Under what has been described as the third generation of human rights,[9]

---

[1] Ed Bates, 'History' in Daniel Moeckli et al (eds), *International Human Rights Law* (Oxford University Press, 2010) 17 (hereafter Bates, 'History').

[2] Ibid, 18.

[3] Peter Baehr, *Human Rights: Universality in Practice* (Palgrave, 2001) 6 (hereafter Baehr, *Human Rights*).

[4] Bates, 'History' (n 1) 20–6.

[5] Micheline R. Ishay, *The History of Human Rights: From Ancient Times to the Globalization Era* (University of California Press, 2008) 64.

[6] Philip Alston and Ryan Goodman, *International Human Rights: The Successor to Human Rights in Context* (Oxford University Press, 2013) 136 (hereafter, Alston, *International Human Rights*).

[7] *Universal Declaration of Human Rights*, GA Res. 217 (III), UN GAOR, 3d Sess., Supp. No. 13, UN Doc. A/810 (1948).

[8] Bates, 'History' (n 1) 37.   [9] Baehr, *Human Rights* (n 3) 6.

The Law of Maritime Blockade: Past, Present, and Future. Phillip Drew. © Phillip Drew 2017. Published 2017 by Oxford University Press.

states have been obligated not only to amend their domestic legislation to meet the requirements of various IHRL conventions, but, in many cases, have accepted supervision mechanisms as created under regional human rights bodies to which they are party.[10]

In recent cases, particularly those emanating from the European Court of Human Rights (ECtHR), some human rights tribunals[11] have been interpreting their jurisdictional clauses in a broad and expansive manner, so as to make the extraterritorial activities of the military forces of states party subject to their oversight,[12] and have read into their constituting statutes the prerogative to interpret issues of humanitarian law.[13] As will be discussed below, the jurisprudence arising from the courts has been inconsistent, and sometimes contradictory, creating an atmosphere of legal ambiguity that has left, 'signatory states unable accurately to include Convention obligations as part of their decisional calculus when assessing the desirability of various extraterritorial undertakings'.[14] In the face of this activism by some tribunals, it is necessary to examine the questions of whether, and to what extent, a human rights tribunal might find jurisdiction to hear an action brought against a state party for its conduct of a maritime blockade.

Jurisdiction and IHRL

At the heart of contemporary IHRL is the obligation of states to ensure that the rights of their residents are respected and protected, and that states' human rights obligations towards their citizens are fulfilled. In accordance with the jurisdictional principles found in IHRL, most international and regional human rights conventions contain language that generally stipulates that countries are accountable for safeguarding human rights within their jurisdiction.[15]

The first use of jurisdictional language in IHRL mechanisms is found in the preamble of the UDHR, which requires member states to:

promote respect for these rights and freedoms and by progressive measures, national and international, to secure their universal and effective recognition and observance, both among

---

[10] Ibid, 82.

[11] See, for example, *Coard et al v United States*, Report No 109/99 [1999] IACHR Case 10.95 (29 September 1999).

[12] *Jaloud v The Netherlands*, no 47708/08 [2014] ECtHR (20 November 2014).

[13] *Al-Skeini v United Kingdom*, no 55721/07 [2011] ECtHR 1093 (7 July 2011) (hereafter *Al Skeini v UK*).

[14] Sarah Miller, 'Revisiting Extraterritorial Jurisdiction: A Territorial Justification for Extraterritorial Jurisdiction under the European Convention' (2009) 20:4 EJIL 1223, 1230.

[15] European Convention for the Protection of Human Rights and Fundamental Freedoms, as amended by Protocols Nos 11 and 14 (4 November 1950) ETS 5, art 1 (hereafter ECHR). For an excellent discussion on this topic, see Marko Milanovic, *Extraterritorial Application of Human Rights Treaties* (Oxford University Press, 2011) (hereafter Milanovic, *Extraterritorial Application of Human Rights Treaties*).

the peoples of Member states themselves and among the peoples of territories under their jurisdiction.[16]

This terminology, which is essentially similar between most IHRL treaties,[17] has two functions. First, it requires member states to respect the human rights processes for its citizens and others in areas wherein the state exercises authority; and, secondly, it protects states against spurious claims from cases in which the state has no ability to influence the rights process. It is commonly understood that 'jurisdiction' encompasses territory, and in some cases, executive acts that occur extraterritorially.[18]

Extraterritorial Application of IHRL

Whether, and to what degree, military forces are required to abide by and uphold their states' international human rights obligations while operating outside of their own borders 'is one of the most controversial and politically charged issues in current human rights discourse'.[19] This issue, which is seen by many as a wedge between the 'closely related, but ... distinct legal systems'[20] of IHRL and IHL, is at the heart of the contemporary exploration of the intersection between the two bodies of law.[21]

The evolution of the notion of extraterritorial jurisdiction in human rights law has been contentious, particularly for states that fall within the jurisdiction of the ECtHR. Over the period of the last three decades, and particularly since the commencement of 'the war on terror', the ECtHR has been expanding the meaning of 'jurisdiction' to encompass a variety of government activities that negatively impact foreign citizens who are affected by individuals outside of the states' sovereign territory, and even outside of Europe.

This issue is fundamentally important to countries that participate in military operations overseas, and has the potential to become a 'dominant constraint on signatory

---

[16] Universal Declaration of Human Rights (adopted 10 December 1948) UNGA Res 217 A(III) (hereafter UDHR) preamble.

[17] International Covenant on Civil and Political Rights (adopted 16 December 1966) UNTS vol 999, 171, art 2 (hereafter ICCPR). See also ECHR (n 15) art 1. 'The High Contracting Parties shall secure to everyone within their jurisdiction the rights and freedoms defined in section I of [the] Convention'; and American Convention on Human Rights (ACHR) art 1, 'The states Parties to this Convention undertake to respect the rights and freedoms recognized herein and to ensure to all persons subject to their jurisdiction'.

[18] *Serdar Mohammed v Ministry of Defence* [2017] UKSC 2, 27–8 (hereafter *Serdar Mohammed v MoD*, UKSC).

[19] John Cerone, 'Human Dignity in the Line of Fire: The Application of International Human Rights Law During Armed Conflict, Occupation, and Peace Operations' (2006) 39 V and J Transnat'l L 1, 5.

[20] Lindsay Moir, 'Decommissioned? International Humanitarian Law and the Inter-American Human Rights System' (2003) 25 Human Rights Quarterly 1, 194.

[21] For a few examples of the large pool of literature on this subject, see Jakob Kellenberger, 'IHL and Other Legal Regimes: Interplay in Situations of Violence' (2003) 85:851 IRRC 645; Naz Moderzideh, 'The Dark Sides of Convergence: A Pro-civilian Critique of the Extraterritorial Application of Human Rights Law in Armed Conflict' (2010) 86 Int'l L Stud 349; Milanovic, *Extraterritorial Application of Human Rights Treaties* (n 15).

states' extraterritorial activities',[22] including, potentially, blockade. One of the countries that has been most affected by this recent trend is the United Kingdom, which has been sued by a number of Iraqi and Afghan individuals who have claimed that their human rights were violated by UK armed forces operating in their countries.

In the 2014 case of *Sedar Mohammed v The Ministry of Defence*,[23] a human rights complaint was brought against the United Kingdom by a Taliban commander who had been captured by British forces and held for more than 100 days. In reaching his decision as to whether the detention was a violation of the Taliban commander's right to liberty under the ECHR, Mr Justice Leggett expressed substantial discomfort with the fact that he was bound to follow the ECtHR's decision from the case of Al *Skeini v the United Kingdom*[24] in which the Court directed that, 'the concept of jurisdiction in Article 1 of the Convention is to be given a much broader meaning, so as to cover a situation where a contracting state exercises physical power and control over an individual outside its territory'.[25] In noting that the path to his decision was 'tortuous', Justice Leggett wrote that, 'It seems evident from the text, interpreted in the light of the *travaux préparatoires* and general principles of public international law, that the term "jurisdiction" in Article 1 is to be understood primarily by reference to the territory over which a state has sovereign authority'.[26]

A review of the *travaux preparatoires* provides substantive insight as to the intentions of the states party in regards to the concept of jurisdiction. As the negotiating parties proceeded through the process of drafting the jurisdictional paragraph of the ECHR, one of the earliest drafts read, 'Every state a party to this Convention shall guarantee to all persons residing within its territory the following rights . . .'.[27] While much discussion was dedicated to the wording of the paragraph, the records of discussion show that the word 'jurisdiction' was chosen because it allowed for a slightly broader interpretation than the term 'residing within its territory'. It was thus determined that the word 'jurisdiction' would allow for the provision of rights to persons that were present on European territory, not just residents of the individual states. Furthermore, the records show that most negotiation around the jurisdiction article focused on the word 'guarantee' and the concerns that parties had regarding the legal implications of the use of that word.

As is clearly illustrated in the *travaux*, one of the reasons that the jurisdiction paragraph was drafted in the form that it was, was to ensure that the Convention would not give 'any collective guarantee . . . to persons and goods of foreign nationals'.[28] For this purpose, the word 'guarantee' was removed from the draft. With respect to the inclusion of the word 'jurisdiction' in later drafts, the following explanation is provided:

The assembly draft had extended the benefits of the Convention to 'all persons residing within the territories of the signatory states.' It seemed to the committee that the

---

[22] Sarah Miller, 'Revisiting Extraterritorial Jurisdiction: A Territorial Justification for Extraterritorial Jurisdiction under the European Convention' (2010) 20:4 EJIL 1223, 1224.

[23] *Sedar Mohammed v The Ministry of Defence* [2014] EWHC 1369 (QB) (hereafter *Serdar Mohammed*).

[24] *Al Skeini v UK* (n 13).   [25] *Sedar Mohammed* (n 23) para 118.

[26] Ibid, para 120.   [27] Ibid, para 1.   [28] Ibid, para 24.

term 'residing' might seem too restrictive. It was felt that there were good grounds for extending the benefits of the Convention to all persons in the territories of the signatory states ... The word ['residing'], moreover, has not the same meaning in all national laws. The Committee therefore replace the term 'residing' by the words 'within their jurisdiction'.

In spite of what states may have intended when they drafted the jurisdictional clauses to the various treaties,[29] there has been, over the past two decades, a broadening of the interpretation of the clauses to the point wherein it is now generally accepted, at least in Europe, that 'In exceptional circumstances the acts of Contracting states performed outside their territory or which produce effects there ("extra-territorial act") may amount to exercise by them of their jurisdiction'.[30]

While the European states are bound by the European Court's peculiar interpretation of jurisdiction, other states, particularly those that are not party to regional human rights instruments, are not subject to the same constraints; at least not yet. Thus far, the International Court of Justice has restricted its interpretation of jurisdiction clauses so as to engage extraterritorial application of human rights treaties only in situations in which 'territories and populations [are] under [the] effective control ... of a foreign state, such as in the course of a military occupation'.[31] From an international law perspective, the discord between the international courts on this issue is problematic, particularly for those countries that are engaged in international military coalition activities. Under the current situation, countries operating within the NATO alliance, but outside of the territory of Europe, have vastly different constraints placed on them based on whether or not they are subject to the oversight of a Court that has unquestionably expanded its own jurisdiction beyond that ever intended by the states that created it.

The broad and expansive interpretation of 'jurisdiction' is a contemporary trend that reflects significant efforts by the human rights community to make states increasingly liable for the activities of their militaries during armed conflict. During the first fifty years of their existence, human rights tribunals treated jurisdictional clauses rather conservatively, adhering to the accepted notions of jurisdiction as reflected in general principles of international law. That is to say, the courts acknowledged that jurisdiction consists of 'prescriptive jurisdiction', which refers to the power of the state to create law and 'enforcement jurisdiction' which is the authority of the state to enforce its laws.[32] Under the traditional model, jurisdiction was held to have

---

[29] Additional evidence as to the territorial intentions of the drafters is found in existence of art 56 of the ECHR, which permits states party to extend the provisions of the ECHR to their overseas territories if they so choose.

[30] *Issa and Others v Turkey* (2004) ECtHR App no 31821/96, para 68 (hereafter *Issa v Turkey*).

[31] *Legal Consequences of the Construction of a Wall in the Occupied Palestinian Territory*, Advisory Opinion [2004] ICJ Rep 136, paras 108–12. See also *Armed Activities on the Territory of the Congo (Democratic Republic of the Congo v Uganda)* Judgment [2005] ICJ Rep 168, para 216.

[32] John H. Currie, Craig Forcese, and Valerie Oosterveld, *International Law: Doctrine, Practice and Theory* (Irwin Law, 2007) 433.

extended only to the territorial boundaries of a country, its embassies and flagged vessels,[33] and in some cases, the actions of its agents.[34]

The extension of the concept of jurisdiction, which has the effect of broadening states' IHRL responsibilities beyond their sovereign borders, began in the late 1990s[35] with the case of *Loizidou v Turkey*.[36] In that case, a Cypriot woman, who had been expelled from her residence during the 1974 Turkish invasion of Cyprus, claimed that by preventing her from returning to her home, Turkey had violated her human rights.[37] Turkey countered her argument by noting that Turkish Republic of Northern Cyprus was not Turkish territory and that in any event, it (the Cypriot Republic) was not a party to the ECHR, and therefore the ECHR could not apply to Turkish actions in the territory. In arriving at its decision that Turkey's actions fell within the jurisdiction of the ECHR, the ECtHR stated that a contracting Party's responsibilities and obligations may be engaged when it, 'exercises effective control of an area outside its national territory... directly, through its armed forces, or through a subordinate local administration'.[38] Thus, the Court found that through its occupation of Northern Cyprus, Turkey exercised control that was sufficient to engage its responsibilities under the Convention. This ruling by the European Court was similar to the current position that the ICJ holds towards the concept of jurisdiction.[39]

The European Court followed its precedent from *Loizidou* in the 2002 case of *Bankovic et al v Belgium et al*,[40] a challenge brought by six citizens of the Federal Republic of Yugoslavia (FRY) against Belgium and the other ECHR member states that had participated in the 1999 NATO bombing of the Radio-Television Serbia (RTS) headquarters building, in which sixteen people were killed and sixteen others injured. The applicants, all of whom were directly affected by the raid, brought an action before the ECtHR, claiming violations of their right to life and their right to freedom of expression.

In its unanimous decision to dismiss the application for lack of jurisdiction, the Court noted that 'extra-territorial jurisdiction by a Contracting state is exceptional',[41] and is limited to circumstances in which a 'state, through the effective control of the relevant territory and its inhabitants abroad as a consequence of military occupation or through the consent, invitation or acquiescence of the Government

---

[33] Peter Malanczuk, *Akehurst's Modern Introduction to International Law*, 7th edn (Routledge, 1997) 190.

[34] For example, see *R v Hape* [2007] 2 S.C.R. 292 (Can.) and *Khadr v Canada* (Prime Minister) [2010] 1 SCR 44, para 3 (Can.).

[35] Note that in the case where police and other officials take their citizens into custody in a foreign country, they are required to abide by the HR obligations of their home state. See, for example, *Sergio Euben Lopez Burgos v Uruguay* (1981) Communication No R.12/52, UN Doc Supp No 40 (A/36/40) 176.

[36] *Loizidou v Turkey* (Preliminary Objections) (1995) ECtHR App no 15318/89 (hereafter *Loizidou v Turkey*).

[37] Ibid.   [38] Ibid, paras 62–4.

[39] See *Legal Consequences of the Construction of a Wall in the Occupied Palestinian Territory*, Advisory Opinion [2004] ICJ Rep 136 (hereafter *The Wall Opinion*).

[40] *Bankovic et al v Belgium et al* (2002) ECtHR App no 52207/99 (hereafter *Bankovic v Belgium*).

[41] Ibid, para 71.

of that territory, exercises all or some of the public powers normally to be exercised by that Government'.[42] Noting that the ECHR 'is a multi-lateral treaty operating, subject to Article 56 of the Convention, in an essentially regional context and notably in the legal space (*espace juridique*) of the Contracting states',[43] the Court ruled that, 'The FRY clearly does not fall within this legal space',[44] and that the 'Convention was not designed to be applied throughout the world, even in respect of the conduct of Contracting states'.[45]

The case of *Issa and others v Turkey*[46] was brought by the spouses of Iraqi Kurdish shepherds who were allegedly killed by Turkish Security forces that had been conducting patrols in Northern Iraq. The case was unique, not only because the alleged killers were conducting operations in another country, but also because they were doing so outside of the boundaries of Europe.

While the Court found that there was no proof that Turkish military personnel were responsible for the deaths of the shepherds, it nonetheless expanded the notion of jurisdiction by remarking that:

a state's responsibility may be engaged where, as a consequence of military action—whether lawful or unlawful—that state in practice exercises effective control of an area situated outside its national territory. The obligation to secure, in such an area, the rights and freedoms set out in the Convention derives from the fact of such control, whether it be exercised directly, through its armed forces, or through a subordinate local administration.[47]

In addition to the statement above, the Court also endorsed a personal model of jurisdiction by stating that:

a state may also be held accountable for violation of the Convention rights and freedoms of persons who are in the territory of another state but who are found to be under the former state's authority and control through its agents operating—whether lawfully or unlawfully— in the latter state.[48]

In this manner, *Issa* was not unlike the case of *Louzidou*. In both cases, the Court held that actions of military personnel and other agents of the state could be imputable to their home state if they exercised sufficient control over an area outside of their national territory. On the other hand, the willingness of the Court to expand its reach beyond *l'espace juridique* foretold the Court's inclination towards judicial activism on this vital issue.

The Court's opportunity to increase its jurisdiction came in the form of the landmark case of *Al-Skeini*. Decided by the ECtHR in July 2011, the case significantly altered the threshold for extraterritorial application of the ECHR.

The complaint in the case of *Al Skeini* was that British soldiers who had been on patrol in the region of Basrah in southern Iraq had shot and killed a number of individuals, one of whom was Mr Al Skeini. The case was first brought before British domestic courts and was ultimately appealed to the ECtHR. In determining

---

[42] Ibid. Note that in *Bankovic* the Court did not discuss the personal model of jurisdiction.
[43] Ibid, para 80.   [44] Ibid.   [45] Ibid.   [46] *Issa v Turkey* (n 30).
[47] Ibid, para 69.   [48] Ibid, para 71.

whether or not Britain could be held responsible for any violation of the rights of Mr Al Skeini and the others, the ECtHR found that:

following the removal from power of the Ba'ath regime and until the accession of the Interim Government, the United Kingdom (together with the United States) assumed in Iraq the exercise of some of the public powers normally to be exercised by a sovereign government. In particular, the United Kingdom assumed authority and responsibility for the maintenance of security in South East Iraq. In these exceptional circumstances, the Court considers that the United Kingdom, through its soldiers engaged in security operations in Basrah during the period in question, exercised authority and control over individuals killed in the course of such security operations, so as to establish a jurisdictional link between the deceased and the United Kingdom for the purposes of Article 1 of the Convention.[49]

As can be noted in the above quoted paragraph, in *Al Skeini* the ECtHR signalled its departure from its singular dependence on 'effective control' and instead created a two-part test for jurisdiction that considers the capacity for a state's agents to exercise public powers and exert personal control over territory and the persons inhabiting it. In arriving at its decision the Court examined whether United Kingdom forces 'exercised of some of the public powers normally to be exercised by a sovereign government'.[50] By adopting this approach, the Court was able to sidestep the issue as to whether the UK forces were occupying Iraq and whether or not they had effective control over the area. The simple fact that they exercised some of the powers usually exercised by the Iraqi government was sufficient. Professor Marko Milanovic has summarized the jurisdictional guidance from the *Al-Skieni* case as follows:

[T]he Court applied a *personal* model of jurisdiction . . ., but it did so only *exceptionally*, because the UK exercised *public powers* in Iraq. But, *a contrario*, had the UK *not* exercised such public powers, the personal model of jurisdiction would not have applied. In other words, *Bankovic* is according to the Court still perfectly correct in its result. While the ability to kill is 'authority and control' over the individual if the state has public powers, killing is not authority and control if the state is merely firing away missiles from an aircraft.[51]

The Extent of Positive IHRL Obligations in Cases of Extraterritorial Jurisdiction

As is noted in the preceding paragraphs, in the case of *Bankovic*, the ECtHR upheld the concept that human rights are 'indivisible and interdependent and interrelated',[52] thus refuting the notion that applicants in human rights cases have the option of picking and choosing which human rights obligations and responsibilities apply as between the individuals and the impugned state. In adopting this position,

---

[49] *Al Skeini v UK* (n 13) para 149.   [50] Ibid, para 149.
[51] Marko Milanovic, 'Al-Skeini and Al-Jedda in Strasbourg' (2012) 23 EJIL 121, 130 (hereafter Milanovic, 'Al-Skeini and Al-Jedda in Strasbourg').
[52] UN General Assembly, *Vienna Declaration and Programme of Action*, 12 July 1993, A/CONF.157/23.

the Court indicated that unless a state was in effective control of an area then it could not be expected to approach human rights obligations and responsibilities in a piecemeal fashion.

The Court's departure from the strict 'all or nothing' approach to human rights began with the case of *Issa*,[53] in which it held that in certain circumstances extraterritorial jurisdiction could apply to military forces. In that case, however, the Court did not elucidate upon its finding that the state has an 'obligation to secure, in such an area, the rights and freedoms set out in the Convention'.[54] Rather, it left that colossal statement completely unexplained.

The Court's further retreat from the principle of indivisibility of human rights was outlined in the case of *Ilascu*, the Court provided some guidance on the issue by finding that the 'scope of a state's positive obligations, regard must be had to the fair balance that has to be struck between the general interest and the interests of the individual, the diversity of situations obtaining in Contracting states and the choices which must be made in terms of priorities and resources. Nor must these obligations be interpreted in such a way as to impose an impossible or disproportionate burden.'[55] This guidance was upheld by the Court in the subsequent case of *Al-Skieni*, in which it stated:

Extraterritorially, a Contracting state is obliged to ensure the observance of all those human rights which *it is in a position to ensure*. It is quite possible to envisage situations in which a Contracting state, in its role as an occupying power, has well within its authority the power not to commit torture or extra-judicial killings, to punish those who commit them and to compensate the victims—but at the same time that Contracting state does not have the extent of authority and control required to ensure to all persons the right to education or the right to free and fair elections: those fundamental rights it can enforce would fall squarely within its jurisdiction . . .[56]

The approach that permits states to be responsible only for those rights and obligations that they can reasonably be expected to manage in given circumstances reflects a pragmatic and positive approach to the issue of extraterritorial jurisdiction. By permitting the rights to be tailored in accordance with a party's ability to affect them, the Court has signalled that people whose rights have been violated by an extraterritorial actor may find a remedy through the ECtHR.

While some national courts, such as the Supreme Court of Canada, have held that domestic rights guarantees do not apply to foreign fighters captured during armed conflict,[57] the European Court's direction in regard to jurisdiction is unlikely to be reversed. All European states, and potentially other states that are party to similar regional IHRL conventions, must be cognizant of the fact that their activities in

---

[53] *Issa v Turkey* (n 30).   [54] Ibid, para 69.

[55] *Ilascu and Others v Moldova and Russia*, no. 48787/99 [2004] VII ECHR (8 July 2004) para 332 (hereafter *Ilascu v Moldova*).

[56] *Al Skeini v UK* (n 13) para 32 (Concurring opinion).

[57] *Amnesty International Canada and British Columbia Civil Liberties Association v Chief of the Defence Staff for the Canadian Forces, Minister of National Defence and Attorney General of Canada*, 2008 FCA 40, leave to appeal to the Supreme Court dismissed, case no 33029.

armed conflict may be increasingly subjected to scrutiny by international human rights tribunals.

Can IHRL be Applied to Blockade?

During the nascent years of IHRL most jurists and practitioners paid little heed to the question of how, or indeed whether, the regimes of IHRL and IHL might interact.[58] As has been discussed in Chapter 7, for many, IHL was simply considered to fall under the umbrella of *lex specialis*.[59] According to their perception of the relationship between IHL and IHRL, any discussion of how IHRL might apply during armed conflict was pointless.

As IHRL matured through the latter half of the twentieth century, and non-international armed conflict became the predominant form of warfare, international tribunals and human rights commissions supported the efforts to enshrine the universality of the principles of human rights. In doing so, they advanced the notion that IHL and IHRL can co-exist in the legal paradigm of armed conflict.[60]

The first decade of the twenty-first century has seen a fundamental shift in the manner with which most jurists and scholars interpret the relationship between IHRL and IHL. With very few exceptions,[61] most international tribunals, and the majority of nations, accept the notion that the two bodies of law have undergone a convergence, co-existing and complementing each other during armed conflict. Thus, in contemporary international law, the primary issues to be resolved rest not in the question of whether IHRL can apply during armed conflict, but rather, when and to what extent IHRL is operative in a particular situation.

The issue of IHRL applicability in the case of maritime blockade is particularly important because of the uncertain scope of the law pertaining to humanitarian assistance during blockade operations. With some asserting that there are no binding obligations that require a state to ensure that the basic needs of an adversary's population are met;[62] others stating that the blockading forces are obligated to

---

[58] Nancie Prud'homme, 'Lex Specialis: Oversimplifying a More Complex and Multifaceted Relationship?' (2007) 40 Isr LR 355, 357 (hereafter Prud'homme, *Lex Specialis*).

[59] See, for example, Bill Bowring, 'Fragmentation, Lex Specialis and the Tensions in the Jurisprudence of the European Court of Human Rights' (2010) Journal of Conflict & Security Law 485 (hereafter Bowring, 'Fragmentation, Lex Specialis') and Prud'homme, *Lex Specialis* (n 58) 359–62.

[60] See, for example, *Legality of the Threat of Use of Nuclear Weapons Opinion*, Advisory Opinion [1996] ICJ Rep 226, 240 (hereafter *Nuclear Weapons* case). For more examples of case law affirming the concurrent operation of IHL and IHRL see discussion below.

[61] Israel, *The Public Commission to Examine the Maritime Incident of 31 May 2010, The Türkel Report* (23 January 2011) para 99 (hereafter Turkel Report).

[62] For a discussion of this issue see Yves Sandoz, Christophe Swinarski, and Bruno Zimmermann (eds), *Commentary on the Additional Protocols of 8 June 1977 to the Geneva Conventions of 12 August 1949* (International Committee of the Red Cross & Martinus Nijhoff Publishers, 1987) paras 2083–123 (hereafter Sandoz, *Commentary*). While AP1 arts 54 and 70 prohibit the deliberate starvation of civilians and obligate the parties to a conflict to provide for relief for the civilian population, the relief is subject to an agreement being reached between the parties. If no such agreement is reached, then there is no obligation for the blockading power to provide relief. In this vein, the non-deliberate starvation of civilians is not necessarily unlawful. For a discussion of this issue see Sandoz, *Commentary*, ibid.

provide humanitarian aid if the population is starving; and still others contending that the blockading force must only permit food to pass in situations in which the damage to civilians would be excessive in relation to the concrete and direct military advantage anticipated from the operation, it is not inaccurate to state that this aspect of blockade law is dysfunctional.

As alluded to above, in order to hear a case respecting extraterritorial jurisdiction, any tribunal would necessarily be required to find that the matter at hand falls within its jurisdiction. According to ECtHR's case of *Al Skeini*, jurisdiction can be established when a state exercises public powers in another state and its agents exercise some control over the lives of the people affected. In order to determine whether jurisdiction might be established as a result of a maritime blockade, an examination of the various potential effects of the action would be necessary.

Amongst the undisputed rules of maritime blockade are the requirements of establishment and effectiveness.[63] Effectiveness implies that the blockading power exercises control over all maritime traffic on, under or above a nation's territorial waters.[64] In so doing, the blockading force displaces the sovereign nation's authority and control over that part of its territory.[65] It can be deduced, therefore, that when a naval force imposes an effective blockade against a state, the blockading force thereby exercises some public powers over the territory of the littoral state.

The case of *Al-Skeini*[66] stands for the proposition that the combination of the exercise of some public powers plus the ability to kill is sufficient to establish jurisdiction[67] (at least for those states Party to the ECHR). As have been proven throughout history, in the right circumstances, blockades can prove deadly for civilian populations. Given the ECtHR's current penchant for finding jurisdiction, particularly in situations 'where a state is prevented from exercising its authority in part of its [own] territory',[68] it is quite conceivable that in the case of an enduring and effective blockade in which the littoral state is no longer capable of providing for its population, a tribunal might find that the blockading power has displaced the littoral state's responsibility to ensure that the human rights requirements of its own population are being met. In such case, a blockading state could plausibly be held responsible for civilian deaths attributable to the blockade.

As the authors of the *Report of the Secretary-General's Panel of Inquiry on the 31 May 2010 Flotilla Incident* have noted, 'there cannot be gaps in the law. In line with the rationale expressed in the Martens Clause—now a part of customary law—it

---

[63] Paris Declaration Respecting Maritime Law—1856 (adopted 16 April 1856), Martens, Nouveau Receuil Général 1st ser, vol XV, UK, HC, c. in *Sessional Papers* vol 66 (1856). (hereafter Paris Declaration).

[64] Every state has the right to establish the breadth of its territorial sea up to a limit not exceeding twelve nautical miles, measured from baselines determined in accordance with UNCLOS art 3. See also Antonio Cassese, *International Law* (Oxford University Press, 2001) 55–65.

[65] Hague Conventions; 18 October 1907, 205 Cons TS 395, (entered into force 26 January 1910) Hague XI, art 3. An example of such control is the current Israeli blockade of Gaza, wherein the government of Israel has restricted all fishing activity to a three-mile coastal strip. This action by Israel is arguably in contravention of international law.

[66] *Al Skeini v UK* (n 13) para 643.

[67] Milanovic, 'Al-Skeini and Al-Jedda in Strasbourg' (n 51).

[68] *Ilascu v Moldova* (n 55) para 312.

must be assured that minimum standards of humanitarian/human rights protection are observed at all times'.[69] While the Secretary General's report is not binding, a number of tribunals have demonstrated that where the protection provisions of IHL are either imprecise or inadequate, they will fill the gaps by imposing and implementing IHRL standards.

Lex Specialis and Blockade Law

> [T]he so-called *lex specialis* argument …, to the effect that applicability of the law of armed conflict excludes the application of human rights norms, is untenable … The normative similarity if not identity between a number of the principles and rules of the two bodies of law should lead to an insight of complementarity, not to mutual exclusion.[70]

The term, *lex specialis derogat legi generali* (*lex specialis*) refers to a process that can be used to interpret law when there is disagreement or conflict either within a law or between two related bodies of law. As described by the International Law Commission (ILC), *lex specialis* 'is a widely accepted maxim of legal interpretation and technique for the resolution of normative conflicts. It suggests that if a matter is being regulated by a general standard as well as a more specific rule, then the latter should take precedence over the former.'[71]

The catalyst for the discussion of *lex specialis* in relation to IHL and IHRL is generally traced to the International Court of Justice and its advisory opinion on the *Legality of the Threat or Use of Nuclear Weapons*[72] in which the Court addressed the issue of whether the use of nuclear weapons would constitute an arbitrary deprivation of life, contrary to article 6 of the ICCPR. In making its decision, the Court was required to assess and balance the two related, yet divergent, bodies of humanitarian and human rights law.

In its deliberations the ICJ was required to address the fact that in accordance with article 4 of the ICCPR, there can be no derogation from the right not to be

---

[69] United Nations, *Report of the Secretary-General's Panel of Inquiry on the 31 May 2010 Flotilla Incident July 2011.* UN <http://www.un.org/News/dh/infocus/middle_east/Gaza_Flotilla_Panel_Report.pdf> 99 (hereafter Palmer Report):

> It is important to stress that it is difficult to make generalized statements on the exact nature of the relationship between human rights law and international humanitarian law. Rather, the application of specific provisions of either legal area depends heavily on the factual context of the situation and has to be assessed accordingly. In any case, there cannot be gaps in the law. In line with the rationale expressed in the Martens Clause—now a part of customary law—it must be assured that minimum standards of humanitarian/human rights protection are observed at all times.

[70] Frits Kalshoven, 'Some Comments on the International Responsibility of States' in Wolff Heintschel von Heinegg and Volker Epping (eds), *IHL Facing New Challenges* (BWV, Berliner Wissenschafts-Verlag, 2007) 210.

[71] International Law Commission, *Fragmentation of International Law: Difficulties Arising from the Diversification and Expansion of International Law: Report of the Study Group of the International Law Commission*, 58th Session, A/CN.4/L.682, (2006) 35.

[72] *Nuclear Weapons* case (n 60).

arbitrarily deprived of life. In order to determine how define what 'arbitrary deprivation of life' means in the context of armed conflict, the Court provided the following guidance:

[T]he protection of the International Covenant of Civil and Political Rights does not cease in times of war, except by operation of Article 4 of the Covenant whereby certain provisions may be derogated from in a time of national emergency. Respect for the right to life is not, however, such a provision. In principle, the right not arbitrarily to be deprived of one's life applies also in hostilities. The test of what is an arbitrary deprivation of life, however, then falls to be determined by the applicable *lex specialis*, namely, the law applicable in armed conflict . . .[73]

In its subsequent advisory opinion on the *Legal Consequences of the Construction of a Wall in the Occupied Palestinian Territory*,[74] the ICJ offered further guidance by finding that:

As regards the relationship between IHL and human rights law, there are . . . three possible situations: some rights may be exclusively matters of international humanitarian law; others may be exclusively matters of human rights law; yet others may be matters of both these branches of international law. In order to answer the question put to it, the Court will have to take into consideration both these branches of international law, namely human rights law and, as *lex specialis*, international humanitarian law.[75]

Finally, in the contended *Case Concerning Armed Activities on the Territory of the Congo*, the ICJ, in response to Uganda's acts of killing, torture, and other forms of inhumane treatment of the Congolese civilian population, ruled that both human rights instruments and IHL could co-exist, stating:

Uganda is internationally responsible for violations of international human rights law and international humanitarian law committed by the UPDF and by its members in the territory of the DRC and for failing to comply with its obligations as an occupying Power in respect of violations of international human rights law and international humanitarian law in the occupied territory.[76]

While in the Uganda case the ICJ did not specifically address the issue of *lex specialis*, it did, through its dicta, elucidate quite clearly that both bodies of law are operative in armed conflict.

Although the ICJ's declaration that IHRL continues to apply during armed conflict was considered to be ground-breaking, the Court has generally been subjected to considerable criticism because of the lack of direction that it has given with respect to how and by whom the converging bodies of law should be interpreted. As a result, there has been a development of conflicting methodologies and analyses for interpreting *lex specialis*. At one end of the spectrum is the theory that *lex specialis* should be interpreted to mean that although the two bodies of law continue to operate in

---

[73] Ibid, para 25.   [74] The *Wall Opinion* (n 39) 94.   [75] Ibid, para 106.

[76] *Case Concerning Armed Activities On The Territory Of The Congo* (*Democratic Republic of the Congo v Uganda*) [2005] ICJ Rep 168, para 220 (hereafter *Armed Activities*). Note that in reaching its decision on the Uganda case, the ICJ was able to do that which regional human rights tribunals cannot, by finding violations of both IHL and IHRL. Whereas the regional tribunals are restricted by jurisdiction clauses as set out in their constituting legislation, the ICJ has no such limitations.

the same paradigm, the principles of IHL are supreme. Under this interpretation, all issues are to be interpreted through the lens of IHL, and IHRL principles will apply only in situations that cannot be addressed through IHL. At the other end of the spectrum, a more cooperative framework is proposed; 'where *lex specialis* is used to interpret the terms of another, more general law ... it does not conflict with nor, *a fortiori*, overrule the norm. Thus ... both the *lex specialis* and the *lex generalis* could be applied side by side, [with] the *lex specialis* playing the greater role of the two.'[77]

Vattel suggests that when determining how to apply lex specialis in the face of two competing regimes, 'we ought ... to prefer the one which is less general, and which approaches nearer to the point in question'.[78] According to this approach, the 'idea that the most closest, detailed, precise or strongest expression of state consent as it relates to a particular factual circumstance, ought to prevail'.[79] The theory follows, therefore, that when dealing with the loss of life in the context of armed conflict, the specialized body of law that regulates how and under what circumstances a civilian might be deprived of his or her life should be the standard for adjudication of the issue, and it is in accordance with this standard that the issue of arbitrary deprivation of life should be determined. This concept, however, is contingent upon there being a clear and understandable standard by which a decision can be rendered under the *lex specialis*.

In the context of blockade operations there has been one attempt to interpret the relationship between IHL and IHRL, the Turkel Commission Report. In the report, the authors addressed the issue of which law should apply to any loss of life that might occur as a result of the Israeli blockade of Gaza. The Commission concluded:

Since there are comprehensive and detailed rules in international humanitarian law regulating the imposition of a naval blockade, the question arises as to what extent the criteria of international human rights law should be taken into account. For example, the rules of the international humanitarian law dealing with a naval blockade, such as the prohibition of starvation or the prohibition of depriving the civilian population of objects essential for its survival and the question of the 'damage' or 'suffering' addressed in article 102(b) of the San Remo Manual, address the right to life, a right that also lies, of course, at the heart of international human rights law.... Since the right of the inhabitants of the Gaza Strip to life is addressed in the *lex specialis* that applies here, namely the rules of international humanitarian law, it is these rules that should primarily be applied.[80]

While the Turkel Commission may have been correct in concluding that there are 'comprehensive and detailed rules in international humanitarian law regulating the

---

[77] Joost Pauwelyn, *Conflict of Norms In Public International Law: How WTO Law Relates To Other Rules Of International Law* (Cambridge University Press, 2003) 410 (hereafter Pauwelyn, *Conflict of Norms*). See also Bowring, 'Fragmentation, Lex Specialis' (n 59) and Francoise Hampson, 'The Relationship Between IHL and Human Rights Law From the Perspective of a Human Rights Treaty Body' (2008) 90:871 IRRC 549.

[78] Emmerich De Vattel, *The Law Of Nations; Or, Principles of the Law of Nature Applied to the Conduct and Affairs of Nations and Sovereigns* (1793) Book Ii, Ch. xvii, paras 311, 316, as cited in Prud'homme, *Lex Specialis* (n 58) 367.

[79] Pauwelyn, *Conflict of Norms* (n 77) 388.   [80] Turkel Report (n 60) 103.

imposition of a naval blockade',[81] it failed to acknowledge that there remains significant discourse on the issues of humanitarian relief and humanitarian action in the law of blockade. In this respect the law is not settled.

Although the Commission placed significant reliance on the provisions from the San Remo Manual to make a number of its findings, it failed to acknowledge that the San Remo Manual is not law, and more specifically, that the blockade provisions of the Manual represent 'a definite departure from traditional law'.[82] By concluding that the law of blockade is settled, and that IHL should be the operative law in maritime blockade, the Turkel Commission thwarted the opportunity to investigate the interrelation of IHL and IHRL in a substantive and meaningful manner.

Significant differences in opinions with respect to the corpus of the customary law of maritime blockade, and a virtual absence of conventional law regulating the practice of blockade has led to uncertainty with respect to obligations for humanitarian protection for civilians who are affected by maritime blockades. International human rights tribunals and international courts have made their positions abundantly clear: '[t]he judicial lodestar, whether in difficult questions of interpretation of humanitarian law, or in resolving claimed tensions between competing norms, must be those values that international law seeks to promote and protect'.[83] As Judith Gardam notes, 'human rights norms can compensate for the deficiencies of IHL'.[84]

How IHRL Might Influence the Law of Blockade

The European Court's finding that when acting extraterritorially contracting states are obliged to ensure the observance of all those human rights which they are '*in a position to ensure*'[85] confirms that when a European state exercises jurisdiction over people in another country, it will be obligated to uphold only those tenets of human rights law that it can reasonably be expected to guarantee. This departure from the historical position that human rights are indivisible has opened the door for the Court to find that extraterritorial jurisdiction applies even when the sending state has limited control over the territory and persons in question. Thus, the threshold for determining extraterritorial jurisdiction has been lowered considerably. Consequently, in reviewing decisions from the ECtHR, it can be deduced that in cases where a blockading force exercises control over the blockaded state's territorial waters, and the blockade has a negative effect on the lives of the civilian

---

[81] As discussed earlier, there is consensus that in order for a blockade to be legally established it must be effective, it must be notified, and it must not bar access to neutral ports.

[82] Louise Doswald-Beck, 'Background—Development of the San Remo Manual and its Intended Purpose—Content of the San Remo Manual' International Review of the Red Cross, No 309. ICRC <http://www.icrc.org/eng/resources/documents/misc/57jmst.htm> accessed 13 May 2017.

[83] *Nuclear Weapons Opinion* (n 60) para 41.

[84] Judith Gardam, 'The Contribution of the International Court of Justice to International Humanitarian Law' (2001) 14 LJIL (2) 350, 353.

[85] *Al Skeini v UK* (n 13) Concurring Opinion of Judge Bonello, para 32.

population, a human rights tribunal might very well hold that the threshold for jurisdiction has been met.

All major IHRL Conventions include the right to life, and most embrace the right to not be arbitrarily deprived thereof.[86] It is generally agreed that in peacetime 'arbitrary deprivation of life' occurs when government actors either kill an individual through 'use of force which was no more than absolutely necessary'.[87] In the case of *Kelly et al v United Kingdom*, the ECtHR determined that the protection against arbitrary deprivation of life, 'covers not only intentional killing but also the situations where it is permitted to "use force" which may result, as an unintended outcome, in the deprivation of life. The deliberate or intended use of lethal force is only one factor however to be taken into account in assessing its necessity. Any use of force must be no more than "absolutely necessary"'.[88]

As enunciated by the ICJ in the *Nuclear Weapons* case, the mechanism by which 'arbitrary deprivation of life' is determined is different for situations that fall under the ambit of IHL:

[T]he right not arbitrarily to be deprived of one's life applies also in hostilities. The test of what is an arbitrary deprivation of life, however, then falls to be determined by the applicable *lex specialis,* namely, the law applicable in armed conflict which is designed to regulate the conduct of hostilities. Thus whether a particular loss of life, through the use of a certain weapon in warfare, is to be considered an arbitrary deprivation of life contrary to Article 6 of the [ICCPR], can only be decided by reference to the law applicable in armed conflict and not deduced from the terms of the Covenant itself.[89]

Considering the Court's dicta, it follows that in order to determine whether the deprivation of life is arbitrary in the case of a maritime blockade, one must refer to the provisions as set out in Part Four of Additional Protocol 1.[90]

The abstruse status of Additional Protocol 1's application in blockade, plus the fact that some nations' military manuals contradict their own countries' statements regarding their interpretation of article 49.3,[91] leaves the issue of starvation during blockade wide open for interpretation. Understanding that there are no provisions for remedies under humanitarian law, and that human rights tribunals are dealing increasingly with issues that intersect both IHRL and IHL, it is conceivable that in

---

[86] See, for example, Council of Europe, European Convention for the Protection of Human Rights and Fundamental Freedoms, as amended by Protocols Nos. 11 and 14 (4 November 1950) ETS 5, art 2; UN General Assembly, Universal Declaration of Human Rights (10 December 1948) 217 A (III) art 3; International Covenant on Civil and Political Rights (16 December 1966, United Nations) 999 UNTS 171, art 6; American Convention on Human Rights, 'Pact of San Jose', Costa Rica (22 November 1969) art 4.

[87] *McCann and Others v United Kingdom* (1995) ECtHR App no 18984/91, 199–201, 213.

[88] *Kelly and Others v UK* (2001) ECtHR App no 30054/96, para 93.

[89] *Nuclear Weapons Opinion* (n 60) 240.

[90] International Committee of the Red Cross (ICRC), Protocol Additional to the Geneva Conventions of 12 August 1949, and relating to the Protection of Victims of International Armed Conflicts (Protocol I) (8 June 1977) 1125 UNTS 3, art 48 (hereafter AP1) arts 48–58. See also Jean-Marie Henckaerts and Louise Doswald-Beck, *Customary International Humanitarian* (Cambridge University Press, 2009) 29 (hereafter Henckaerts, *Customary Law Study*) Rules 11–20.

[91] See, for example, UK Ministry of Defence, *The Manual of the Law of Armed Conflict* (Oxford University Press, 2004) 21 (hereafter, UK Manual).

the future civilian victims of a blockade may seek remedies through international human rights tribunals.[92] As some commentators have stated, human rights tribunals are generally not particularly adept[93] at dealing with issues that fall within the *lex specialis* of IHL,[94] and 'that teaching IHL to human rights professionals or discussing human rights law with military personnel can seem like speaking Dutch to the Chinese or vice versa'.[95] Additionally, it has been observed that when dealing with cases in which they are required to deal with both bodies of law, human rights tribunals are inclined to demonstrate a 'clear bias in favor of [Human Rights Law]'.[96] Understanding that human rights tribunals have the specific mandate to adjudicate matters arising from the human rights conventions over which they have jurisdiction to preside, it is not surprising that their judgments will often reflect their areas of specific expertise. In this respect, a state party responding to a claim in a human rights tribunal as a result of an act that occurred during armed conflict, may find it difficult to base the defence for their action in humanitarian law, particularly if the defence is grounded in customary law that is unsettled or otherwise ripe for judicial consideration.

As has been noted, while there is significant consensus regarding the requirements for the establishment of a blockade, there is significant disagreement regarding the legal requirement to permit humanitarian access and assistance during maritime blockade. There are currently three main arguments regarding the issue:

1. There is no obligation for a blockading party to allow humanitarian goods to pass through a blockade;[97]

2. A blockade will be legal so long as its primary purpose is not to cause starvation amongst the civilian population;[98] or

3. A blockade will be unlawful if the damage to the civilian population is, or may be expected to be, excessive in relation to the concrete and direct military advantage anticipated from the blockade.[99]

---

[92] Shana Tabak, 'Ambivalent Enforcement: International Humanitarian Law at Human Rights Tribunals' (2016) 37:4 Michigan Journal of International Law 661, 672 (hereafter Tabak, 'Ambivalent Enforcement).

[93] Ibid, 684.

[94] Samuel Hartridge, 'The European Court of Human Right's Engagement with International Humanitarian Law' in Derek Jinks et al (eds), *Applying International Humanitarian Law in Judicial and Quasi-Judicial Bodies* (Asser Press, 2014) 268.

[95] N. Lubell, 'Challenges in Applying Human Rights Law to Armed Conflict' (2005) 860 IRRC 737, 744.

[96] Tabak, 'Ambivalent Enforcement' (n 92) 683.

[97] See The United Kingdom of Great Britain and Northern Ireland, reservation declaration 2 July 2002. Online: ICRC <http://www.icrc.org/ihl/NORM/0A9E03F0F2EE757CC1256402003FB6D2?OpenDocument > accessed 9 October 2017. See also France, Réserves Et Déclarations 11 Apr 2001. Online: ICRC <http://www.icrc.org/applic/ihl/ihl.nsf/Notification.xsp?action=openDocument&documentId=D8041036B40EBC44C1256A34004897B2> accessed 9 October 2017.

[98] Louise Doswald-Beck (ed), *San Remo Manual on International Law Applicable to Armed Conflicts at Sea* (Cambridge University Press, 1995) 102 (hereafter SRM).

[99] Ibid.

Because of the uncertain nature of the obligations regarding humanitarian requirements in maritime blockade, the uncertain applicability of blockade law during non-international armed conflict, and disagreement respecting other aspect of the law, it is impossible to state with any certainty that there is settled customary international law to which any tribunal can refer if faced with a case arising from harm caused by a blockade. Without such guidance, any court that deals with the issue will find it ripe for judicial consideration, and wide open to judicial interpretation and activism.

One of the fundamental differences between IHL and IHRL is the fact that IHL is a set of rules and laws that are designed 'to be applied prospectively [in] a framework to guide decision making. . . .[while] IHRL concentrates on the intrinsic value of the persons themselves . . . is framed in terms of general obligations, and tends to be directed towards post hoc application.'[100] Insofar that maritime blockade law, in its current state, does not provide a standard framework upon which commanders may rely for all aspects of the conduct of a blockade, its value as a legal instrument is severely limited. It would indeed be difficult for a country to defend its actions during blockade through reference or reliance on the provisions of this body of law.

One of the ways in which states can reduce their exposure to human rights tribunals is through the creation of an agreed set of rules for humanitarian access in maritime blockades. It is in this area that the current framework for the law of blockade is most unsettled, and correspondingly, the area under which harm to civilians is most likely to manifest.

Professor Heintschel von Heinegg is a proponent of the notion that 'if the establishment of a blockade causes the civilian population to be inadequately provided with food and other objects essential for their survival, the blockading party must provide for free passage of such essential supplies'.[101] His approach is correct in the contemporary humanitarian law paradigm. By accepting his approach, and building the requirement for humanitarian access, with appropriate limitations regarding the distribution of humanitarian goods to the military, into the law of blockade, an effective, realistic, and defensible framework can be achieved.

---

[100] Samuel Hartridge, 'The European Court of Human Rights Engagement With International Humanitarian Law' in Derek Jinks et al, *Applying International Humanitarian Law in Judicial and Quasi Judicial Bodies* (Springer, 2014) 260.

[101] Wolff Heintschel von Heinegg, 'The Law of Armed Conflict at Sea' in Deiter Fleck (ed), *The Handbook of International Humanitarian Law* (Oxford University Press, 2008) 555.

10

Conclusion

Despite its use as an instrument of naval warfare over the period of the past four and a half centuries, substantive aspects of the law remain contentious and unsettled. While it is accurate to state that some of the basic rules regarding blockade are widely recognized as being settled in customary international law, it is equally apparent that 'there is a need to strengthen the law in the light of humanitarian problems and related normative "weaknesses" and "gaps". Strengthening the law may mean reaffirmation of existing law in situations where it is not properly implemented and its clarification or development when it does not sufficiently meet the needs of the victims of armed conflict.'[1]

Confronting the Humanitarian Challenges of Blockade

It is a basic principle of humanity that the outside world does not stand idly by while the civilian population in a country is suffering, starving and being deprived of basic supplies.[2]

Blockade is an insidious method of warfare whose true nature generally remains hidden until such time as its effects create a humanitarian crisis. The globalization of economies, growth of urban population centres, and the move away from agrarian-based economies have made most modern economies particularly vulnerable to the effects of economic warfare. Insofar as very few modern coastal states can sustain their populations or agricultural sectors without access to foreign markets and suppliers, blockade is, and will remain, a method of warfare that has the potential to cause severe humanitarian consequences.

While it is true that the adoption of Additional Protocol 1[3] in 1977 brought significant advances in the protections offered to civilians affected by armed conflict, the construction of article 49.3[4] has created uncertainty as to whether or not the protective principles of the Protocol apply during maritime blockade. Whereas some

---

[1] Knut Dörmann,'Detention in Non-International Armed Conflicts' (2012) 88 Int L Stud 347, 358.
[2] Michael Bothe, 'The Law of Neutrality' in Dieter Fleck (ed), *The Handbook of International Humanitarian Law*, 3rd edn (Oxford University Press, 2008) 433.
[3] International Committee of the Red Cross (ICRC), Protocol Additional to the Geneva Conventions of 12 August 1949, and relating to the Protection of Victims of International Armed Conflicts (Protocol I) (8 June 1977) 1125 UNTS 3 (hereafter AP1).
[4] Ibid, art 49.3.

consider it untenable that any interpretation of article 49.3 can be interpreted so as to exempt blockade from the protections against starvation provided in Additional Protocol 1,[5] the stark reality is that during the negotiations for the Protocol some states specifically intended to ensure that blockade would be unchanged by its implementation.[6] This is reflected in the words that stipulate that the provisions of Section 1 to Part IV, which covers articles 48–68 of the Protocol, 'do not otherwise affect the rules of international law applicable in armed conflict at sea'.[7] Insofar as the wording of article 49.3 is deliberate, and that some of the world's largest naval powers designed it that way, this section of the Protocol is contentious. This holds particularly true in light of the fact that a number of countries do not agree on the scope of article 49.3.[8] A prime example of a differing position can be found in the German Navy's Kommandanten-Handbuch, which states that, 'If there is a shortage of foodstuffs ... or other essential items for the civilian population in the blockaded area, the blockading state is obligated to authorize the passage of relief consignments'.[9]

The absence of consistent and identifiable rules for humanitarian protection in blockade is problematic, particularly for states that may find their actions subjected to review by human rights bodies. Recent case law from the European Court of Human Rights (ECtHR) has shown that in situations in which humanitarian law on a specific topic is not clear, the Court will move with alacrity to fill the gaps. Certainly, as the cases of *Al Skeini*[10] and *Jaloud*[11] have demonstrated, the Court will find extra-territorial jurisdiction in situations that defy the common understanding of the term. Additionally in situations in which the provisions of the law of armed conflict are not precise, the Court will supplant IHL with IHRL, and/or interpret any ambiguities from the perspective of the IHRL specialists that the judges are. As Professor Hampson notes, allowing human rights tribunals to determine how IHL may or may not govern the conduct of state militaries 'is a remarkably arbitrary and haphazard way of working out ... the relationship between two bodies of [law]'.[12]

In its current state, the law of maritime blockade is vulnerable to incursions from human rights tribunals, principally because of its inherent humanitarian gaps. One

---

[5] Wolff Heintschel von Heinegg, 'The Law of Armed Conflict at Sea' in Deiter Fleck (ed), *The Handbook of International Humanitarian Law* (Oxford University Press, 2008) 555.

[6] The United Kingdom of Great Britain and Northern Ireland, reservation declaration 2 July 2002. ICRC <http://www.icrc.org/ihl/NORM/0A9E03F0F2EE757CC1256402003FB6D2?OpenDocument> accessed 13 May 2017. See also France, Réserves Et Déclarations 11 Apr 2001. Online: ICRC <http://www.icrc.org/applic/ihl/ihl.nsf/Notification.xsp?action=openDocument&documentId=D8041036B40EBC44C1256A34004897B2> accessed 13 May 2017.

[7] AP1 (n 3) art 49.3.

[8] Diplomatic Conference on the Reaffirmation and Development of International Humanitarian Law Applicable in Armed Conflicts (Geneva, 1974–1977) Committee Three Records, Official Records Volume III, 255 (hereafter CDDH/III/67).

[9] *Unbehau, Kommandanten-Handbuch—Rechtsgrundlagen für den Einsatz von Seestreitkräften* (Bundessprachenamt—Referat, 2002) 156 (hereafter German Handbook).

[10] *Al-Skeini, v United Kingdom*, no. 55721/07, [2011] ECtHR 1093 (7 July 2011) (hereafter *Al Skeini v UK*).

[11] *Jaloud v The Netherlands*, no. 47708/08 [2014] ECtHR (20 November 2014).

[12] Francoise Hampson, 'The Relationship Between IHL and Human Rights Law From the Perspective of a Human Rights Treaty Body' (2008) 90:871 IRRC 549, 559.

of the best ways to reduce states' exposure to such bodies is to ensure that the *lex specialis* of blockade law is better defined and reflective of the principles of twenty-first-century humanitarian law.

A Role for the UN Security Council

In the years since the end of the Second World War, the United Nations Security Council has made regular use of sanction and blockade-type operations in efforts to maintain or restore international peace and security.[13] Given that these tools provide the UN with coercive means of encouraging compliance without necessarily employing direct force against impugned states, it is highly likely that these types of operations will continue to be utilized for the foreseeable future.

It is widely acknowledged that the de facto naval blockade against Iraq triggered a humanitarian crisis. As a result of lessons learned from this fiasco, the UN has, in recent years, taken positive steps towards ensuring that in future operations of a similar nature, humanitarian considerations are taken into account. Accordingly, in the naval interdiction operations that the UN authorized against Yugoslavia (1992)[14] and Libya (2011),[15] the Security Council included provisions for humanitarian assistance, and established sanctions committees to oversee the operations. By ensuring that humanitarian issues were addressed in those resolutions, the Security Council demonstrated its determination to avoid repeating the humanitarian disaster that was inflicted on Iraq as a result of the UN sanctions regime.[16]

The United Nations, more so than any other organization, institution, or individual state, is in a position to take a strong and effective leadership role in outlining a modern humanitarian legal regime for maritime blockade and sanctions. By ensuring that properly administered humanitarian assistance can be permitted to flow to civilians before they begin to starve, unnecessary suffering and harm to the civilian population can be avoided. In consistently setting such an example, the UN can establish the standard for the conduct of future blockades and other similar operations.

A Role for States

The primary responsibility for developing international law rests with sovereign states.[17] While over the period of the last few decades there have been several notable

---

[13] Charter of the United Nations (adopted 24 October 1945), 1 UNTS XVI, arts 41 and 42 (hereafter UN Charter).

[14] UNSC Res 787 (16 November 1992) UN Docs S/RES/787.

[15] UNSC Res 1970 (26 February 2011) UN Docs S/RES/1970 (hereafter S/RES/1970).

[16] Ala'din Alwan, 'Health in Iraq: The Current Situation, Our Vision for the Future and Areas of Work', 2nd edn, December 2004 (Iraq Ministry of Health).

[17] Peter Malanczuk, *Akehurst's Modern Introduction to International Law*, 7th edn (Routledge, 1997) 36–8.

advances in humanitarian law, such as the Ottawa Treaty[18] and the Rome Statute,[19] there has also been a trend by some states to assiduously avoid becoming party to international treaties that will restrict their options. In some cases, states that do not engage in treaty making have shown a distinct preference to support 'soft law' initiatives aimed at either creating or supporting their interpretations of customary law on specific issues.[20] While such projects can be helpful and practical stopgap measures, they are not, and should not be seen as, long-term solutions to serious or contentious issues of international law.

The inclusion of starvation rules into the blockade provisions in the San Remo Manual in 1992 is an example of the use of a soft law approach to addressing the issue of starvation during blockade. While the intentions of the drafters were laudable, the formulation that they set out, while reproduced in a number of military manuals, has not been universally embraced; some states have adopted the San Remo Manual scheme verbatim,[21] some have adopted them with revisions,[22] whilst others have rejected the initiative as being inconsistent with their nations' interpretations of article 49.3 of Additional Protocol 1.[23]

The indeterminate nature of blockade law renders it difficult for states and their naval forces to engage in a blockade with the confidence that they are conducting their operations in accordance with international law. Additionally, the uncertainty surrounding the scope and application of humanitarian provisions leaves states vulnerable to potential claims by individuals who believe that their human rights have been violated. The best defence for such countries is to demonstrate compliance with the law. However, in order to comply with an international law there must first be a law that is internationally recognized and accepted. Such is not the case with the law of maritime blockade.

The adoption and implementation of a universally acceptable model that would outline the fundamental principles of blockade, to include provisions for humanitarian assistance, would not only create a new framework for a law of blockade, but also develop a basis from which states, and potentially individuals, could defend their actions.

---

[18] United Nations, *Convention on the Prohibition of the Use, Stockpiling, Production and Transfer of Anti-Personnel Mines and on Their Destruction* (adopted 18 September 1997) 2056 UNTS 211 (hereafter Ottawa Treaty).

[19] *Rome Statute of the International Criminal Court* (18 December 1998) 2187 UNTS 90.

[20] See, for example, Michael N. Schmitt (ed), *Tallinn Manual 2.0 on the International Law Applicable to Cyber Operations* (Cambridge University Press, 2017).

[21] Canadian Forces Joint Doctrine Manual, Law of Armed Conflict at the Operational and Tactical Level (Canadian Forces, 2001) para 850.

[22] German Handbook (n 9) para 300.

[23] The United Kingdom of Great Britain and Northern Ireland, reservation declaration 2 July 2002. ICRC <http://www.icrc.org/ihl/NORM/0A9E03F0F2EE757CC1256402003FB6D2?OpenDocument> accessed 13 May 2017. Of note, the UK Manual on the Law of Armed Conflict does not reflect the official position of the government of the United Kingdom.

The Challenge

The lack of clarity and common understanding of the law maritime blockade was evident in the nature, quality, and conclusions of the various reports that were written in the aftermath of the Israeli interception and opposed boarding of the *Mavi Marmara*. If there was a positive aspect to the *Mavi Marmara* incident, it was that the issue of maritime blockade was, at least for several news cycles, pushed briefly to the forefront of international humanitarian law.

The fact that the various commissions that investigated the *Mavi Marmara* incident arrived at such vastly different conclusions, while purportedly relying on the same facts and law, is of little surprise. Because of its infrequent application, blockade law is generally not discussed outside of a small community of scholars until such time as a crisis occurs. When such situations do arise, those who are tasked to investigate often have very little guidance or understanding of maritime blockade law.

Recent decisions from international human rights tribunals and some domestic courts[24] indicate that the current trend is for some tribunals to use human rights standards to interpret and influence the ever-changing interrelationship between international human rights law and international humanitarian law. As the relationship between IHRL and IHL continues to evolve in the courts, it is highly probable that the trend towards the 'humanization' of IHL will persist. Any court that attempts to deal with blockade will face the same challenges that were encountered by the commissions that examined the *Mavi Marmara* incident. Uncertain law lends itself to misinterpretation, confusion, and manipulation.

Maritime blockade can be an incredibly beneficial method of warfare. While it has been shown through history that a blockade can play an effective role in undermining a state's ability to sustain military operations, history has also shown that blockades can cause severe damage to affected civilian populations. The continuing viability of blockade as a military strategy will require a substantive and meaningful evolution of the law of maritime blockade. In order to meet the requirements of the contemporary IHL paradigm, it will be crucial for the law to include clear, meaningful, operationally realistic, and unambiguous measures for humanitarian assistance and protection. If this can be accomplished, blockade will continue as an effective strategy that can influence the outcome of a conflict without causing unnecessary suffering and harm to the civilian population.

---

[24] *Serdar Mohammed & Others v Secretary of State for Defence* [2015] EWCA Civ 843.

Suggested Guidance for Maritime Blockade

Part One: Definitions and Application

Article 1: Definitions

1. Blockade—an *in bello* military operation by which one or more parties to an armed conflict seek to prevent all vessels and aircraft, other than certified humanitarian relief vessels, from entering or exiting specified ports, airfields, or coastal areas belonging to, occupied by, or under the control of an opposing belligerent.
2. Blockading Force—the naval and air forces of the Blockading Power
3. Blockading Power—the state or organized armed group that is conducting blockade operations against a blockaded area.
4. Blockaded Power—the state or organized armed group that is being blockaded by the Blockading Power.
5. Certified Humanitarian Relief Vessel—a vessel that is certified by the Blockading Power or the Protecting Power as carrying only humanitarian goods and personnel.
6. Hospital Ship—a ship built or equipped by specially and solely with a view to assisting the wounded, sick and shipwrecked, to treating them and to transporting them.
7. Prize Court—a court in which decisions respecting the capture of vessels, cargo and individuals are determined.
8. Protecting Power—a neutral and impartial state or international organization, appointed by the Blockading Power and acceptable to the Blockaded Power, that is responsible for determining and overseeing the requirement and provision of humanitarian relief to the civilian population of the blockaded state.
9. Warship—for the purpose of this Guidance, means a ship belonging to the armed forces of a belligerent Party to an armed conflict, or an organized armed group in an armed conflict not of an international nature. A warship must bear the external marks distinguishing such ships of its nationality or association to the organized armed group, be under the command of an officer duly commissioned by the belligerent Party and whose name appears in the appropriate service list or its equivalent, and manned by a crew which is under regular armed forces discipline.

Article 2: Scope of Application

1. This guidance shall apply in the situations referred to in Article 2 and Article 3 common to the Geneva Guidances of 12 August 1949, and to situations as described in paragraph 1 of Article 1 of Additional Protocol II to those Guidances.
2. This guidance shall not apply to situations of internal disturbances and tensions, such as riots, isolated and sporadic acts of violence, and other acts of a similar nature, as not being armed conflicts.

3. An organized armed group (non-state Party) may lawfully engage in blockade operations against a state if the following conditions are met:
   a. There is, within the state an armed conflict of a general nature between the regular armed forces of the state and an organized armed group;
   b. The organized armed group exercises such control over a part of its territory as to enable it to carry out sustained and concerted military operations;
   c. Any vessels used by the maritime forces of the organized armed group must be warships;
   d. The organized armed group must be under responsible command and conduct its hostilities in guidanceance with the law of armed conflict; and,
   e. The organized armed group must accede to this Guidance in its entirety.
4. Nothing in this Guidance shall be invoked for the purpose of affecting the sovereignty of a state or the responsibility of the Government, by all legitimate means, to maintain or re-establish law and order in the state or to defend the national unity and territorial integrity of the state.
5. The application of the provisions of this guidance to non-state parties to a conflict shall not change their legal status, or the legal status of a disputed territory.
6. A party that desires to adhere to this guidance may notify its intention in writing to all Parties to the armed conflict and to all neutral powers that may be affected.

Part Two: Blockade—Operational Principles

Article 3: General Provisions

1. A blockade may be imposed by parties to an armed conflict against the specified ports, airfields, or coastal areas belonging to, occupied by, or under the control of an opposing belligerent.
2. Only warships and military aircraft belonging to parties to an armed conflict may engage in blockade operations.
3. A Blockading Force may employ all lawful means and methods of warfare in conducting and enforcing a blockade.
4. A Blockading Force may suspend rights of innocent passage through the territorial sea of a Blockaded Party for such time as a blockade is in effect.

Article 4: Declaration of Blockade

1. A blockade must be declared by the Blockading Power.
2. A declaration of blockade is made either by the Blockading Party or by the naval authorities acting in its name. A declaration must specify:
   a. the date when the blockade begins;
   b. the geographical limits of the coastline under blockade;
   c. the geographical limits of the blockade area; and
   d. the period within which neutral vessels may come out of neutral ports.

Article 5: Notice

1. A declaration of blockade is notified by the Blockading Power by means of all of the following forms of communication:
   a. Notice to the United Nations Security Council;
   b. Notice to the International Maritime Organization;

    c. Notice to mariners and airmen;

    d. Notification posted on official government web sites of the Blockading Power; and

    e. Daily radio broadcasts on regular marine frequencies at 0000 hrs, 0600 hrs, 1200 hrs and 1800 hrs GMT.

2. A vessel that is equipped with a radio that has access to normal shipping communication channels will be presumed to have notice of a blockade.

3. If a vessel approaching a blockaded area has no knowledge, actual or presumptive, of the blockade, the notification must be made to the vessel itself by an officer of one of the ships of the blockading force. This notification should be entered in the logbook of the breaching vessel, and must state the day and hour, and the geographical position of the vessel at the time.

Article 6: Effectiveness

1. A blockade, in order to be binding, must be effective; that is to say, it must be maintained by a force that is sufficient to prevent ingress to and egress from the blockaded area.

2. A Blockading Force shall consist of at least one naval vessel that is capable of conducting interception, boarding and search operations against vessels.

3. The question whether a blockade is effective is a question of fact.

4. A blockade is raised when the Blockading Force is unable to effectively maintain it.

5. A Blockading Force may, without affecting the status of the blockade, temporarily suspend boarding and search operations in situations of dangerous weather.

6. A maritime blockade is not rendered ineffective if it does not stop the delivery of transhipped items to the Blockaded Power.

7. The fact that goods flow into and out of a Blockaded state via land or air transport does not render a blockade ineffective.

Article 7: Impartiality

1. A blockade must be applied impartially to the vessels and aircraft of all states.

2. In circumstances of distress, acknowledged by an officer of the Blockading Force, a neutral vessel may enter a place under blockade and subsequently leave it, on the condition that it neither discharges nor takes on any cargo there.

Article 8: Area of Operations

1. Blockading Forces may board and search vessels reasonably suspected to be operating in breach of blockade anywhere in the blockade area.

2. A blockade area may not extend more than 1000 nautical miles from a blockaded coast.

3. Vessels may not be captured for breach of blockade except within the Exclusive Economic Zone of the Blockaded Power, or the Exclusive Economic Zone of a state from which a cargo will be transhipped to a blockaded area.

4. Blockading Forces must not enter neutral territorial waters or airspace.

5. Blockading Forces must not bar access to neutral ports, coasts or airfields.

Article 9: Breach of Blockade

1. A breach of blockade occurs when a vessel attempts to enter or depart a blockaded coast or port, or has entered into or departed from a blockaded coast or port. A vessel that is within

the EEZ of a Blockaded Power with the intention of entering the territorial waters of the Blockaded Power is in breach of a blockade.

2. The liability of a vessel to capture for breach of blockade is contingent on its knowledge, actual or presumptive, of the blockade.
3. A vessel may be boarded if there are reasonable grounds for suspecting that it is breaching or about to breach a blockade.
4. Vessels intending to breach a blockade, but are outside of the EEZ of the Blockaded Power, may be diverted and warned to not attempt to breach the blockade.
5. A vessel found to be in breach of blockade inside of the EEZ of the Blockaded Power may be diverted or captured.
6. A vessel that that has been warned but continues to evade Blockading Forces within the EEZ of the Blockaded Power may be stopped by force.
7. If the Master of a vessel that is within the EEZ of the blockaded state has resisted all requests and attempts by the Blockading Force to stop the vessel, the Blockading Force may use all lawful force to stop the vessel.
8. A vessel that has breached a blockade outwards, or which has attempted to breach a blockade inwards, is liable to capture so long as it is pursued by a warship of the Blockading Force. If the pursuit is abandoned, or if the blockade is raised, the breaching vessel may not be captured.
9. Vessels that have been seized, their cargo, crew and passengers will be delivered to the nearest port of the Blockading Power. If the Blockading Power is a part of a coalition Force, a captured vessel, crew and passengers may be delivered to the nearest port of a coalition member state.
10. Evidence of an attempt to breach a blockade is established through the following:
    a. The breaching vessel's bill of lading;
    b. Actual knowledge of the intent of the shipper or Master;
    c. Reasonable belief that the shipper or Master intends to breach the blockade.

Article 10: Coastal Fishing Vessels

1. Vessels used exclusively for fishing along the coast or small boats employed in local trade are exempt from capture, as well as their appliances, rigging, tackle, and cargo.
2. Blockading Forces shall not prohibit local fishing vessels from fishing within the Exclusive Economic Zone of the blockaded state.
3. Individual vessels engaged in fishing or coastal trade cease to be exempt from capture as soon as they take any part whatever in hostilities.

Article 11: Certified Humanitarian Relief Vessels

1. Vessels with cargo consisting only of relief consignments, humanitarian equipment and humanitarian assistance personnel may be certified by the Blockading Force, its agents or the Protecting Power as being Certified Humanitarian Relief Vessels.
2. Certified Humanitarian Relief Vessels engaging in their normal duties are not subject to capture.
3. A Blockading Force must allow and facilitate passage of Certified Humanitarian Relief Vessels.

Article 12: Internationally Protected Vessels

1. Vessels flying the flag of the United Nations are not subject to capture.
2. Vessels flying the flag of the International Committee of the Red Cross are not subject to capture.
3. Hospital ships, that is to say, ships built or equipped specially and solely with a view to assisting the wounded, sick and shipwrecked, to treating them and to transporting them, may in no circumstances be attacked or captured, but shall at all times be respected and protected.

Part Three: Humanitarian Assistance to the Civilian Population

Article 13: Protecting Power

1. The establishment of a blockade that has a goal or effect of starving the civilian population is unlawful.
2. Before a blockade is commenced, a Protecting Power must be appointed. The Protecting Power shall be neutral and impartial as between the belligerent parties.
3. The responsibility to identify and nominate potential Protecting Powers lies with the Blockaded Power.
4. The responsibility to appoint a Protecting Power rests with the Blockading Power.
5. The Blockading Power shall not arbitrarily reject a state or organization that has been nominated as a Protecting Power.
6. The Protecting Power shall be responsible for determining requirements for humanitarian assistance, facilitating humanitarian access, and ensuring that humanitarian aid is not diverted to the armed forces of the Blockaded Power.

Article 14: Humanitarian Assistance

1. If, as a result of the blockade, the civilian population is suffering undue hardship owing to a lack of the supplies essential for its survival, such as foodstuffs and medical supplies, relief actions for the civilian population which are of an exclusively humanitarian and impartial nature, and which are conducted without any adverse distinction, shall be permitted by the Blockading Power.
2. The Protecting Power shall assess and determine the requirement for humanitarian assistance.
3. When the Protecting Power has informed the Blockading Power that humanitarian relief is required in the blockaded area, the Blockading Power shall immediately permit the passage of humanitarian goods.
4. The Blockading Power retains the right to prescribe the technical arrangements, including inspection, under which passage of relief supplies is permitted.
5. The distribution of relief supplies may be made subject to the condition that it will be carried out under the local supervision of the Protecting Power or a humanitarian organization that offers guarantees of neutrality and impartiality.
6. Each belligerent party must, to the fullest extent practicable, assist relief personnel in carrying out their relief mission. Only in case of imperative military necessity may the activities of the relief personnel be limited or their movements temporarily restricted.

7. Humanitarian relief personnel, acting within the prescribed parameters of their mission, must be respected and protected. The protection extends to humanitarian vessels, transports, installations and goods.

Article 15: Civilians Displaced by Armed Conflict

1. A vessel carrying only civilians who are displaced by armed conflict shall not be subject to capture.
2. A Blockading Power that encounters a vessel carrying civilians who are displaced by armed conflict shall advise the Protecting Power of the location of the vessel.

Article 16: Diversion of Humanitarian Aid

1. Under no circumstances shall the Blockaded Power divert or otherwise transfer humanitarian goods to its armed forces or other government departments or agencies.
2. In the event that the Blockaded Power diverts or otherwise transfers humanitarian goods to its armed forces or other government departments or agencies, the Blockading Force may halt humanitarian access until such time as the diversion of such material stops.

Part Four: Prize Courts

Article 17: Establishment of Prize Courts

1. Blockading Powers must establish prize courts that have the capacity to adjudicate prize cases in accordance with international standards.
2. Prize courts shall have jurisdiction to determine all matters arising from this Guidance.
3. In the event that an international prize court is established, the international prize court shall have absolute jurisdiction to deal with all prize matters arising from this guidance.

Article 18: Penalties for Breach of Blockade

1. A vessel found guilty of breach of blockade, is liable to condemnation unless it is proved that at the time of the breach the owner neither knew nor could have known of the intention to break the blockade.
2. The owner of a vessel found guilty of breach of blockade shall be liable to a fine not exceeding $5 000 000.00, unless it is proved that at the time of the breach the owner neither knew nor could have known of the existence of the blockade.
3. A Master of a vessel convicted for breaching a blockade shall be liable to a fine not exceeding $100 000.00, unless it is proved that at the time of the breach the Captain neither knew nor could have known of the existence of the blockade.
4. Individual crew members and individual passengers of a vessel convicted of breach of blockade shall be liable to a fine not exceeding $10 000.00, unless it is proved that at the time of boarding the vessel they neither knew nor could have known of the intention to break the blockade.
5. If the prize court does not uphold the capture of a vessel or goods, or if the prize is released without any judgment being given, the injured parties have the right to compensation, unless the court determines that there were good reasons for the capture.

Bibliography

PROCLAMATIONS, ORDERS IN COUNCIL, AND GOVERNMENT PAPERS

Abraham Lincoln: 'Proclamation 81—Declaring a Blockade of Ports in Rebellious States' 19 April 1861 online: Gerhard Peters and John T. Woolley, *The American Presidency Project* <http://www.presidency.ucsb. edu/ws/?pid=70101>.

British Order in Council in Furtherance of Her Majesty's Declaration of March 28, 1854 Respecting the Trade of Neutrals and British Subjects—April 15, 1854.

Correspondence with the Italian Government Regarding the Exercise by His Majesty's Government in the United Kingdom of their Belligerent Rights at Sea (1940) Cmd. 6191

George R.I., Proclamation 4 August 1914 (1914) London Gazette 6163.

George R.I., Proclamation 4 September 1939, *A Proclamation Specifying the Articles to be Treated as Contraband of War* (1939) London Gazette 6051.

George R.I., Order in Council (1940) London Gazette 34195, 4800.

Victoria R.I., Proclamation 14 May 1861, *Proclamation of Neutrality* (1861) London Gazette 2046.

BOOKS

Addison, Paul and Jeremy A. Crang (eds). *Firestorm: The Bombing of Dresden, 1945* (Random House 2006).

Australian Defence Force, *Executive Series: Law of Armed Conflict* (Defence Publishing Service 2006).

Bane, Suda Lorena. *The Blockade of Germany After the Armistice: 1918–1919* (Stanford University Press 1942).

Boothby, William. *Weapons and the Law of Armed Conflict* (Oxford University Press 2009).

Bothe, Michael, Karl Josef Partsch, and Waldemar A. Solf. *New Rules for Victims of Armed Conflicts: Commentary on the Two 1977 Protocols Additional to the Geneva Conventions of 1949* (Martinus Nijhoff Publishers 1982).

Bourne, John M. *Britain and the Great War, 1914–1918* (Edward Arnold 1983).

Brewer, John. *The Sinews of Power: War, Money and the English State: 1688–1783*. (Alfred A. Knopf 1989).

Burt, Raymond A. *British Battleships: 1919–1939* (Arms and Armour Press 1993).

Canadian Forces. *The Law of Armed Conflict at the Operational and Tactical Levels* (Department of National Defence 2003).

Carroll, Francis M. *Athenia Torpedoed: The U-Boat Attack that Ignited the Battle of the Atlantic* (Naval Institute Press 2012).

Cassese, Antonio. *International Law*, 2nd edn (Oxford University Press 2005).

Catterton, E. *The Big Blockade* (Hurst & Blackett Ltd 1932).

Chadwick, Elizabeth. *Traditional Neutrality Revisited: Law, Theory and Case Studies* (Kluwer Law International 2002).

Chickering, Roger and Stig Förster (eds). *Great War, Total War: Combat and Mobilization on the Western Front, 1914–1918* (Cambridge University Press 2000).

Clark, G.N. *The Dutch Alliance and the War Against French Trade: 1688–1697* (The University Press 1923).

von Clausewitz, Carl. *On War* (trans. J.J. Graham). New and Revised edition with Introduction and Notes by F.N. Maude (Kegan Paul, Trench, Trubner & Company 1918).

Cole, Alan, Phillip Drew, Robert McLaughlin, and Dennis Mandsager. *International Institute for Humanitarian Law Rules of Engagement Handbook* (International Institute for Humanitarian Law 2009).

Cullen, Anthony. *The Concept of Non-International Armed Conflict in International Humanitarian Law* (Cambridge University Press 2010).

Currie, John H., Craig Forcese, and Valerie Oosterveld. *International Law: Doctrine, Practice and Theory* (Irwin Law 2007).

Davison, Charles Stewart. *The Freedom of the Seas* (Moffat, Yard and Company 1918).

Deane, James Parker. *The Law of Blockade: As Contained in the Report of Eight Cases Argued and Determined in the High Court of Admiralty on the Blockade of the Coast of Courland, 1854* (Butterworths 1855).

de Beer, Lydia (ed). *The Hague Conventions: A Compilation of Documents* (Wolf Legal Publishers 2011).

de Madariaga, Isabel. *Britain, Russia and the Armed Neutrality of 1780* (Yale University Press 1962).

Department of the Navy. *Instructions for the Navy of the United States Governing Maritime Warfare: June 1917* (Government Printing Office 1917).

Dinstein, Yoram. *The Conduct of Hostilities Under the Law of International Armed Conflict* (Cambridge University Press 2004).

Döenitz, Karl, *Memoirs: Ten Years and Twenty Days*, English translation by R.H. Stevens (Da Capo Press 1959).

Doswald–Beck, Louise (ed). *San Remo Manual on International Law Applicable to Armed Conflicts at Sea* (Grotius Press 1995).

Ehrman, John. *The Navy in the War of William III: 1689–1697* (Cambridge University Press 1953).

Elleman, Bruce A. and S.C.M. Paine (eds). *Naval Blockades and Seapower: Strategies and Counter-Strategies 1805–2005* (Routledge 2006).

Fleck, Dieter and Michael Bothe. *Handbook of International Humanitarian Law*, 2nd edn (Oxford University Press 2008).

Ford, Paul Leicester. *The Works of Thomas Jefferson, Federal Edition Vol. 7* (G.P. Putnam's Sons 1905).

Gantenbein, James W. *The Doctrine of Continuous Voyage Particularly as Applied to Contraband and Blockade* (Keystone Press 1929).

Gardam, Judith. *Necessity, Proportionality and the Use of Force by States* (Cambridge University Press 2004).

Goldsmith, Jack L. and Eric A. Posner. *The Limits of International Law* (Oxford University Press 2005).

Goodspeed, D.J. *The Road Past Vimy: The Canadian Corps 1914–1918* (MacMillan of Canada 1969).

Government of Australia. *The Law of Armed Conflict* (Defence Publishing Service 2006).

Grotius, Hugo. *The Law of War and Peace, Book III*, translated by Jean Barbeyrac (The Liberty Fund Inc 2005).

Gutman, Roy and David Rieff (eds). *Crimes of War* (W.W. Norton and Co. 1999).

Guzmán, Andrew T. *How International Law Works: A Rational Choice Theory* (Oxford University Press 2008).

Hale, William Bayard. *American Rights & British Pretensions on the Seas: The Facts and the Documents, Official and Other, Bearing upon the Present Attitude of Great Britain toward the Commerce of the United States* (Robert M. McBride & Company 1915).

Hart, Liddell. *History of the First World War* (Pan Books Ltd 1982).

Heintschel von Heinegg, Wolff and Hans-Joachim Unbehau. *Kommandanten-Handbuch— Rechtsgrundlagen für den Einsatz von Seestreitkräften* (Bundessprachenamt—Referat 2002) (Translation).

Henckaerts, J.-M. and L. Doswald-Beck (eds). *Customary International Humanitarian Law* (International Committee of the Red Cross 2005).

Herstlet, Edward. *The Map of Europe by Treaty: Political and Territorial Changes Since the General Peace of 1814* (Butterworths 1875).

Higgins, A. Pearce. *The Hague Peace Conferences and Other International Conferences concerning the Laws and Usages of War. Texts of Conventions with Commentaries* (Cambridge University Press 1909).

Horne, Charles F. and W.F. Austin (eds). *The Great Events of the Great War*, vol 2 (The National Alumni 1920).

Hufbauer, Gary Clyde et al. *Economic Sanctions Reconsidered*, 3rd edn (Peter G. Peterson Institute for International Economics 2007) 5.

Hyde, Charles Cheney. *International Law, Chiefly as Interpreted and Applied by the United States*, vol 3, 2nd edn (Little, Brown and Company 1922).

Hyde, Charles Cheney. *International Law Chiefly as Interpreted and Applied by the United States*, vol 1, 2nd rev edn (Little, Brown and Company 1947).

Jacques, Richard (ed). *Maritime Operational Zones* (United States Naval War College 2006).

Jessup, Phillip and Francis Deak. *Neutrality: Its History, Economics and Law, Vol I, The Origins* (Columbia University Press 1935).

Kalshoven, F. (Frits) and Liesbeth Zegveld. *Constraints on the Waging of War: An Introduction to International Humanitarian Law*, 4th edn (Cambridge University Press 2011).

Keegan, John. *The Second World War* (Viking 1990).

Kennan, George Frost. *The Decline of Bismarck's European Order: Franco–Russian Relations, 1875–1890* (Princeton University Press 1979).

Kissinger, Henry. *White House Years* (Little, Brown and Company 1979).

Kleen, Richard. *De la Contrebande De Guerre et des Transports Interdits Aux Neutres D'Apres les Principes du Droit International Contemporains* (J. Lebegue and Co. 1893).

Kraska, James and Raul Pedrozo. *International Maritime Security Law* (Martinus Nijhoff 2013).

Kulsrud, Carl. *Maritime Neutrality to 1780* (Little, Brown and Company 1936).

Lauterpacht, H. *Recognition in International Law* (Cambridge University Press 1948).

Lauterpacht, H. *Oppenheim's International Law*, 7th edn (Longmans Green and Co 1952).

Lauterpacht, Hersch. *International Law: Vol 5, Disputes, War and Neutrality*, Parts IX–XIV (Cambridge University Press 2004).

Library of Congress, *Letters and Other Writings of James Madison Fourth President of The United States*, vol 2, 1794–1815 (J.B. Lippincott and Co. 1815).

Lloyd George, David. *Memoirs of Lloyd George: 1918* (Little, Brown and Company 1937).

Mahan, Alfred T. *The Influence of Sea Power Upon the French Revolution and Empire*, vol II (Sampson, Low, Marston & Company 1892).

Malanczuk, Peter. *Akehurst's Modern Introduction to International Law*, 7th edn (Routledge 1997).

Milanovic, Marko. *Extraterritorial Application of Human Rights Treaties: Law, Principles and Policy* (Oxford University Press 2011).

Moore, John Bassett. *A Digest of International Law*, vol 7 (Government Printing Office 1906).

Moorehead, Caroline. *Dunant's Dream: War, Switzerland and the History of the Red Cross* (Carroll & Graf 1999).

Ortolan, Théodore. *Règles internationales et diplomatie de la mer*, vol 2 (Cosse et Delemotte 1845).

Pares, Richard. *Colonial Blockade and Neutral Rights 1739–1763* (Clarendon Press 1938).

Parmelee, Maurice. *Blockade and Sea Power: The Blockade of 1914–1919 and its Significance for a World State* (Hutchison and Co 1924).

Patrick, Christine Sternberg and John C. Pinheiro (eds). *The Papers of George Washington, Presidential Series*, vol 12, 16 January 1793–31 May 1793 (University of Virginia Press 2005).

Pauwelyn, Joost. *Conflict of Norms in Public International Law: How WTO Law Relates to Other Rules of International Law* (Cambridge University Press 2003).

Perreau-Saussine, Amanda and James Bernard Murphy (eds). *The Nature of Customary Law* (Cambridge University Press 2007).

Piggott, Francis. *The Declaration of Paris, 1856* (University of London Press 1919).

Politakis, George P. *Modern Aspects of the Laws of Naval Warfare and Maritime Neutrality* (Kegan Paul International 1998).

Proctor, Tammy. *Civilians in a World at War, 1914–1918* (New York University Press 2010).

Provost, René. *International Human Rights and Humanitarian Law* (Cambridge University Press 2002).

Ravasi, G. and G.L. Beruto. *IHL and Other Legal Regimes: Interplay in Situations of Violence* (Nagard 2005).

Roberts, Adam and Richard Guelff. *Documents on the Laws of War*, 2nd edn (Oxford University Press 1989).

Ronzitti, Natalino (ed). *The Law of Naval Warfare: A Collection of Agreements and Documents with Commentaries* (Martinus Nijhoff 1988).

Sandoz, Yves, Christophe Swinarski, and Bruno Zimmermann (eds). *Commentary on the Additional Protocols of 8 June 1977 to the Geneva Conventions of 12 August 1949* (International Committee of the Red Cross & Martinus Nijhoff Publishers 1987).

Schabas, William. *The Universal Declaration Of Human Rights: The Travaux Préparatoires*, vol 1, October 1946 to November 1947 (Cambridge University Press 2013).

Schmitt, Michael N. *Blockade Law: Research, Design and Sources* (William S. Hein and Co 1991).

Schmitt, Michael N. *Essays on Law and War at the Fault Lines* (Asser Press 2012).

Schmitt, Michael (ed). *Tallinn Manual 2.0 on the International Law Applicable to Cyber Operations* (Cambridge University Press 2017).

Schmitt, Michael and Jelena Pejic (eds) *International Law and Armed Conflict: Exploring the Faultlines* (Martinus Nijhoff 2007).

Scott, James Brown. *The Armed Neutralities of 1780 and 1800: A Collection of Official Documents Preceded by the Views of Representative Publicists* (Oxford University Press 1918).

Scott, James Brown. *The Declaration of London February 26, 1909: A Collection of Official Papers and Documents Relating to the International Naval Conference Held in London December 1908–February 1909* (Oxford University Press 1919).

Shennan, J.H. *International Relations in Europe: 1689–1789* (Routledge 1995).

Smart, Nick. *British Strategy and Politics During the Phony War: Before the Balloon Went Up* (Praeger 2003).

Smith, Andrew F. *Starving the South: How the North Won the Civil War* (St. Martin's Press 2011).

Solis, Gary. *The Law of Armed Conflict: International Humanitarian Law in War* (Cambridge University Press 2010).

Speer, Albert. *Inside the Third Reich* (The Macmillan Company 1970).

Strachan, Hew. *The First World War* (Oxford University Press 2001).

Tooze, Adam. *The Wages of Destruction: The Making and Breaking of the Nazi Economy* (Allen Lane 2006).

Tucker, Robert W. *The Law of War and Neutrality at Sea* (United States Government Printing Office 1957).

Turlington, Edgar. *Neutrality: Its History, Economics and Law in Four Volumes: III the World War Period* (Columbia University Press 1936)

United Kingdom Ministry of Defence. *The Manual of the Law of Armed Conflict* (Oxford University Press 2004).

United States Naval War College. *Annotated Supplement to the Commanders Handbook on the Law of Naval Operations* (Naval Publication Library 2007).

United States Department of the Army. *FM 27-10: The Law of Land Warfare* (Department of the Army 1976).

Vattel, Emerich. *The Law of Nations, or, Principles of the Law of Nature, Applied to the Conduct and Affairs of Nations and Sovereigns*, 1797 edn, translated by Joseph Chitty (T. & J. W. Johnson 1853).

Vincent, C. Paul. *The Politics of Hunger: The Allied Blockade of Germany, 1915–1919* (Ohio University Press 1985).

Volkov, Shulamit. *Walther Rathenau: Weimar's Fallen statesman* (Yale University Press 2012).

Walzer, Michael. *Just and Unjust Wars: A Moral Argument with Historical Illustrations*, 2nd edn (Basic Books 1992).

Watkin, Kenneth. *Fighting at the Legal Boundaries: Controlling the Use of Force in Contemporary Conflict* (Oxford University Press 2016).

Weeks, William Earl. *The New Cambridge History of American Foreign Relations: Dimensions of the Early American Empire 1754–1865* (Cambridge University Press 2013).

Welch, David. *Germany, Propaganda and Total War, 1914–1918* (Rutgers University Press 2000).

Westlake, John. *International Law: Part Two—War* (Cambridge University Press 1907).

ARTICLES

'American Civil War: The Blockade and the War at Sea' online: Military History Encyclopedia on the Web <http://www.historyofwar.org/articles/wars_americancivil_war09_waratsea.html#intro>.

Atherley-Jones, L.A. 'Contraband of War' (1915) 20:12 The Virginia Law Register 881.

Australian Broadcasting Corporation. 'Rudd Condemns Aid Flotilla Violence' online: ABC <http://www.abc.net.au/news/2010-06-01/rudd-condemns-aid-flotilla-violence/849712> (video).

Bancroft Davis, J.C. 'Geneva Arbitration' in Lalor, John J. (ed). *Cyclopædia of Political Science, Political Economy, and the Political History of the United States* (Maynard, Merrill & Co. 1899) online: Library of Economics and Liberty <http://www.econlib.org/library/YPDBooks/Lalor/llCy497.html>.

Barnidge, Robert P. Jr. 'The Principle of Proportionality Under IHL and Operation Cast Lead' in William C. Banks (ed). *New Battlefields/Old Laws* (Columbia University Press, 2011).

Bellinger, John B. and William J. Haynes, 'A US Government Response to the International Committee of the Red Cross Study Customary International Humanitarian Law' (2007) 89:866 Int'l Rev Red Cross 443, 445.

Bingham, Tom. 'The Alabama Claims Arbitration' (2005) 54:1 International and Comparative Law Quarterly 1.

Bowring, Bill. 'Fragmentation, Lex Specialis and the Tensions in the Jurisprudence of the European Court of Human Rights' (2010) 15:3 Journal of Conflict & Security Law 485.

Bridgeman, Tess. 'The Law of Neutrality and the Conflict with Al Qaeda' (2010) 85 NYULR 1186.

Briggs, Herbert W. 'Neglected Aspects of the Destroyer Deal' (1940) 34:4 AJIL 569.

Byron, Christine. 'A Blurring of the Boundaries: The Application of International Humanitarian Law by Human Rights Bodies' (2007) 47:4 Va J Int'l L 839.

Blum, Gabriella. 'Laws of War and the "Lesser Evil"' (2010) 35:1 Yale J Int'l L 1.

Cable News Network online: CNN <http://edition.cnn.com/video/#/video/politics/2010/06/01/bts.clinton.israel.gaza.flotilla.cnn?hpt=T1 (video).

Castren, Erik. 'Recognition of Insurgency' (1965) 4 Indian J Int'l L 443.

Cerone, John. 'Jurisdiction and Power: The Intersection of Human Rights Law & the Law of Non-International Armed Conflict in an Extraterritorial Context' (2007) 40 Isr L Rev 72.

Cerone, John. 'Human Dignity in the Line of Fire: The Application of International Human Rights Law During Armed Conflict, Occupation, and Peace Operations' (2006) 39 Vanderbilt Journal of Transnational Law 1.

Chan, Steve and A. Cooper Drury. 'Sanctions as Economic Statecraft: An Overview' in Steve Chan and A. Cooper Drury (eds). *Sanctions as Economic Statecraft: Theory and Practice* (Palgrave 2000).

Charbonneau, Louise. 'Collective Punishment for Gaza is Wrong: UN' (18 January 2008) online: Reuters <http://www.reuters.com/article/2008/01/18/idUSN18343083>.

Crouzet, Francois. 'Wars, Blockade and Economic Change in Europe, 1792–1815' (1964) 24:4 The Journal of Economic History 567.

De Montmorency, J.E.G. 'The Principles Underlying Contraband and Blockade' (1916) 2 Problems of the War, 21–30.

Dennis, Michael J. 'Application of Human Rights Treaties Extraterritorially in Times of Armed Conflict and Military Occupation' (2005) 99 AJIL 119.

Dinstein, Yoram. 'The Right to Humanitarian Assistance' (2000) 53:4 USNWC Rev 77.

Doswald-Beck, Louise. 'Background—Development of the San Remo Manual and its Intended Purpose—Content of the San Remo Manual,' International Review of the Red Cross, No 309 online: ICRC <http://www.icrc.org/eng/resources/documents/misc/57jmst.htm>.

Doswald-Beck, Louise. 'Some Thoughts on Computer Network Attack and the International Law of Armed Conflict' in Michael N. Schmitt and Brian T. O'Donnel (eds), *Computer Network Attack and International Law: War Studies*, vol 76 (US Naval War College, 2002) 163–85.

Doswald-Beck, Louise and S. Vité, 'IHL and Human Rights Law' (1993) 293 IRRC 94.

Dormann, Knut. 'Applicability of the Additional Protocols to Computer Network Attacks' International Expert Conference on Computer Network Attacks and the Applicability of International Humanitarian Law, Stockholm, 17–19 November, 2004. on line:<http://www.icrc.org/eng/resources/documents/misc/68lg92.htm>.

Droege, Cordula. 'Elective Affinities? Human Rights and Humanitarian Law' (2008) 90 IRRC 501.

Farrant, James. 'Modern Maritime Neutrality Law' (2014) 90 Int'l L Stud 198.

Fassbender, Bardo. 'The United Nations Charter as Constitution of the International Community' (1998) 36:3 Columbia Journal of Transnational Law 529.

Fenrick, William J. 'The Rule of Proportionality and Protocol I in Conventional Warfare' (1982) 98 Mil L Rev 91.

Fenrick, William J. 'The Exclusion Zone in the Law of Naval Warfare' (1986) 24 Canadian YBIL 91.

Fink, Martin. 'Contemporary Views on the Lawfulness of Blockade' (2011) 1 Aegean Rev Law Sea 191.

Fraunces, Michael G. 'The International Law of Blockade: New Guiding Principles in Contemporary State Practice' (1992) 101:4 Yale LJ 893.

Gardam, Judith. 'The Contribution of the International Court of Justice to International Humanitarian Law' (2001) 14:2 LJIL 350.

Garraway, Charles. 'The Use And Abuse Of Military Manuals' (2004) 7 Yearbook of International Humanitarian Law, 425.

Goldstone, Richard. 'Human Rights in Palestine and Other Occupied Arab Territories: Report of the United Nations Fact-Finding Mission on the Gaza Conflict' A/HRC/12/48, 25 September 2009.

Gordon, Joy. 'Smart Sanctions Revisited' (Fall 2011) 25:3 Ethics & International Affairs, 315.

Guilfoyle, Douglas. 'The Mavi Marmara Incident' (2011) 81:1 BYIL 171.

Hall, Hubert, 'The League of Armed Neutrality' (1915) 108 Contemporary Review 166.

Hampson, Francoise. 'Means and Methods of Warfare in the Conflict in the Gulf' in P. Rowe (ed), *The Gulf War 1990–91 in International and English Law* (Routledge 1993) 89, 92.

Hampson, Francoise. 'The Relationship Between IHL and Human Rights Law from the Perspective of a Human Rights Treaty Body' (2008) 90:871 IRRC 549.

Heintschel von Heinegg, Wolff. 'The Current State of the Law of Naval Warfare: A Fresh Look at the San Remo Manual' (2006) 82 Int'l L Stud

Heintschel von Heinegg, Wolff. 'Blockade' in R Wolfrum (ed), *The Max Planck Encyclopedia of Public International Law* (Oxford University Press 2012) online edition, [http://opil.ouplaw.com/view/10.1093/law:epil/9780199231690/law-9780199231690-e252?rskey=fmmbBq&result=1&prd=EPIL].

Heintschel von Heinegg, Wolff. 'Naval Blockade' (2000) 75 International Law Studies 207.

Heintschel von Heinegg, Wolff. 'The Law of Armed Conflict at Sea' in Deiter Fleck (ed), *The Handbook of International Humanitarian Law* (Oxford University Press, 2008) 463.

Heller, Jeffrey. 'Israel Said Would Keep Gaza Near Collapse: Wikileaks' (5 January 2011) online: Reuters <http://www.reuters.com/article/2011/01/05/us-palestinians-israel-wikileaks-idUSTRE7041GH20110105>.

Himmelfarb, Gertrude. 'The Idea of Compassion: The British vs. The French Enlightenment' (2001) 145 Public Interest 3.

Holman, Brett. ' "Bomb Back, and Bomb Hard": Debating Reprisals During the Blitz' (2012) 58 Australian Journal of Politics & History 394.

Howard, N.P. 'The Social and Political Consequences of the Allied Food Blockade of Germany 1918–1919' (1993) 11 German History 161.

ICRC. 'Founding and Early Years of the ICRC (1863–1914)' online: ICRC <http://www.icrc.org/eng/who-we-are/history/founding/overview-section-founding.htm>.

ICRC. 'The Martens Clause and the Laws of Armed Conflict' online: ICRC <http://www.icrc.org/eng/resources/documents/misc/57jnhy.htm>.

Jones, Thomas David. 'The International Law of Blockade—A Measure of Naval Economic Interdiction' (1983) 26 Howard LJ 759.

Kaeckenbeeck, Georges. 'Divergences Between British and Other Views on International Law' (1918) 4 Transactions of the Grotius Society, Problems of the War: Papers Read Before the Society in the Year 1918, 213.

Kalshoven, Frits. 'Some Comments on the International Responsibility of States' in Wolff Heintschel von Heinegg and Volker Epping (eds), *IHL Facing New Challenges* (BWV, Berliner Wissenschafts-Verlag, 2007) 207.

Kennedy, William R. 'Some Points in the Law of Blockade' (1908) 9:2 Journal of the Society of Comparative Legislation 239.

Kraska, James. 'Rule Selection in the Case of Israel's Naval Blockade of Gaza: Law of Naval Warfare or Law of the Sea?' (2010) 13 Yearbook of International Humanitarian Law 367, 388.

Lindroos, Anja. 'Addressing Norm Conflicts in a Fragmented Legal System: The Doctrine of Lex Specialis' (2005) 74 Nordic J Int'l L 27.

Lowe, Vaughan and Antonios Tzanakopolous. 'Economic Warfare' in R Wolfrum (ed), *The Max Planck Encyclopedia of Public International Law* online: Oxford University Press <http://www.mpepil.com/subscriber_ article?script= yes&id=/epil/entries/law-9780199231690-e292&recno=5&search Type=Quick&query=Blockade>.

Lubell, N. 'Challenges in Applying Human Rights Law to Armed Conflict' (2005) 860 Intl Rev Red Cross 737.

Malkin, H.W. 'The Inner History of the Declaration of Paris' (1927) 8 BYIL 1.

Marsden, R.G. 'Naval or Victualling Stores: The Right of Pre-Emption' (1902) 4:1 Journal of the Society of Comparative Legislation 45.

McCormack, Timothy L.H. and Paramdeep B. Mtharu. 'Expected Civilian Damage and the Proportionality Equation—To What Extent Should the Mid to Longer Term Consequences of Explosive Remnants of War be Taken into Consideration in the Proportionality Assessment? online: <https://disarmament-library.un.org/UNODA/Library.nsf/95c7e7dc864dfc0a85256bc8005085b7/2e8cc7f7dbf63f648525794300554815/$FILE/CCW-CONFIII-WP9.pdf.>

McLaughlin, Rob. 'United Nations Mandated Naval Interdiction Operations in the Territorial Sea?' (2002) 51(2) ICLQ 249.

McLaughlin, Rob. 'Legal-Policy Considerations and Conflict Characterisation at the Threshold Between Law Enforcement and Non-International Armed Conflict' (2012) 13 Melb J Int'l L 94.

McLaughlin, Rob. 'The Law Applicable to Naval Mine Warfare in a Non-International Armed Conflict' (2014) 90 Int'l L Stud 475.

McNulty, James F. 'Blockade: Evolution and Expectation' (1980) 62 Int'l L Stud 172.

Meron, Theodor. 'The Humanization of Humanitarian Law' (2000) 94 AJIL 239.

Milanovic, Marko. 'Al-Skeini and Al-Jedda in Strasbourg' online: EJIL <http://ssrn.com/abstract=1917395>.

Milanovic, Marko. 'Norm Conflicts, International Humanitarian Law and Human Rights Law' (2010) online: SSRN <http://ssrn.com/abstract=1531596>.

Miller, Sarah. 'Revisiting Extraterritorial Jurisdiction: A Territorial Justification for Extraterritorial Jurisdiction under the European Convention' (2010) 20:4 EJIL 1223.

Moir, Lindsay 'Decommissioned? International Humanitarian Law and the Inter-American Human Rights System' (2003) 25:1 Human Rights Quarterly 182.

Montmorency, J.E.G. 'The Principles Underlying Contraband and Blockade' (1916) 2 Problems of the War: Papers Read Before the Society in the Year 1916, 21.

P.F.N. 'International Law, Contraband and the Confiscation of Vessels Carrying Contraband' (1917) 65:4 University of Pennsylvania Law Review and American Law Register 374.

Parks, W. Hays. 'Linebacker and the Law of War' (1983) 34 Air University Review 2.

Parks, W. Hays. 'Air War and the Law of War' (1990) 32:1 Air Force L Rev 1.

Phillips, George I. 'The Declaration of Paris: 1856' (1918) 34 LQ Rev 63.

Phillips, George I. 'Economic Blockade' (1920) 36 LQ Rev 227.

Powers, Robert D. 'Blockade: For Winning Without Killing' (1958) 84:8 US Naval Inst Proc 63.

Provost, Rene. 'Starvation as a Weapon: Legal Implications of the United Nations Food Blockade Against Iraq and Kuwait' (1992) 30 Colum J Transnat'l L, 577.

Prud'homme, Nancie. 'Lex Specialis: Oversimplifying a More Complex and Multifaceted Relationship?' (2007) 40:2 Isr L Rev 355.

Ranking, D.F.D.L. 'Contraband of War and the Right of Search' (1900) 7:39 The New Century Review 175.

'Report of The Committee On Neutrality And Naval Warfare' (1996) 67 Int'l L Ass'n Rep Conf 367.

'Report on Expert Meeting "Targeting Military Objectives"' (12 May 2005) Geneva, University Centre for IHL.

Richmond, A.A. 'Napoleon and the Armed Neutrality of 1800. A Diplomatic Challenge to British Sea Power' (1959) 104 Journal of the Royal United Service Institution 186.

Roach, J. Ashley. 'The Law of Naval Warfare at the Turn of Two Centuries' (2000) 94:1 AJIL 64.

Roberts, Anthea Elizabeth. 'Traditional and Modern Approaches to Customary International Law: A Reconciliation' (2001) 95:4 AJIL 757.

Ronzitti, Natalino. 'Naval Warfare' in R Wolfrum (ed), *The Max Planck Encyclopedia of Public International Law* online: Oxford University Press <http://www.mpepil.com/subscriber_article?script=yes&id=/epil/entries/law-9780199231690-e334&recno=3&searchType=Quick&query=Blockade>.

Roscini, Marco. 'Targeting and Contemporary Aerial Bombardment' (2005) 54:2 Contemporary Law Quarterly 411.

Rose, Gregory. 'Updating IHL and the Laws of Armed Conflict for the Wars of the Twenty-first Century' (2007) 14:3 Defender: The National Journal of the Australian Defence Association 21.

Saint-Brice, M. 'French Statement on the Blockade of Neutral Commerce to Germany' in Charles F. Horne and Walter F. Austin (eds), *The Great Events of the Great War*, vol 2 (The National Alumni 1920) 36.

Sassoli, Marco, 'Military Objectives' in R Wolfrum (ed), *The Max Planck Encyclopedia of Public International Law* online: Oxford University Press <http://www.mpepil.com/subscriber_article?script=yes&id=/epil/entries/law-9780199231690-e334&recno=3&searchType=Quick& query=Blockade>.

Schmitt, Michael N. 'Aerial Blockades in Historical, Legal and Practical Perspective' (1991) 2 USAF Acad J Legal Stud 21.

Schmitt, Michael N. 'Faultlines in the Law of Attack' in Susan Breau and Agnieszka Jachec-Neale (eds), *Testing the Boundaries of International Humanitarian Law* (British Institute of International and Comparative Law 2006) 277.

Schmitt, Michael N. 'Military Necessity and Humanity in International Humanitarian Law: Preserving the Delicate Balance' (2010) 50:4 Va J Int'l L 795.

Schmitt, Michael N. 'Wired Warfare: Computer Network Attack and Jus in Bello' (2002) 84 IRRC 846, 365.

Spelman, Elizabeth. 'The Legality of the Israeli Blockade of the Gaza Strip' (2013) 19:1 Web JCLI.

Stockton, Charles H. 'The Declaration of Paris' (1920) 14 AJIL 3, 356.

Strachan, Hew. 'Strategic Bombing and the Question of Civilian Casualties up to 1945' in Paul Addison and Jeremy A. Crang (eds), *Firestorm: The Bombing of Dresden, 1945* (Random House 2006) 1–18.

'Supplement: Diplomatic Correspondence Between the United States and Belligerent Governments Relating to Neutral Rights and Commerce' (1915) 9:3 AJIL 1.

Surdam, David G. 'The Union Navy's Blockade Reconsidered' (1998) 51:4 Naval War College Review 85.

'The Declaration of Paris' *The Saturday Review*, 22 July 1876, 96.

Thirlway, Hugh. 'Reflections on *Lex Ferenda*' (2001) 32 Netherlands Yearbook of International Law 3.

Thomas, Ward 'Victory by Duress: Civilian Infrastructure as a Target in Air Campaigns' (2006) 15:1 Security Studies 1.

Ticehurst, Rupert. 'The Martens Clause and the Laws of Armed Conflict' (1997) 37 IRRC 317, 125.

United States Department of State. *Treaty of Alliance* and *Treaty of Amity and Commerce* dated 6 February 1778. See, *Milestones 1776–1783: Diplomacy and the American Revolution* online: Office of the Historian <http://history.state.gov/milestones/1776-1783>.

United States Department of Defense. *United States Joint Publication 3-13: Information Operations* (2006) online: Joint Electronic Library <http://www.dtic.mil/doctrine/new_pubs/jp3_13.pdf>.

Urquhart, Conal. 'Gaza on Brink of Implosion as Aid Cut-Off Starts to Bite' online: Guardian <http://www.guardian.co.uk/world/2006/apr/16/israel>.

Walker, Jeffrey. 'Strategic Targeting and International Law: The Ambiguity of Law Meets the Reality of a Single-Superpower World' (2006) 80 Int'l L Stud 121.

Walker, Paul A. 'Rethinking Computer Network Attack: Implications for Law and US Doctrine' (2010) online: SSRN <http://ssrn.com/abstract=1586504>.

Walker, Wyndam L. 'Recognition of Belligerency and Grant of Belligerent Rights' in *Transactions of the Grotius Society, Vol. 23, Problems of Peace and War, Papers Read before the Society in the Year 1937* (Cambridge University Press, 1937) 177.

Watkin, Ken. 'Assessing Proportionality: Moral Complexity and Legal Rules' (2005) 8 Yearbook of International Humanitarian Law 3.

Winter, J.M. 'Britain's "Lost Generation" of the First World War' (1977) 31:3 Population Studies 449.

Woolsey, Lester. 'Government Traffic in Contraband' (1940) 34:3 AJIL 498.

RESEARCH PAPERS, COMMISSION REPORTS, AND OTHER GOVERNMENTAL DOCUMENTS

Action on Armed Violence 'Air Power in Afghanistan: How NATO Changed the Rules 2008–2014' online: Action on Armed Violence <https://aoav.org.uk/wp-content/uploads/2015/03/AOAV-Air-Power-in-Afghanistan.pdf>.

Ala'din, Alwan. 'Health in Iraq: The Current Situation, Our Vision for the Future and Areas of Work', 2nd edn, December 2004 (Iraq Ministry of Health).

Boone, Peter, Haris Gazdar, and Athar Hussain. 'Sanctions Against Iraq: The Cost of Failure' (1997) Center for Economic and Social Rights online: CESR<http://www.cesr.org/downloads/Sanctions%20Against%20Iraq%20Costs%20of%20Failure%201997.pdf>.

Bossuyt, Marc. 'The Adverse Consequences of Economic Sanctions on the Enjoyment Of Human Rights', *United Nations Economic and Social Council* (2000), E/CN.4/Sub.2/2000/33

House of Lords Select Committee on Economic Affairs, 2nd Report of Session 2006–07, *The Impact of Economic Sanctions*, vol 1 (The Stationery Office Ltd 2007).

Hudson-Phillips, Karl T. *Report of the International Fact-Finding Mission to Investigate Violations of International Law, Including International Humanitarian and Human Rights Law, Resulting from the Israeli Attacks on the Flotilla of Ships Carrying Humanitarian Assistance*, UNHRC, 15th Sess, UN Doc A/HRC/15/21 (2010).

International Law Commission, *Fragmentation of International Law: Difficulties Arising from the Diversification and Expansion of International Law: Report of the Study Group of the International Law Commission*, 58th Session, A/CN.4/L.682, (2006).

Israel Ministry of Foreign Affairs. 'Security Cabinet Declares Gaza Hostile Territory' (19 September 2007) online: Israel Ministry of Foreign Affairs <http://www.mfa.gov.il/MFA/Government/Communiques/2007/Security+Cabinet+declares+Gaza+hostile+territory+19-Sep-2007.htm>.

International Security Assistance Force Afghanistan Directive (6 July 2009) online: NATO ISAF HQ <http://www.nato.int/isaf/docu/official_texts/Tactical_Directive_ 090706. pdf>.

ISAF statement on Air Dropped Munitions online: NATO ISAF HQ <http://www.isaf.nato.int/article/isaf-releases/isaf-statement-on- air-dropped-munitions.html>.

Israel. The Public Commission to Examine the Maritime Incident of 31 May 2010, *The Türkel Report* (23 January 2011).

National Archives of the United Kingdom, *Spotlights on History: The Blockade of Germany*, The National Archives <http://www.nationalarchives.gov.uk/pathways/firstworldwar/spotlights/blockade.htm>.

National Archives of the United Kingdom, 'Memorandum to Cabinet In Regard to the Present Position of The Blockade, January 1st, 1917' online: The National Archives <http://www.nationalarchives.gov.uk/pathways/firstworldwar/transcripts/spotlights/cabinet_memo_blockade.htm>.

'President Ends Economic Sanctions Against South Africa' (1991) 2:1 Foreign Policy Bulletin 52–3 online: <https://www.cambridge.org/core/journals/foreign-policy-bulletin/article/president-ends-economic-sanctions-against-south-africa/296A92143448A611F5E5656705E9DCEF>.

Public Broadcasting System. 'Casualty and Death Tables: World War One' online: PBS <http://www.pbs.org/greatwar/resources/casdeath_pop.html>.

Turkey. 'Turkish National Commission of Inquiry: Interim Report On The Israeli Attack on The Humanitarian Aid Convoy To Gaza on 31 May 2010' online: Turkish Ministry of Foreign Affairs <http://www.mfa.gov.tr/data/Turkish%20Interim%20Report.pdf>.

'United Kingdom House of Commons Research Paper 98/28' (1998) HC Debates c990.

United Kingdom Parliamentary Papers (House of Commons and Command), (1856) 1856 Paris Declaration Respecting Maritime Law, vol 66.

United Nations. *Report of the Secretary-General's Panel of Inquiry on the 31 May 2010 Flotilla Incident July 2011* online: UN <http://www.un.org/News/dh/infocus/middle_east/Gaza_Flotilla_ Panel_ Report.pdf>. [Palmer Report].

United Nations Children Emergency Fund (UNICEF). 'Iraq Surveys Show "Humanitarian Emergency"' online: UNICEF <http://www.unicef.org/newsline/99pr29.htm>.

United Nations Human Rights Committee. 'General Comment No 6: The Right to Life (Article 6)' in *Compilation of General Comments and General Recommendations Adopted by Human Rights Treaty Bodies* (1994) UN Doc HRI/GEN/1/Rev.1 at 6.

United Nations Office for the Coordination of Humanitarian Assistance. 'Blockade of Gaza Denies Palestinians "Humanity and Dignity" Says UN Special Rapporteur' online: UNOHCHR <http://www.ohchr.org/en/NewsEvents/Pages/Display News. aspx?NewsID=11179&LangID=E>.

United Nations Office for the Coordination of Humanitarian Assistance. 'Farming Without Land, Fishing Without Water: Gaza Agriculture Sector Struggles to Survive' (May 2010) online: UNOCHAOPT <http://www.ochaopt.org/documents/gaza_agriculture_25_05_2010_fact_sheet_english.pdf>.

United Nations Office for the Coordination of Humanitarian Assistance. *Locked In: The Humanitarian Impact of Two Years of Blockade on The Gaza Strip* (UN 2009).

United Nations Office for the Coordination of Humanitarian Assistance. *The Humanitarian Monitor* (UN 2010).

United Nations Security Council Document S/22366 dated 20 March 1991. Report to the Secretary-General on Humanitarian Needs in Kuwait and Iraq in the Immediate Post-Crisis Environment by a Mission to the Area led by Mr. Marti Ahtisaari, Under-Secretary-General for Administration and Management, dated 20 March 1991.

United States Strategic Bombing Survey 1946 (reprinted) (Air University Press 1987).

World Health Organization. 'World Health Organization: Gaza Health Fact Sheet' online: WHO <http://unispal.un.org/UNISPAL.NSF/0/80E8238D765E5FB7852576B1004EC498>.

World War One Document Archive. 'US Protests Against Maritime Warfare: December 26, 1914' online: Brigham Young University <http://wwi.lib.byu.edu/index.php/U.S. Protests_Against_Maritime_ Warfare>.

Index